Home Coming

Book II

God's Miracles
in
Lives of Regular People

TRILOGY

BOOK II

Home Coming

By Angelic Tarasio

iUniverse

GOD'S MIRACLES IN LIVES OF REGULAR PEOPLE

HOME COMING

Graphic Design Credits: Johny Ivanov

iUniverse books may be ordered through booksellers or by contacting:

iUniverse
1663 Liberty Drive
Bloomington, IN 47403
www.iuniverse.com
1-800-Authors (1-800-288-4677)

ISBN: 978-1-5320-9243-5 (softcover)
ISBN: 978-1-5320-9244-2 (e-book)

Print information available on the last page.

iUniverse rev. date: 02/03/2020

I dedicate this book to all victims of Stalin repressions, and particularly to my Mother-in-law Countess Maria Kotyk-Kurbatov and her family. Their lives, freedom, loves, childhood, youth and happiness were destroyed by the evil totalitarian regime. I also dedicate this book to you, my reader. You are blessed not to experience the terror of inquisition and humiliation. Praise the Lord for being protected.

Author Angelic Tarasio

Foreword

God's Miracles will inspire a profound sense of gratitude in almost any reader: 'There but for the Grace of God go I'. Superficially, it is a harrowing tale of unimaginable suffering and human tragedy. But this is no sob story. What prevails is an astonishing and uplifting tribute to the enduring strength of the human spirit, the triumph of love over hatred, faith over despair, light over darkness.

I've known Angelic Tarasio personally for 15 years. Her own life has been filled with hardship most of us would find unbearable. And yet she embodies the courage and unwavering faith of her protagonist, and mother-in-law, Maria. Tarasio's muse in writing this trilogy, and her unique insight which brings the story alive, flow from the blessing that her own life was touched and changed forever by this extraordinary woman - by Maria's indomitable faith and capacity to shine in spite of all adversity.

In this second volume, Maria returns home, heavily pregnant, after escaping the horrors of the Nazis, only to be separated from her husband by zealous revolutionaries and dispatched to a remote corner of Siberia to serve a 12-year sentence in Stalin's Gulag. We see clearly how <u>the roots</u> of human cruelty sprout from our sinful human hearts, far deeper than any allegiance to intellectual constructs such as Fascism or Communism. Tarasio's vivid narrative also gives the reader a deep insight into a paradox which inhabits the Russian soul and pervades its history to the present day: the coexistence of breathtaking brutality alongside incredible humanity. (As a lifetime Russianist, it's never seemed accidental that the Russian version of "Hope springs eternal" is "Hope dies last".)

Above all, the story of Mother Maria's life, like the author's, inspires and reassures us that no matter what storms rage around us, we retain ultimate sovereignty over our inner worlds. If through faith, we can keep the lights of hope and love burning inside, darkness doesn't stand a chance.

Peter Minet
Family friend, Parent,
Vipassana Meditator, Finance Professional
London, January 2020

Preface

In my dedication to the book "***Home-Coming***" I named Mother-in-law's family and millions of other people who underwent the terror of Stalin's repressions in 1930-50s in the USSR and other countries. Up to the present time, the Stalin's terror had not received comparable recognition, as Nazism, Holocaust or atomic bombing of Hiroshima and Nagasaki. The world has to learn more facts of the most suppressed democracy in human history. The documents of NKVD crimes are not exposed to the right extent in the historical museums and educational programs in different countries in order to teach new generations the danger of forceful communist or socialist dictatorships.

In late 1980s, Russia experienced upsurge of communist memory, as did most European states. Moreover, Moscow was an initiator of restoration of truth when opened the archives of NKVD in 1992, published Solzhenitsyn's books, invited Andrei Sakharov to talk to the Congress of the People's deputies in Moscow, and supported the restoration of hundreds of churches, cathedrals, synagogues and mosques. May God bless a new country, developing the humanistic democracy and wellbeing of people!

The family of my Mother-in-law, as many other families in the USSR, got into the fire of Stalin's repressions and while working at this book, I understood the necessity to bring additional historical facts in order to prove the viciousness of *red octopus* - the soviet surrogate of the communist leadership, voiceless government and brutal security system. I showed how the terrifying soviet *red octopus* kept millions of their own citizens and people of other countries half-paralyzed due to fear of physical annihilated.

In this introduction I used family and authentic historical facts to illustrate how the soviet totalitarian communist regime affected the life of millions of people. I spent hours, days and weeks with the research of the historical material which factiously describes an alarming period in history of mankind. Besides my mother-in-law journals and knowledge of the family history, there are many books which describe the absurdity and cruelty of the soviet dictatorship of proletariat. There was no other state structure in the world that in reality was so much against the growth of welfare of their citizens. There was not any other political system that ratified its power through the repeal of all the human laws, humiliation and slaughter of their own population, as the soviet surrogate of the communist party, government and forceful GPU/NKVD/KGB security departments.

The authors of “Black Book of Communism” mentioned that communism and Nazism are two slightly different totalitarian structures. Both regimes were ***genocidal***. The communist regimes have killed more than 100 million people in USSR and other countries, in contrast to the approximately 25 million victims of Nazis. Both communists and Nazis labeled “a huge part of human population unworthy of existence”. The primary difference is that the communist model is based on the class system while the nazi model on race and nationalities.

Who was involved in the revolution of 1917 that made Russia the poorest nation in Europe for a rather long time period? The revolution was driven more than anything else by hatred and envy of *illiterate workers, homeless, unemployed people* and some part of the *poorest landless peasants.* The revolution was against the “***class enemies***”, who Stalin identified later, as the “***people's enemies***”. Who belonged to those “*people's enemies* or *class enemies*”? Nobles, aristocrats, clergy, landowners, owners of the banks, companies, plants and factories, shop and hotelkeepers, ex-policemen, ex-tsarist civil offices, ex-tsarist military officers, ex-members of bourgeois parties and government.

The new rulers took fast measures to “*liquidate their enemies, as a class*”. Since revolution of 1917-28 the government took the following discriminatory measures:

- fired thousands of “class enemies” from their jobs;

- denied civil rights to those people;
- deprived them of ration/food cards in order their families and they starved and died;
- denied them the right to receive medical care;
- evicted them out of their own homes and apartments or left just one room for the entire family and resided "revolutionaries" in the rest of the house.

The communist party and Stalin gave voice to the most despotic tyranny and dictatorship that ever existed. It *was forbidden to think differently.* Stalin demonstrated his oppressive mentality when he stated, "Ideas are more powerful than guns. We would not let our enemies have guns. Why should we let them have ideas?" What democracy could survive under the leadership of such a ruler?

Entrepreneurs or socially undesirable elements

In 1929 Stalin had become the supreme leader of the USSR. Beginning in early 1930s, the demonic regime initiated a campaign to get the country rid of *"entrepreneurs"* – mostly self-employed shopkeepers and craftsmen, who operated tiny, one-person businesses. They were by no means wealthy people and 93.3% had no employees at all. However, as "capitalists", they were regarded as "*socially undesirable elements*" and were punished by a tax hike of 1,000%, as well as the confiscation of their business inventory. A December

1930 decree designated more than 30 different categories of citizens to be deprived of their civil rights, housing rights, access to health care and ration/food cards.

The system grew a special category of *"spy" neighbors / informers*, who were scared to death by the security organs and submitted their reports about "the forbidden underground activity of their neighbors." My aunt had three children and a sick husband. She was a professional designer of clothing and a tailor. Considering the fact that, at that time, there was impossible to find any ready-made clothing for adults and children at the stores, she could hardly find the possibility to make some income, working at home. The customers brought the fabric and my poor aunt worked secretly in constant fear for bread, flour, milk and potato that the women paid her with. I remember, how in 1950s, she continued to keep her old Singer sewing machine hidden from the eyes of inspectors in the basement in order not to protect her five-member family from starvation.

Total collectivization of the peasant farmers created famine

The utopist idea of Marx' *social equality* and *social justice* meant in practice that ***25 million*** peasant farmers would not be paid their wages for their labor but would instead produce the agricultural output entirely for the state, which would in turn allow them to keep a modest share for their own survival needs. How was it achieved in reality?

In practice, this meant that a nation which had been *Europe's breadbasket* under the tsarist regime, experienced famine and chronic agricultural scarcity until the system collapsed in1980s. The peasant farmers were completely demoralized by Stalin's 1932 decree for *total collectivization.* The commissars took away cattle animals, horses and poultry from the farmers, as well as the families' lands, grain and potato supply for a new farmers' year. More than 12 million peasants flooded Russian cities, as homeless and beggars.

The following example is from life history of my family. As my grandmother described, "In 1930s we were driven by the only thought - finding some food for children, because our poor *kids were dying fast from starvation.* We suffered for two years in our village, buried our daughter and decided to move to the city in order to save the lives of four other children. Nobody was allowed to move anywhere without passports. My brother from Kursk helped me and four children to escape, while my poor husband Adrian could hardly survive another year in the village. After three years of famine, barely 30% of population managed to survive there. When I arrived secretly to take my husband to Kursk, I discovered that many people perished, and some families escaped from our formerly beautiful and prosperous village."

Collectivization of peasant farms had its most cataclysmic effect *in Ukraine*, where in 1932-1933 Stalin turned famine into a tool of ***genocide***. Identifying relatively rich Ukrainian peasantry, as an enemy to proletarian revolution, he sent the special units of NKVD and army to Ukraine, Caucasus and the lower Volga river region to confiscate the peasants' lands, supply, and intentionally create famine throughout the ethnic-Ukrainian areas. This resulted in the death of more than ***10 million*** Ukrainian people. The communist government followed one purpose in this calamity: they wanted to break the resistance of Ukrainian farmers to the confiscation of their lands, cattle, horses and poultry farms and force them to accept the socialism.

Exactly at that time, Stalin and NKVD created the infamous ***GULAG*** archipelago, a chain of ***slave labor camps*** in ***Siberia***. Mass number of peasants was sent there or executed by soviet henchmen. Another huge number of farmers' families were deported to remote wild regions of the country, where before them humans had never inhabited. It was understandable that few people could survive. Here are the facts from life history of my husband's family. The cousin of my mother-in-law Gregory was deported with his parents and other prosperous farmer families from Odessa region to Siberia in February 1934. Many years passed but Gregory could not recollect this story without tears.

"The cargo train stopped at the end of the railway, and the guards opened the doors. They stood in the deep snow, looking at us and laughing loudly. They were completely drunk. We were ordered to jump down. When we were in the snow, they locked the doors and the train moved back, leaving more than two hundred people to die. The cold hands of the women could hardly carry their babies and children.

We did not know where to go. The thick forest shrouded us on both sides of the railway road and, as we found later, it was its dead end and the trains did not go anywhere further. Somebody suggested moving inside of the forest. We could not move from the spot they left us on, sinking into the deep snow. Thank God, two men brought the axes with them, hiding them under the clothing, and one of the exiled men wrapped his torso with a manual hand saw.

The men decided to make wooden posts, pikes and some kind of shovels in order to clean a small meadow from the snow. While the men were cleaning the meadow from the snow, the women, children and older people gathered wood and brushwood around the meadow, making a huge fire on the spots of the meadow cleaned from snow. The fire melted the icy soil and after that, the younger men were using sharp wooden spears to hollow out the soil, in order to place the posts for the tent. We had to set fire two or three times in order to melt the ever-frozen soil and hollowed it out to the necessary depth. Then we collected a huge heap of fir branches and twigs and covered the prepared space with them. Using the posts, the men built the hut and covered it with fir branches, as well. By the end of the day, the women with children and old people were hidden in the hut under the second vast layer of fir branches. The vast levels of fir twigs had wonderful feature to produce natural warmth and gave people the possibility of not freezing at night.

As for men, we were working at the constructing of two more huts to the morning of the next day. Thank God that there were several people among us with rich experience of winter hunting! The Creator took care of our group, giving us cherished knowledge of surviving in the condition of wild nature. We had to change the fir branches every two days and built the small fireplaces in the middle of the huts. The people-on-duty were not asleep at night, taking care of the fire inside of the huts.

The worst thing in our expulsion was the absence of food. Hunting without rifles did not bring a lot. We found the oak trees, cleaned the snow around them and ate the acorns. It was more difficult with children. The absence of pots did not allow us to make some hot food or tea. In a day we found a small river in the forest, crashed the ice and caught some fish using our bare hands and sticks. We cooked it on the fire for children but knew that in order to survive, we had to cook hot food for everyone. Three days after our arrival, we decided to send several groups of younger men to find the villages of old-believers (Christians who exiled there due to some differences in religious concepts and rituals). One more thing we wanted to know – where the location of our banishment was.

As we found the old-believers, they helped our people with some food and clay pots for cooking. They allowed seven women with smallest babies to move to their village. The most important gift from old-believers was a rifle. That was not life, it was a nightmare. We lost many people, especially old during the initial three months of exile. The temperature in the hut was still freezing and they could not move sufficiently to warm themselves. It was awful, but we were unable to prevent their dying in freezing temperature and food deprivation. I lost my parents there, because they refused to take any food from the family saving it for the grandchildren when they got sick…"

Between August 1932 and December 1933 more than 125,000 people were arrested and sentenced; about ***5,400*** were ***executed***. It was the beginning of *mass deportation* of people to GULAG. Records show that in 1932, some 71,236 "specially displaced deportees" were sent to the camps. In **1934** this number climbed to ***268,091***.

The NKVD commissars and soviet inspectors continued their search for hidden grains and produce. They were allowed to torture people. The documents of the GPU/NKVD mentioned that among their methods of torturing were the following:

- the suspected victims were always unmercifully beaten;
- the peasants were stripped bare and exposed to freezing temperatures;
- sometimes they were stretched out and scalded on white-hot stove before being placed in freezing temperatures;
- the peasants' feet and clothing were doused with gasoline and set ablaze; the flames were then snuffed out and this procedure was repeated

until they were burnt to the level of fatal damage, or they revealed where the grain was hidden;
- groups of peasants were lined up against the wall in front of their families and neighbors for simulated and rather often real execution.

The communist party and soviet government *suspended the sale of railway tickets in regions affected by the famine.* Their aim was to trap people inside the hunger zone, with no chance to escape, and let them slowly starve to death.

One of the regions affected most severely by the famine was the Ukrainian city of Kharkov. An *Italian consul* stationed there described in horrific detail the events that took place in that city: "Along with peasants who flock to the towns because there is no hope for survival in the countryside, there are also children who are simply brought here and abundant by their parents, who then return to their villages to die. Their hope is that someone in the city will be able to look after their children..." The children were collected and taken to the nearest militia stations.

An Italian consul stated the following: "That's where all the children who are found in stations and on trains, the peasant families, the old homeless people and all the peasants that were picked up during the day are gathered together... A medical team does a sort of selection process... Anyone who is not yet swollen up from starvation and still has a chance of survival is directed to a specific area. People who already started to swell up are moved out on goods trains and abundant about 40 miles out of town, so that they can die out of sight. When they arrive at the destination, huge ditches are dug, and the dead and half dead are carried out of the wagons."

The artificially created famine affected *40 million of people*, including those who *died* from it and those who suffered through it and survived.

In 1934 for one year and two months ***6,500*** people were sentenced for the crime of terrorism and *immediately* ***executed***. In 1935, 1936 and 1937 the astronomical numbers of sentences handed down by NKVD: 267,000 in 1935; 274, 000 in 1936 and in a single operation in 1937 more than 259,000 people were arrested and nearly ***73,000*** were ***executed***.

According to soviet nuclear physicist and academician Andrei Sakharov, more than 1.2 million members of the communist party were arrested between 1936 and 1939; of these, at least ***600,000*** *were* ***killed*** *through torture, execution, and confinement* in the concentration camps of GULAG.

Stalin's repressions also sent thousands of scientists, writers, publishers, journalists, theater directors, actors, ballet dancers, high-ranking officers of the Red army, doctors, and engineers to Gulag, prisons, exiles in ever-freezing zones, or executioners. They were sentenced for the "*wrong political or philosophical views*".

What is “militant atheism”?

In the latest pre-war wave of terror in 1940-41, soviet authorities provided the “***complete liquidation** of the clergy*”, a mission under the satanic slogan of ***militant atheism.*** They have started this evil mission right after the revolution and continued throughout the late 1920s. The purge against the clergy and the religion in general, as the communists considered, the poisonous “opium for the masses”, resulted in the arrests of thousands of priests, rabbis and nearly all bishops. *Most* of them were ***executed*** and the rest sent to forced labor camps of GULAG.

The statistics of ***1936*** show that **21,000** churches and monasteries were active in the USSR and, in the beginning of ***1941***, fewer than **914** were functioning. The number of officially registered clerics nationwide declined from over 24,000 in 1936 to about 5,665 in early 1941. The priests who were allowed to provide the church services signed the agreement with NKVD that obliged them to record all the names of the participants and report to local NKVD and communist committee about those who participated in religious services, such as church and synagogue marriages, baptizing or circumcision of children, or burial services.

Executions of innocent people

During 1937-1938, the NKVD arrested 1,575,000 people. My grandfather Adrian was among them.

1,345,000 received some sentence. 85.4% were ***executed***. This was an average of more than **20,000** executions **monthly**.

For death sentences no appeals were permitted and the executions were usually carried out within a few days. The number of political prisoners in Gulag grew significantly. In 1929 there were approximately 55,000 prisoners; in 1935 their number reached to 965,000 prisoners; in 1941 the Gulag population doubled from 1935 to nearly 2 million, to be more accurate it was 1,930,000 people. In addition to that number the political prisons were packed with 462,000 criminal inmates.

When WWII started, the difficult conditions of prisoners in Gulags deteriorated. The camps commonly did not receive any food supplies for weeks or months. During the winter of 1942-43, **25%** of all **Gulag** prisoners **died** from ***starvation***. Over the entire war more than **2 *million*** prisoners of Gulags perished in Siberian camps. Somewhere **20-35%** of the prisoners were ***released each year***, BUT it did not mean a genuine freedom, in most of the cases it was ***house arrest*** or ***exile***.

Soviet Terror in Annexed Countries

In ***1940*** NKVD ***deported*** from the occupied territories of ***Lithuania, Latvia*** and ***Estonia*** more than ***60,000*** people.

The post-war period was not much easier for the population of the USSR and especially the population of new annexed lands of Baltic republics – ***Latvia, Lithuania*** and ***Estonia***, as well as ***Western Ukraine***. These territories were fighting for their independence. None of the annexed lands wanted communist regime. The NKVD was given all the rights for arrests, interrogations, inquisition and extirpation of the local population of wild eastern lands in order to break the resistance.

Soviet ***archival data*** states that on ***October 9, 1944***, 1 NKVD Division, 8 NKVD brigades, and NKVD cavalry regiment with the total number of 26,304 NKVD soldiers were stationed in Western Ukraine. In addition, 2 regiments with 1,500 and 1,200 persons, 1 battalion (517 men) and 3 armored trains with 100 additional soldiers each, as well as 1 border guard regiment and 1 unit were relocated to reinforce them.

Mass arrests of suspected UPA (Ukrainian Partisan Army) members, their informants or family members were conducted among the civil population. Between February 1944 and May 1946, over ***250,000*** were arrested in ***Western Ukraine***. All the arrested underwent *beating* and *tortures*. The reports exist of the facts when the suspected prisoners were *burnt alive*. Many arrested women believed to be affiliated with UPA were subjected to *torture, deprivation* and *rape* at the hands of NKVD in order to force them to reveal UPA members' identities and locations or to turn them into soviet double-agents. *Mutilated corpses* of captured rebels were put on *public display*. Ultimately, between 1944 and 1952, more than ***600,000*** were *arrested* and more than ***200,000*** were ***executed*** in annexed zones. The rest were imprisoned in Gulags or exiled. The resistance of Western Ukrainians continued in some arias until 1957. The last deportations by NKVD were directed against clergy and farmers.

When WWII was over Stalin announced that ***all the soviet citizens*** who had been *detained in foreign prisons, concentration and labor camps*, as well as those who were forcefully taken by Nazis to slavery work in Germany during the war should now be ***classified*** *as* ***traitors*** and should be ***executed*** *or* ***deported*** *to the Gulags*. Thus some ***1.5 million*** new ***innocent*** victims were shipped straight to Gulags by 1945.

The intense ***Russification*** program and ***propaganda*** for ***communism*** and ***militant atheism*** was implemented in schools of all levels. The religious families were strictly persecuted, priests were murdered and nearly all the churches were closed or turned into the storage depots and clubs. In all the annexed territories tribunals were set up to sentence "*traitors to the people*" and "*people's enemies*" and provide their *prompt liquidation*. The Russification program included massive immigration in the Baltic countries and Western Ukraine. Hundreds of thousands of migrants were relocated from different parts of the Soviet Union "to assist" with industrialization, collectivization and militarization of the annexed countries.

For two Soviet occupations approximately ***150,000*** *Latvians ended up in exile in Arctic, Siberia Gulag* or in *Kazakhstan uncivilized areas*. More than ***200,000***

Estonians were deported during pre-war and post-war Soviet occupations. In addition, at least ***75,000*** *Estonians* were sent directly to *Gulag*. More than ***157,000*** *of Lithuanians* were arrested, part of them was murdered and the rest deported to Gulags or the areas where the surviving was extremely difficult. No wonder that half of the deported perished during the initial years of hardships. The other half were not allowed to return to their native lands until the early ***1960s***. By that time most of the people died in exile.

One week before Hitler attacked the USSR, over ***30,000 Ukrainians*** were taken ***in one night*** from Bessarabia and Bukovina, recently annexed by the USSR lands, and deported to frozen wastelands of Siberia and Kolyma, the "land of gold and death". Those families, as the family of my mother-in-law Countess Maria Kotyk-Kurbatov, who were not familiar with the soviet regime until 1940, and their first meeting with horrifying *"red octopus"* did not leave misfortunate Ukrainian people any chances to escape.

Crime against the Polish officers in 1940

Recently we learned the horrible facts about ***secret assassinations, arrests*** and ***death sentences for 25,000 Polish people, mainly Polish officers,*** who "disappeared" from the annexed territories of Poland and Baltic countries.

In April 1940, NKVD ***shot 11*** Polish generals, ***1*** admiral, ***77*** colonels, ***197*** lieutenant colonels, ***541*** majors, ***1,441*** captains, ***6,061*** lieutenants and other ranks, ***18*** chaplains, the ***chief rabbi*** *of the Polish army*, together with *Polish civil service representatives* and *bourgeoisie*. There were also a few women among secretly deported victims and one of them was Janine Lewandowska, the Polish aviator. In Kiev and Moscow trails, the arrested Polish individuals were charged with "*struggling against the international communist movement*" and found guilty.

The Katyn massacres are the examples of senseless and brutal crimes of the socialist regime, in which NKVD murdered ***22,000 polish*** officers, policemen, clergy and civil servants. The prisoners were transported to the execution sites in the forest around Katyn. The eliminating contingent of NKVD was equipped with German weapons and ammunition. A total of fifty executioners were used and each evening a victim count was telegraphed to Moscow. These victims of NKVD could be lost forever, but 4,143 bodies were exhumed by the German occupants in 1943.

These ***victims suffered***: they were forced to stand in groups by open pits, many of them had their hands bound with barbed wire and some had nooses around their necks. Others, particularly the clergy, were not taken to the forests, they were shot in Smolensk prison in an underground execution chamber, and their bodies stacked in pits. In October the chief of NKVD Beria rewarded the executioners with an extra month salary, and the organizers of massacres were awarded with medals and other kinds of state awards.

As the shooting ended in mid-April, the unsuspecting families were sent to the Arctic zone to build a railway to cold mines of Vorkuta.

140,000 Polish citizens were sent to *Kolyma, as Stanislaw Kowalski named "the land of gold and death"*, to the *permafrost area.* Their ***wives*** and ***children*** were exiled for 10 years to Kazakhstan in April 1940. Until June 1941, Poles, Ukrainians, Latvians, Lithuanians and Estonians were railroaded east to Siberia and wilderness of Komi soviet republic.

Intrusion of the USSR in Spain in 1930s

The ***soviet atheistic propaganda*** worked ***internationally*** to the degree that even Spanish leftists became evil and took a photo that later was word-spread, as the Soviet anti-religious propaganda. The picture was taken during the civil war in Spain in 1930s, at the moment, when a group of Spanish demonic men was shooting the stature of Jesus Christ. I doubt that it could be possible in the country of faith in 1930s even in the fire of Civil war without satanic propaganda of the USSR. The leaders of the proletarian revolution provoked the political fight in Spain, involving the International communist brigades from the other countries.

The Soviet historical books, magazines and newspapers described how the poor population of Spain suffered from clergy and landowners. They used the Russian scenario of revolution. So, the republicans consisted of communists, unemployed workers, landless peasants and revolutionary anarchists. They were called "the reds", as the revolutionary forces in Russia. All those forces were gathered under the Republic Army, which was *supported* by military specialists and *"volunteers"* from the Soviet Union with brand new *multiple pilot escadrilles, tank units* and *other weapons.*

The soviet communist propaganda worked so well that Mexican and international brigades from other countries arranged their intrusion into the sovereign country and participated in Spanish Civil war. Roughly 30,000 communists, trade unionists and foreigners of 53 nations fought in Spain. They were guided and controlled by Moscow NKVD. None of them considered that it was illegal and scandalous intrusion in the life of a country with its history, strong faith and culture. Spain became the land of hatred, treachery of God, and destruction. At least half a million people were killed during the civil war and about 7,000 of them were clerics. Churches, convents and monasteries were attacked and destroyed. ***Thirteen bishops, 4,184 priests, 283 nuns, 2,365 monks*** were ***killed*** during the war. Numerous repressive actions were organized, financed and committed by the USSR.

At the beginning, none of the countries wanted seriously intervene in the senseless war. On the contrary, in the early days of the war, NKVD and Spanish leftists *arrested* and ***executed*** over ***50,000 innocent people*** just because they *were* found on the "*wrong*" side of the fronts and refused to support the ***reds*** in their fight.

During the Spanish civil war, NKVD agents, acting in conjunction with the communist party of Spain, exercised substantial control over the republican government, using soviet military aid for further influence. The ***NKVD*** established *numerous* ***secret prisons*** *around Madrid*, which were used to detain, torture, and murder hundreds of NKVD enemies, initially focusing on Spanish Nationalists and Catholics.

From late 1938, the anarchists and Trotskyites became the objects of NKVD persecution. In June of 1937, ***Andres Nin***, the secretary of the anti-Stalinist Marxist party, was tortured and murdered in NKVD prison. Many interesting facts were discovered and opened in ***1992***, when the archive of NKVD/KGB was released. Two Canadian journalists prepared a documentary on Nin's assassination. They found two letters of Alexander Orlov, the chief of Soviet NKVD in Spain, who fled to Canada after Spain, where he was granted the political asylum. One letter was dated May 23, 1937 and explained how *the material* linking Nin to the fascists was *fabricated.* The other letter, dated July 24, 1937, gave detailed report on ***NKVD involvement*** in the ***torture*** and ***killing*** of **Nin**, who being a Marxist, provided criticism of Stalin's dictatorship. The second letter written after Nin's death identified the place where the victim's body lay. Nobody had known before that the NKVD buried his mutilated corpse between two highways in Spain, as told in the letter.

The Repressions of the USSR in Eastern Europe

Not so many people are familiar with the policy of the USSR provided in the countries liberated from Nazi Germany. The USSR considered itself the only winner in the WWII and had not presented a liberal and humane policy to many of the European countries. Shortly after the end of the war, the NKVD created ***a chain of internment camps in Europe***. In *Eastern Germany* of **11** *NKVD camps*, 4 were established in former Nazi camps, including ***Buchenwald***, which was re-named, as Special camp #2. Camp inmates were primarily members of the Nazi party, the SS, members of the previous government, nobility, landowners, clergy and owners of the factories, plants, banks, stores, and railroads.

In less than 12 months, all the camps were jam-packed with former Social democrats, communists, critics of the Socialist Unitary Party and the relatives of SED members. Author Norman Naimark labeled those camps, as ***"death camps"***.

According to NKVD records, they imprisoned the total 120,000 inmates, and ***42,907*** Germans ***died*** in the camps in the period running from 1945-1949. This number is huge. Nevertheless, Author Norman Naimark did not believe in these numbers, presented in the reports of NKVD, and considered that they were different and achieve 120,000 to 140,000 individuals perished in the camps, out of a greater number of imprisoned people. Only uranium mining alone had killed enormous number of inmates. The project of nuclear weapons was under the watchful eye of Beria, the head of NKVD. Soviet authorities employed the forced labor of imprisoned German scientists and workers. Nobody was allowed to check the work conditions on the object of top secrecy, and the inmates were buried without coroner's examinations and recording.

The civil population of Eastern Germany, who did not leave their homes, suffered by taking the burden of Red army rules: ***murder, rape, robbery*** and ***expulsion***. For example, in the East Prussian city of Konigsberg, in August 1945, approximately 100,000 Germans lived there. After the Red army conquered the city, only 20,000 were still there in 1948. After the Soviet capture of Berlin in 1945, one of the largest and most horrible cases of ***mass rape*** occurred. Tens of thousands of women and girls were raped until winter 1947-48, when the soviet occupation authorities confined the Soviet troops to strictly guarded military posts and bases, completely separating them from the residential population of Eastern Germany.

The Soviet Union did not recognize the entry of the tsarist Russia to the Hague Conventions 1899 and 1907, as binding for itself and refused to sign it until 1955. This resulted in ***barbaric treatment of POW*** (prisoners of war). Throughout the WWII, more than **300,000** German, French, Romanian, Hungarian and other captives **died**. The POW were not released right after the war, but instead they were kept until 1956 under similar conditions as before.

The soviet totalitarian policy in Hungary

The Soviet Union demonstrated its totalitarian policy regarding any political changes in the policies of the "satellite countries". ***The Hungarian revolution of 1956*** was a spontaneous nationwide revolt against the pro-Stalinist communist government of Hungary. The revolt began as a massive student demonstration moving through central Budapest to the Parliament building. A student delegation entered the radio building with an attempt to broadcast their demands. The delegation was detained. The demonstrators insisted in the release of their delegators. The State Security Police answered with fire from within the radio building.

The revolt spread quickly through Hungary, and the government fell. Pro-Soviet communists were executed, or imprisoned, and former political prisoners were released and armed. On November 4, 1956 the Soviet army invaded Budapest and other regions of Hungary. The resistance of Hungarians lasted until November 10. Over 2,500 Hungarian and 700 Soviet troops were killed in the conflict, and about 200,000 Hungarians fled, as refugees, escaping the purges of KGB. Mass arrests and demonstrations continued for months after. By January 1957, the new Soviet-installed government had suppressed the public opposition, and the democratic block was deprived to provide any changes.

The communist dictatorship of the USSR in Czechoslovakia

The experience of the Soviet Union in establishment of the communist dictatorship in other countries had a long history. Another example is the Soviet intrusions in the life and political structure of the ***Czechoslovakia***. The country underwent serious losses during the WWII. The Soviet Union prepared the members of the communist party of Czechoslovakia for leading the country under red banner of communism. In 1948 the communists took power in the country under the ideological orientation of the USSR. The country was declared, as a people's republic – the first step toward socialism and communism.

Dissident elements, including Catholic priests and monks were purged from all levels of society organizations. The entire educational system was separated from the church and submitted to antireligious state control. The private ownership in all the fields of social life was eliminated. Czechoslovakia became a satellite of the Soviet Union.

A new constitution was passed through the National Assembly of Czechoslovakia, and the communists took complete control. Stalin's paranoia resulted in ***periodical cleansing the parties*** of the Soviet Union and the satellite countries. In all the countries, they accused opponents of ***"high treason"*** in order to remove them from the position of power. The NKVD and local security services provided large-scale arrests of communists with "an international background, veterans of Spanish war, Jews and Slovak "bourgeois nationalists". The arrests were followed by show trails.

Rudolf Slansky, the first secretary of the communist party, was ***executed*** and in November and December 1952, 13 other prominent communists were sentenced ***to death*** or forced labor in prison camps. In March 1948, approximately **2.5 million** people began to be subjected to merciless scrutiny. By 1960, the membership of the communist party in Czechoslovakia was reduced to 1.4 million.

The Soviet Union insisted in providing the policy of ***total collectivization of agriculture in Czechoslovakia***. The United Agricultural cooperatives were founded on supposed "*voluntary*" basis. The scenario of the USSR suggested implementing discriminatory policies to ruin the wealthy and hardworking peasants. The collectivization was completed by 1960, and agricultural production declined seriously, as the main inhuman and senseless policy of the USSR collectivization was fulfilled. The country was cleared from wealthy individuals in all the aspects of the social life.

In **1959,** the pre-war level of production was not met. The communist policy destroyed the most experienced and productive farmers and provoked the peasantry of Czechoslovakia for sabotage. Nobody wanted to work hard, without receiving anything for their work.

The Constitution of Czechoslovakia in 1960 declared the victory of socialism and proclaimed Czechoslovakia Socialist Republic. In reality, in early

1960s, the economy of the country was stagnant, and the industrial growth rate was the lowest in Europe. In 1963, a large number of communists insisted in providing the **reforms** in the country. The reform-minded communists expressed criticism of economic planning, bureaucratic control of the communist party and ideological conformity.

The leaders of the communist party of Czechoslovakia arranged the consultations with Brezhnev, a new general secretary of the communist party of the Soviet Union and the head of the USSR. Brezhnev, being a new leader of the country, saw the picture a little bit different from Stalin, and some hardliners were replaced by younger and more liberal communists in the government of Czechoslovakia. Democratic centralism was redefined, placing a stronger emphasis on democracy. The leading role of the communist party was reaffirmed but limited.

For some time, the soviet leaders watched the development of Czechoslovakia. In August 1967, Soviet troops enter the country. KGB ordered to arrest the leader of the country **Dubcek,** and he was delivered to Moscow for "*negotiations.*" The outcome was the Brezhnev's doctrine of "limited sovereignty", which requested the strengthening of the communist party, strict party control of the media, and full suppression of Czechoslovak Social Democratic party. The Soviet troops remained stationed in Czechoslovakia, as in all satellite countries, until the crush of the Soviet empire when those countries finally received their independence.

Why did the soviet communist empire collapse?

Few people concentrated their attention to this question: ***Who*** or ***what made possible the collapse of the terrifying empire of viciousness?*** It was one of the strongest countries with its demonically built totalitarian structure, and, all of a sudden, it was demolished to the ground without war and other objective reasons for it.

The answer is rather simple: ***the angelic patience of our Creator was overwhelmed*** with ferocity of revolution, humiliation, annihilation, forced deportation of millions of innocent people and their family members to GULAG, endless executions, forceful and inhuman policy toward the population of the annexed countries and domineering policy toward the sovereign countries of the world… The list of crimes is endless.

When nobody expected the collapse of the USSR, ***the Divine forces*** *destroyed the empire of viciousness.* Nobody could predict the ***peaceful*** transition toward independence and democracy of all the countries, earlier subjugated or kept under soviet communist control. ***The world was blessed for these peaceful changes, but never was grateful enough to our Lord for justice that triumphed.***

Not all the criminal facts of the totalitarian Soviet communist regime could be mentioned in one article. It was not my major objective to name all the crimes of the terrible soviet "red octopus". We know about multiple intrusions of the USSR in the countries of Africa, Middle East and Asia. I wanted the readers to understand the dangerous environment and circumstances the main character Maria Kurbatov-Kotyk encountered in USSR in September of 1946.

The end of the soviet empire of viciousness gave the possibility for a new democratic Russian government to open the archives of the communist party and its security service GPU/NKVD/KGB. The fact, that chronological records of political crimes were released to the mankind, demonstrates the difference between new Russia and old totalitarian secret structure of the USSR. We hope that our Creator would not allow any country of the world to step on the road of suppressive and totalitarian policy toward others.

What should we understand in order to achieve peace, happiness and success?

The world needs peace. We must be friends, remembering that ***we all*** are ***children*** of ***ONE CREATOR*** and ***responsible*** for peaceful ***development*** of this ***world***. Only the complete understanding of this phenomenon can give us a chance of finding peace, happiness, love and success in the hardships of modern life.

Now, it is the right time to understand that only with ***Blessing from Above*** we can achieve the progress in different aspects of our life, and successfully overcome any personal or Global crises. The history of already non-existing empire of the USSR demonstrated the unshakable power and righteous will of our Lord. He is patient to us at this difficult time, giving a chance for *understanding our karmic mission* and *awakening of real faith. During our human life, we should fulfil our Divine purpose, and become incredible in faith, tolerance, compassion, integrity and professionalism.*

During many years of my practice, I met thousands of different people. When I have met them for the first time, many of them were discontented, seriously ailing, depressed and completely lost in chaos of modern world. Not all of them were familiar with God's presence in human life. With God's blessing, they learned spirituality and enlightenment that brought them to health, happiness and success. They have recognized the major law of human life - ***"With God All Things are Possible".***

Author Angelic Tarasio
Florida, USA.

Introduction

I still consider myself a happy person. My life isn't easy. However, all the challenges from youth to the present moment did not break me physically, spiritually and psychologically. God blessed me to pass one life test after another, and every time, my relatives and friends asked the same question: How could I manage?

They saw that all my hardships were resolved at the end with miraculous results. Sometimes, it has already happened, but it was difficult for the regular observers to believe that I was able to go through sufferings again. My dear readers, I am close to sharing my secret with you. I learned from my mother-in-law Countess Maria Kotyk-Kurbatov to accept nearly everything, not as God's punishment, but as His will. Sometimes, it is difficult to follow this rule, especially when something unexpected and tragic happens with your family.

I've learned from my rather long-life experience that there is nothing can happen that we cannot stand or overcome. We need to preserve the connection with the Divinity and receive the support from Above. We need to feel that we are not alone and lost in our chaotic world, everything is placed on our life path to make us stronger and wiser.

As you saw in the first book, my mother-in-law's Faith kept her alive in the most life-threatening situations. She had never judged people and always felt sorry for atheists, considering them deaf and blind to the Divine providence and miracles of life. She asked me to understand the difference between a spiritual person and atheistic one, in order I can help the atheists to find the healing connection with the Divinity. For me it was quite understandable. I was from nonbelievers and repeated like a parrot Karl Marx's conception that religion was an opiate for people.

I remember my mother-in-law's saying, "When you want to be happy in your life, preserve Faith, Health and Loyalty. Life and love last forever, when people are blessed with true Faith. Help each other to fulfil God's mission." Being young, I was sure that nothing could be changed in our personal lives. However, everything is possible, and we overcome the changes easier, when we accept it as God's will.

When Mother Maria mentioned to me that her children did not like the idea of her writing the journals, I could not comprehend: why? Then she explained, whatever she truthfully recorded about the life in the USSR, it could bring her again into the force labor camp. The children did not want to lose their mother. It was the first reason but not the only one. The second was in her uneasy emotional state, when she registered the events. The whole picture of the tragic event was recalled in her memory, and Mother Maria cried, as if it happened to her or her beloved at that very moment, when she recorded it in her journal.

Nearly every night, Mother Maria secretly described her thorny life under the nazi and communist regimes, hiding the dated records under the armrests of the sofa. Who could imagine that she staffed the armrests with her journals? When I began to read the journals, I checked the data with reliable sources. What was my surprise? Mother Maria's memory was always sharp, but it was difficult to imagine the accuracy of the facts and dates, she mentioned in her journals.

I remember, how the information that I've learned from Mother Maria's diaries, turned up-side-down my understanding of life in the whole world. All the knowledge of history after the university studies did not give us the truth that I found in my mother-in-law's journals. Only after the brake-up of the USSR, the information that was covered up was unveiled and introduced to the public.

When Mother Maria saw that I read every part of her journal with interest and sincere compassion to her, Mother Maria brought the idea of writing a book out those dry chronological facts about the life of her family. She knew that there was no way to publish the book in the communist country. When God gave us the opportunity to leave the USSR, she brought the journals again one week before our departure, and we read them together with her personal explanations of the data.

I understood the records much better after her interpretations. I knew that in the country of red octopus, the authorities kept everyone under control. They would never like her writing, although she recorded the events without emotional or self-pitying description.

She provided me with the main concept of the book: "I want the book to be written in such a way that people believe that God's miracles happen in the lives of regular people. Otherwise, how can you explain the fact that we have met and are all together in this life? Only Divine forces did not allow the evil to destroy our family."

Upon arriving to the United States with an attempt to save my daughter's life, the life became extremely busy and the possibility to write a book was delayed. Many years passed, before I sensed a persistent desire to write a book about God's miracles with which three generations of our family were blessed, including myself. My mother-in-law's dream came true. Being a linguist, but not a professional writer, I did my best. My book is a work of not a complete fiction. I used the dated chain of events from Mother Maria's records and described them using her interpretation of the facts and my imagination. The true story of my mother-in-law became the foundation of the trilogy. The chain of miraculous events happened, as described. However, most of the names and places I used fictitiously, and any resemblance to actual living or diseased person, as well as the places of the events are entirely coincidental.

Author Angelic Tarasio

Chapter 1

The train Brest-Lvov arrived at Lvov railway station at 11:15 a.m. on Tuesday, October 1, 1946. The long Kurbatovs' journey was over. The arrival made Maria happier. She did not complain out loud, but it was not easy in her condition on the sixth month of pregnancy, to sit for five days in a train compartment. They ate a light breakfast in the restaurant, took a taxi, and went home to her Blue Creeks.

Alexander noticed,

"Marie, you do not feel well, do you?"

"I am fine, Alex" Maria answered quietly. "I am just a little bit tired of staying in a closed compartment."

She did not mention to him, but she regretted about her stubbornness and arrival to Creeks during pregnancy. She had to wait, probably, for another year.

They arrived at her family's place around 2 p.m. The beautiful gates with the family coat of arms were broken and thrown behind the servants' lodge. Both statues from either side of the gates were damaged. The central fountain was destroyed. Yellow leaves were strewn all over the yard and in the fountain water. The leaves made the water in the fountain green and unclear. Maria thought, "It's obvious that nobody has taken care of the mansion for a long time." The door of the house was left wide opened. There was a sign near the door, "NKVD – the national committee of the internal affairs."

Maria read it twice and a fearful thought appeared in her mind, "Where is my family? It does not look like they reside here. It was the war. God forbid, something bad had happen to them. Lord, have mercy!"

Maria entered the vestibule of the house. It was no longer her home, everything looked so different inside. The people in military uniforms were sitting, talking, and smoking in every room. No one paid attention to Maria and her husband. A strange thought came to her mind: "Run away, Marie. Take your husband and disappear. Do it now." Maria looked around and smiled to Alexander. Then she whispered,

"I heard a voice, Alex. It took many years to arrive here, and all of a sudden, that voice suggested me to run away or even disappear from here."

Alexander did not have a chance to answer. Somebody opened the door of the former living room and noticed them in the vestibule. The officer asked in Russian,

"What do you need?"

Maria answered,

"I am looking for my family."

The officer let them in. Alexander introduced himself and Maria, explaining the reason of their arrival. The officer did not introduce himself. He wrote something on a sheet of paper and called in a loud voice for someone to come. The younger officer entered the room and took the paper.

Then the older officer said with an unpleasant smile on his lips,

"We'll arrange everything for you. You'll see your father and siblings soon. I am more than sure about it. Leave your passports, entry documents, and tickets here on the table. I need to call to Lvov and arrange the transportation for you to deliver you to your father."

The Kurbatovs sensed sarcasm in his words and his eyes radiated inhuman coldness. When the Kurbatovs were leaving the room, Maria asked the man if she could use a restroom in the house. He said that the restrooms in the house were out of order after the war, and she could use one outside. Maria was surprised, and asked Alexander,

"Why didn't they repair the restrooms in the house? If even the pump system or pipes broke during the war, why didn't they fix them for a year?"

Alexander went with her to find the lavatory behind the house. It was made of wooden boards with holes between the boards. There was no electricity inside. It was very dirty, and the odor was so strong that there was no way to be in there. Maria felt nauseous and vomited.

"You were right, darling. We should not come here, Alex. I mean, we shouldn't arrive now, when I am pregnant."

When they returned to the house, the man was talking on the phone. They were waiting until the end of his conversation. The doors were closed, but they heard his sarcastic voice and loud laugh.

"I am afraid, Alex. Let us go somewhere, let us run to my grandpa's lodge."

Alex replied, "Marie, it is dusk already and the lodge is many miles away. The officer promised to arrange everything tonight. We are citizens of France. They cannot do any harm to foreigners."

Maria asked,

"Why did he take away our passports?"

"I wish I knew, Marie."

They sensed with every inch of their skin that they were in a dangerous trap. They tried to find the way out but could not. The major took away their entry documents, tickets and passports. They could not go anywhere without them.

"Calm down, Marie. You cannot be nervous because of the pregnancy. You know well that our son does not like it."

Alexander touched Marie's belly, and stroked it gently. He felt the motions of his son inside.

"He is too little to go through stress. Try to stay calm, darling."

Maria started to pray, "Lord, have mercy. Lord, have mercy. Lord …" Her prayer was interrupted by the heavy footsteps that were approaching the door. The door was opened, and they were 'invited' with the motion of the head to enter the room.

"Everything is arranged for you, Count and Countess Kurbatov. The transportation is coming, and you are going back to Lvov. There you'll be happy to meet your father."

"What does he do in Lvov? Does he work in Lvov hospital?" Maria asked.

There was no clear answer.

Alexander inquired,

"What does he do there? Is he all right?"

The man's face shifted, and Maria saw his demonic smile. She was frightened and stepped backward, thinking:

"Oh, Lord! Is he a demon? A real demon?"

Marie's heart raced. She was about to faint. Marie heard again the voice of her guardian angel,

"Not now, Marie. Be strong."

She turned slowly to her husband and noticed that he was tense. Marie thought,

"He must notice that face shift as well."

Marie was frightened even more. Then the face of the officer became normal again, and he suggested Marie a glass of cold water. It was just what she needed at that moment. The water was from their well. She remembered that taste. It was the taste from her childhood.

"I had been hungry or tired, and whatever I saw was definitely a kind of hallucination."

It seemed to Marie that she found a plausible explanation for the horrible officer's facial shift that she noticed two minutes ago. The thought calmed her down.

Lord, have mercy!

Chapter 2

Maria and Alexander waited outside for the transportation to Lvov. While walking around the property, she could hardly recognize her former home. Some of the structures were destroyed to the point that they were unusable, particularly the summer kitchen and the house for seasonal workers.

All the statues along the lime tree alley were completely damaged or deeply scratched. Maria saw only fragments of two colorful stone amphorae on the ground around their pedestals. Dr. Kotyk brought this beauty in mid-1930s from Greece. The war completely crashed the central part of the Garden fountain with a huge statue of Neptune. All formally white benches around the fountain presented a sorry spectacle as well.

Maria stopped at the entrance to the white, lace-like gazebo in the garden. It used to be one of her favorite places. Alexander asked her,

"Did you like to sit here? What did you like to do in the gazebo? Let me guess: to read."

Maria had not answered at once. The roof of the gazebo was destroyed, and some pieces of it were on the ground around and inside gazebo. She stepped carefully in and answered,

"I liked to hide here and dream. My younger brothers could not find me. Nobody could. Here I prayed and dreamed."

Alexander recognized his Marie. It was Marie, the young lady, who lived in her dreams, when he first met her in Paris.

"What were your dreams about, mon cher?"

She answered immediately,

"At ten or eleven, they were about Maman and her return home. At sixteen, I dreamed about you, a handsome prince with blue eyes. Alex, it seemed to me that I saw precisely you in my dreams."

They were returning to the house along the old lime trees alley. The trees were losing their yellow leaves, and Maria liked the sound of the dry leaves under their feet. It was obvious that no one had cleaned the park in over a year.

Alexander paid attention to an elderly woman in black shawl who stopped near the broken gate of the mansion. The woman stared fixedly at his wife, who wandered with him along the alley. Alexander asked,

"Who is that woman that looks intently at you, Marie?"

Maria turned to the gates and stood frozen.

"Ganja? Is that you, Ganja?"

She rushed to the old woman and hugged her.

"Pannochka (Ms.-Ukr.) Maria, what are you doing here? Why did you come?" The elderly woman burst into tears.

"I am looking for my father, my brothers, and Jenny. Do you know anything about them? Where are they?"

The woman was sobbing and shaking,

"Please leave, run away. They killed your father. They took your brothers and a sister away. I wanted to protect my Jenny and, look, they broke my arm. Run from this place, Pannochka Maria. I can see you are expecting your child to come. Why did you arrive? You cannot help your poor family. You should not come to this horrible place."

Ganja motioned toward the house and added,

"Do not trust them! They have no mercy."

Maria was stood still as a stone for some time. Then she felt like something cracked inside of her and she started to cry,

"Papa, oh my God, Papa…"

Alexander tried to calm her down, but it did not work. Maria complained,

"Ganja, can you imagine, they promised to arrange our meeting with Papa."

The poor woman did not know what to do.

"Alex, ask them to return our documents and we'll leave."

Alexander went to the office again. He thought,

"What a situation! I anticipated that there was some kind of danger in this trip, but I was not at all ready for this."

All the doors in the house were closed. There were voices in the former living room. Alexander knocked at the door. The person-on-duty did not allow interruption of the meeting. He commanded to Alexander in a rude way,

"Sit and wait."

Meanwhile, Maria continued talking to Ganja. Alexander returned without passports and entry documents. Maria did not ask about the papers. All of a sudden, she surprised everyone with her request,

"I am so hungry, Ganja. Can you bring my husband and me anything to eat? We ate last time in Lvov around 11 o'clock in the morning."

Ganja replied,

"I am sorry Pannochka Maria, but I have only bread and potatoes. Will you eat it?"

"Yes, please."

The old woman ran away. Maria asked Alexander about the documents. He did not have a chance to answer because at that moment they noticed two officers coming in their direction. Maria stood in front of her husband, thinking that her pregnancy would protect them. The men were arguing about something, and when they came up to the Kurbatovs, they were quiet again.

"Who was the woman that you talked to?" The younger officer asked.

"A nanny of my younger sister Jenny," Maria answered honestly.

"I wonder, what did the old frog tell you about your family?"

The man sounded rude.

Alexander was the first who answered.

"Not much. My wife is hungry. She asked the woman to bring her something to eat."

"The transportation from Lvov cannot be here before eight o'clock in the morning. We'll put you in one of the rooms of your house, Madam. And your husband will be next door to you. You will be happy to sleep one more night at home. Am I right?"

Alexander asked,

"Why cannot we stay together? My wife is pregnant, and she might need my help at night."

"Vassily, can count Kurbatov stay with his wife in one room?"

"I don't think that Madam will feel lonely at night. But if they want to be together, who could mind it?"

Maria heard again the sarcastic tone and leaned towards her husband. She was shaking. She turned to Alexander and whispered,

"Why do they do all this to you and me, Alex? Why do they scare us?"

Alexander suggested,

"We would like to sleep at nanny Ganja's house."

Maria added,

"She will give us something to eat tonight and tomorrow in the morning. It would be better for me to go there and to eat some fresh homemade food."

Both men were looking at her with great surprise. At that moment they were thinking alike,

"This countess is definitely too naïve and cannot or does not want to see the danger in her arrival."

Then the senior officer said firmly,

"You will stay in your house, Madam. We will feel better about you in your own house. No other alternatives."

The two scary men went back to the house, neighing loudly and clapping hands, like they were expecting something extremely funny.

"Alex, they are ugly. I am afraid of them."

Alexander answered,

"I am not fond of them either. The situation is not clear, mon amour."

"Alex, I do not feel safe here. I wish we were back in Germany. I know that those people have killed my father, yet they pretend that they are polite and care about us. Why didn't I listen to you, darling? Why did I put you and our child in danger? Why did the Lord allow me to challenge our life, peace, and happiness?"

Maria burst into tears.

Alexander tried to find the right words to calm her down.

"My angel, you worry too much. We do not have their citizenship, and they have no right to arrest us. We came here as citizens of France. Nevertheless, you are right, even in Germany we felt more secure. Listen, Marie, maybe the Soviet authorities have another understanding of ethics and diplomacy?"

At that moment Ganja brought their supper. Maria was so exhausted and hungry that she could not help waiting for food and rest. They sat at the porch table, eating bread and boiled potatoes. Ganja brought some goat's milk, and Alexander gave his portion of milk to his wife.

"Ganja, where is my Grandpa?"

"I do not know for sure, but people met him in the woods."

"Where did they take the boys? Is Jenny together with them? Do the boys have the opportunity to see and protect her?"

Maria wanted to know everything about her family.

"I do not think so, Pannochka Maria. They took the boys the next day after they killed your father. Jenny was with me for two more months."

"How did they kill Papa?"

It was so difficult for Maria to comprehend that the civilized people, who were sitting in her house, had killed Papa and could do the same to her husband and her.

Ganja made her conclusion, "They are here for torture and execution. They cannot live without it. People know everything about them: they arrest people, make their own stories and execute without true reason for it."

"Why did they kill Papa? What did poor Papa do to them?"

"Nobody knows. People said that doctor came to pick up his surgical instruments from the home office. They just pulled him out and shot on this porch. Later, I've heard that they had learned about German burgomaster that Dr. Kotyk successfully operated on and decided to kill him for it. You know, Pannochka

Maria, they killed many nice people. They killed our priest Bogdan and his sons in the church during an evening service. They insulted his daughter and beat his wife to death when she was trying to protect her daughter from being raped. The priest's wife passed away on the second day."

Ganja crossed herself and continued.

"They also murdered the mother of Pan (Mr. – Ukr.) Gachevsky. Do you remember the owner of the sugar factory? Thank God, both of his sons and he stayed in Czechoslovakia at that time. They left for Prague for the funeral of old Pan Gachevsky and never came back. Pannochka Maria, it is very bad that you are here, especially in your condition."

Ganja looked at Maria with love and pity. Maria sent old woman back home.

"Pray for us, Ganja. Pray for us, please!"

It was chilly outside, but Maria was afraid to step inside the house.

Maria could not get rid of that terrifying thought,

"They want to separate me from Alex. Why?"

Lord, have mercy! Lord, have mercy! Lord, have mercy!

Chapter 3

Alexander and Maria sat side by side on the porch. Both of them sensed danger, and they could not understand what scenario those people were writing for them. The Kurbatovs thought,

"We did not do any harm to anyone in this country. Well, they should not do any harm to us."

Maria was grateful to God that she did not mention in her papers her work at the Linden hospital during the war. Did she want to work there? Definitely not, but the life- threatening circumstances forced her to be there. If they knew, nobody would allow them to sit on the porch. By this time, they could execute her and her Alexander.

Maria tried to recollect a strange conversation of two high-rank officers in the train restaurant. After the WWII, Stalin instructed NKVD to consider people who were deported by Nazis for forceful labor in Germany and those who were captured and worked in German concentration or labor camps - traitors of Motherland USSR. NKVD was responsible for deporting those people from Germany directly to Siberia labor camps. Maria was sitting with her back to the officer that was making the explanation of a new instruction to another colonel. She overheard everything well. It was hard to believe in cruelty of a new law and that was why Alexander was sure that she misunderstood something.

"Alex, it was good that I told them just about my work at the farm and restaurant. These people would never understand the sternness of life circumstances. If they shot my father for saving the life of one Nazi officer, they would never forgive me my work at the military hospital."

Alexander did not answer her, listening to the noise on the road. The noise became louder and louder.

"It's a big truck there. Must be passing by…"

He intuitively hugged Maria. In this motion was all his desire to protect her and their son.

"I love you, Marie. It was my sin from the very beginning, that I love you more than anybody or anything in my life. Your strong desire to help your family made me weak."

Maria asked,

"Why do you think that it was your sin?"

Alexander explained.

"I forgot about our Lord, and He forgot about me. I was too happy during the last year. That's why we have arrived here and are staying among enemies."

Maria replied,

"People cannot be too happy, Alex."

Alexander sighed and continued.

"For the years of war, I was thinking of you all the time. I prayed to God, asking Him to keep you alive and out of danger. Then I found you and forgot about Him. I did not thank Him enough for seeing you every day, breathing in the smell of your hair, touching you, kissing you and just melting in you. I forgot to tell Him, how grateful I was for the child He was presenting us."

He kissed Maria's tiny hand and continued with his confession.

"I was watching you praying every night, and sometimes it irritated me that you talked to the Lord for so long and asked for forgiveness and mercy. I thought that we did not need any mercy after we had found each other. I thought it was not nice even to ask for mercy when we were blessed with love, health, jobs, and financial stability. Wrong! Now I understood it was wrong. People need to ask Him for mercy every single day of their lives because every day we think, feel, or do something wrong, accumulating the sins and challenging God's patience."

Maria interrupted her husband.

"Alex, my dear Alex, it was me, it's my fault that we came here. Olesya, my cousin from Poland, insisted in her letters that I'd rather stay away from this country. And the Schulenburgs as well wanted me to wait. Deportation is the least of unpleasant things that they can arrange for us."

The Kurbatovs kept silence for a while when they heard the noise of the truck again. It was nearer and nearer, and in a couple of minutes they could see the beam of lights on the road. Maria and Alexander stood up when the truck turned to the estate. The driver stopped the truck in front of the fountain. Six military men jumped out of the truck. They went in the direction of the house. Two ugly men went out to the porch to meet them.

"Cold?" asked the chief authority in his sarcastic tone.

He looked like an older demon, again with horrible shifts in his face.

"A little bit," answered Maria.

"They came here to warm you, Madam." Answered the younger officer and laughed in her face. Maria picked up a strong odor of alcohol and flinched from him.

The group of young military men came up to the porch. The assistant to the authority stopped laughing and turned to the group. He acted as a clown, and announced aloud in a theatrical manner,

"Let me introduce the owners of this estate, Madam Kurbatov and her husband Mousier Kurbatov, who came here to meet her father and to ask his permission for their marriage and making children."

"Why do you do this?" Alexander asked.

The face of the older demon shifted again, and he hissed in their faces,

"We have not done anything yet, but now we'll do everything, trust me."

He pulled Maria inside of the house so fast that Alexander did not have a single chance to stop him. She screamed in the hands of a monster and Alexander rushed inside. They stopped him in the entrance with a strong blow to his face. Alexander did not feel his pain; he heard Maria's piercing scream and shouted,

"Stop it! She is pregnant! She is six months pregnant."

Somebody laughed demonically on the second floor where two demons pulled Maria.

"People, we did not do any harm to you. I beg you; please do not touch my wife." Another blow was stronger that the first one and Alexander stopped hearing the voices. He fainted and tumbled down on his back, as a big, young, and beautiful oak-tree that was crashed with satanic tornado. They continued to beat him with their boots, smashing every part of his body and face with demonic force.

Nobody tracked how long they beat him. His blood was on all of chastisers, the walls, and furniture. When they got tired of beating Alexander, they turned him, hit him two times on his head, and went to the former dining room to rest. The squad leader said, catching his breath,

"It was good. We'll murder this way all the spies and terrorists, in order that the capitalists do not even try to send them here."

They were sitting in the living room that had its new name, Red Corner, where they exhibited the *historical* materials and photos on the walls about the heroism of the NKVD detachment - before, during, and after the war. The slogan on the top of the wall appealed "Be pitiless to the enemies of the soviet regime!" It was true - they were pitiless, and not only to the enemies.

The two demons that pulled Maria to the second floor came downstairs, giggling. The older one asked,

"What do you think we need to do with those French frog eaters? Maybe we'll finish them here and not even write the transcription of interrogation."

The younger monster agreed,

"Let us finish them and send them to the river to feed frogs. Let the frogs enjoy them. They have to be punished for all the frogs they have eaten in their lives."

Demonic spirits were flying in the old house. The demons arranged their meal, chewing like pigs. Then they were discussing the strength of vodka in the bottle. From time to time, the walls and window glass were shaken by their inhuman neighing.

Being barely conscious, Alexander moaned and called to Maria with a weak voice. He was lying in the middle of the entrance hall with his face in a pool of his own blood, breathing it in and out. Once he tried to open the eyes and fainted again. There was no power in the whole world that could come and save them from the demons.

The demons had finished their food and vodka. They had to do something with those people from the *other world.* At first, they examined their documents and diplomas. The interpreter was sent to Blue Creeks from Lvov, together with five soldiers to check and translate the documents of the *spies and terrorists.* He was the only officer who did not take part in the brutality. Capitan Novikov knew French and German and was a corps interpreter during the war. He was impressed that Alexander was born in France, graduated from Sorbonne as a surgeon, and spoke Russian fluently.

The older demon started to write the interrogation report. All the answers were written quickly, with the signs of supposed proof that Alexander Kurbatov was a dangerous enemy who arrived into the country on a serious spy and terrorist mission. He brought his assistant, a pregnant woman, for easier legalization, due to her Ukrainian origin. All the military men who were present in the room accepted the information without hesitation. Only the interpreter, who did not belong to the local committee asked questions,

"How did you find out that they are real spies? Where is the evidence that they are terrorists?"

Demonic neighing was the answer.

The report about Maria's mission was written even easier. She was the one who *confessed sincerely in their spy mission and terroristic plans* because she wanted to save the life of her future child. The younger demon said in his sarcastic voice,

"She was not very cooperative and a little bit skinny, but now we'll go upstairs again and sign the confession of committed crime or an attempt to commit the crime."

Lord, have mercy! Lord, have mercy! Lord, have mercy!

Chapter 4

Maria was sitting at the edge of her bed, crying bitterly and hugging her belly with both arms. She wrapped herself with a tablecloth. It was the only thing she found in a dresser. Those two demons tore off her dress and underwear, as they raped her.

Maria looked around the room. She was conceived in that bed. She was born in it nine months later. She slept in it from ten years of age since her mother left. And tonight: she was raped by two huge demons in her bedroom and in her bed. She found strength to go to the bathroom and to take a shower afterwards.

"I am a sinner,"

Maria thought.

"It's not because I was raped by those demons, but because I have killed my husband, and nobody knows what can happen to our child."

She felt the baby's motion again, as if he tried to calm his mother and to show her that he was alive.

"Why was I so stupid and stubborn? Why couldn't I listen to my husband? Why did the war and suffering not teach me to be careful with all my decisions? I survived through four years of war due to my cautious behavior. Why did I suddenly lose that intuition?"

Then she answered.

"The war was over, there was no martial law announced."

She stopped wiping her tears as they continued pouring, dripping on the tablecloth that covered her with her baby.

Maria's thoughts were interrupted by loud voices and footsteps of the monsters coming up. She jumped off the bed and stood near the window. They switched on the light. The older demon came up to her wearing a disgusting smile and pulled her hair.

"Oh, Madam, you took a shower in order that we can enjoy you better."

He turned to his group and asked

"Do you mind, if I am the first?"

Maria was about to faint. The man was pulling her to the bed. She begged him,

"No, please, do not touch me again."

The men around were neighing. She saw their eyes and understood that it was her end. But what about her baby?

"People, have mercy. Have mercy upon my baby! Oh, my God!"

Two other men threw her down on the bed and another two pulled her legs apart. The older demon leaned heavily on her body and she fainted. She regained consciousness when the other one turned her on her right side and tried to get in her anus. It was so painful that she screamed again. He did it, and after a couple of pushes, he jumped off.

"Look, what she did!"

Maria realized that something warm and sticky was coming out of her anus.

"It's blood. It is blood and shit. Look what she did!"

He hit her in her face, and Maria fainted again.

She did not see the moment he pressed the pistol to her belly. It was her child, who was moving all the time, disturbing the monster, and pushed him off. That's why he decided to turn her on the right side and to finish his lusty job from the back.

"Stop it! Stop it now! Do not put all of us in trouble. Clean yourself and leave her alone."

They did not even notice that the interpreter came up to the bedroom. The voice of the officer sounded firm enough and his pistol was ready, as well.

"Move, lieutenant, and follow my order fast."

Then he turned to the older demon and said,

"If you want to sign a document, go downstairs and do it now. Her husband is conscious at the moment."

In two minutes, a group of demons was around Alexander's body. The old demon handed a paper to sign. Alexander could not see anything there because he was not able to open his eyes. He knew that his signature could kill him and Maria. His thoughts were mixed up. He dropped the paper on the floor, pretending that he was unconscious again.

The older demon looked at the watch and made his demonic conclusion.

"We cannot wait until he signs. We'll sign."

He looked outside at the interpreter who was smoking on the porch.

"I do not want this intelligent interpreter to know how this German, French, or whatever resident signed the paper. He is too *loyal.* If I was in Germany during the war…" he tightened his fists.

At that moment he looked like a real demon with his fists tightened. He jumped to Alexander, stepped on his arm above the wrist, and pulled the right hand up with his demonic strength. Everyone in the room heard the sound of broken bones. Alexander groaned and fainted for real.

The demon grinned and said,

"Who is he? A surgeon? He'll fix it, I guess."

Then he took a report and signed *Count Alexander Kurbatov.*

"Who will doubt that it is not his original signature in Russian? He would never be able to sign in any language again his original signature with his hand broken."

The squad was silently watching their commander. One of the monsters asked,

"How could he sign if his hand was broken?"

The older demon had his explanation ready.

"He signed, tripped on the porch, and fell down. Poor man, he fractured his right hand."

The demonic neighing brought the interpreter in.

The older demon showed him the signed paper and asked to go upstairs and check whether the countess would *like* to sign the report about her mission. Capitan Novikov asked,

"Why should I go and persuade her to sign anything?"

The old demon answered,

"She is too fragile and shitty. I would ask you to go there."

The captain took the interrogation report and went upstairs. Maria was sitting again at the edge of the bed, covered with the tablecloth. The dirty soldier's blanket was removed from the bed. The window was opened to let the fresh air in, and she was washed again.

She jumped up from the bed and screamed in agony,

"Not again! My Lord, not again!"

Her Angel switched on her French.

"I beg you, officer, do not touch me again!"

He looked at her with pity and introduced himself,

"Captain Novikov, the interpreter."

Then he answered Maria in French,

"I am here not to touch you, Madam Kurbatova. I want you to sign this document. Your husband has already signed. Now, it's your turn."

The officer allowed her a minute. She read *her* answers in the interrogation report and realized that she was signing her death sentence.

"Thank you, Lord!" Maria blessed herself with the cross. She smiled at her thought and pronounced out load,

"It is more merciful to be executed than tortured, as they tortured me at night."

Then she turned slowly to the officer and asked,

"Will you execute us now? Can I see my husband before the execution?"

The interpreter did not have an answer for her. Then she looked frightened again.

"Is my husband alive?"

She started to cry.

"I killed him, I know. It was me who wanted to go home after the war. I wanted to see my family. I missed my Papa, my old grandpa, my brothers, and my little sister Jenny. It is terrible, what I did. Please, let me see my husband before the execution: I must ask him to forgive me."

Maria burst into sobbing.

The officer was a little bit confused.

"Where is your home, Madam Kurbatova?"

He looked at Maria and continued asking,

"This particular estate and house were your family home, wasn't it? You belong to Dr. Kotyk's family, don't you? You must be his daughter, am I right?"

Maria just nodded her agreement.

Captain Novikov continued asking.

"Did you give them yesterday the answers that you are supposed to sign today?"

Maria shook her head,

"Nobody asked. But what's the difference now?"

She signed the document. The puzzle was completed.

The interpreter turned to leave. Then he stopped at the doorway and asked: "Where are your clothes?"

Maria looked at him and answered,

"They tore off my clothes and destroyed them yesterday. We have our suitcases somewhere on the first floor, maybe in the room where Alexander is now. Brown is mine."

The interpreter saluted, turned around and left. Maria thought,

"It is strange, but he does not look like a demon. Maybe not all of them are demonic. But who cares now about the difference?"

She looked out of the window: it was sunrise. Maria thought,

"Today is October 2, 1946. The demonic night is over. God sent us a new day, probably the last day in our lives."

Lord, have mercy!

Chapter 5

Captain Novikov did not like from the very beginning the tale about those *spies* and *terrorists*. When he collected all the pieces of the puzzle, the picture looked absolutely ugly.

"Poor lady, she does not even know that her husband was beaten mercelessly and for the whole night lay unconscious on the floor near the entrance door."

Novikov, personally, did not believe that the Kurbatovs were spies and terrorists.

"I have to talk to somebody in Lvov. There is something wrong. The local committee of internal affairs seems to have allowed itself too much."

He brought the suitcase upstairs and put it on the bed. Maria thanked him and asked him to stay in her room until she was dressed.

"I am afraid that they can come again."

She could barely move. He watched her open the suitcase. She was very, and her hands shook. The interpreter helped her with the locks. Maria opened the case and started to take out the clothing. She was talking to herself.

"Everything is jammed and wrinkled. I did not have the chance to take it out and to hang it in the wardrobe."

Maria tried to look up at the officer but could not do it. Her head spun around and she felt nauseous again.

She rushed to the bathroom and vomited. When she was back, she looked a little bit better. She chose the clothes and went to the bathroom again. She was there for quite some time, and the officer was not sure whether she was well or not. He knocked on the door, and Maria opened it immediately.

The lady looked absolutely different in her clothing. She had an elegant burgundy cashmere dress on and a pair of beautiful black, low heel shoes. The child was moving all the time under her dress. She put her hand on her belly, as she wanted to calm down the baby's motions. Her hair was well done and if not for her bluish paleness and a big purple bruise on the left cheekbone, she could be considered a very beautiful lady.

Maria said,

"I want to die in this dress. Maybe you can allow my sister's nanny to bury me in it. They can put us together in one grave: my husband and me with our baby. I am sure that we'll be always together - here and there."

She spoke calmly about death, as she would talk about a book she recently finished reading or a movie she saw last week.

Being an interpreter during the war, Captain Novikov saw commanders who were not ready to die. That's why he watched the tiny woman with amazement and respect. He thought,

"How is it possible at her age to be ready to die?"

Maria read his mind and answered,

"People are afraid to die when they are sinners. My worst sin was to bring my husband and future son to this Godforsaken country. I hope I have paid for my sin this night."

The officer looked at the delicate lady with admiration.

"She does not pretend. She has zero fear of death. She is talking about her own death at age 27, without agony. She believes that God will take care of her and her family. She is a strange woman, more exactly – an unearthly woman."

Maria concluded,

"It is better to die than to go through all this again."

Maria could not walk downstairs by herself. She was too dizzy and weak. It was good that the demons were on the porch, smoking. The translator helped her, holding her under the arm and bringing her suitcase to the first floor.

When Maria was downstairs, captain Novikov opened the door to the vestibule area and Maria stopped frozen, as she saw the body of her husband there. She kneeled near her husband and burst into tears.

"Dear Lord, what have they done? Alex, what have they done to you?"

It looked like Maria did not have enough air to breathe. She leaned over her husband's body and, even through the strong flow of her tears, the poor woman saw clearly what her husband had gone through. The man on the floor was mutilated so much that Captain Novikov could hardly recognize the gentleman he met yesterday. The interpreter felt guilty in a way and left.

Maria was examining her husband's body. Everything was swollen. There was no more her handsome husband. The appearance of the man was severely mutilated. They broke all his teeth and the lips were bruised and torn. The nose was fractured and twisted to the right so much that it nearly touched the cheek. His ear, nose, and left eye were still bleeding. The blood glued the eyelashes and the swelling of the face was enormous. It looked like the skin was ready to burst any moment.

Maria cried bitterly, touching the face of her husband. She gently unbuttoned his mackintosh, jacket and vest. Then she untied his favorite tie with blue and gray strips and palpated the chest. Two right side ribs were fractured and moved with terrible cracking sound under her light touches. Alexander was unconscious, however Maria's touch triggered cough, bubbling and suffocation. She saw how he suffered, trying to catch his breath. The symptomatic picture clearly manifested serious damage of his lungs. Maria suspected that the lung tissues were inflamed and accumulated a lot of fluid.

Maria examined Alexander's arms and found the right wrist fractured and misaligned upward. She did not find visual fractures of the legs, but it was difficult to make the exact conclusions with the concise examination. The position of the whole body was abnormal, and her conjecture was that Alexander's spinal column was also injured. The results of her short and snappy evaluation made Maria desperate. For her, as a physician, it was absolutely clear– her beloved Alexander was dying.

Maria could not keep quiet. She began sobbing loudly, and the NKVD bandits on the porch were neighing, listening to the cry and praying of the misfortunate woman. Maria repeated constantly,

"O, God, be merciful to us, sinners. O Lord Jesus Christ, Son of God, for the sake of the prayers of Thy most pure Mother and all the saints, have mercy on us. Amen."

The chief deputy of the local NKVD "commented" Maria's praying with sarcastic and dirty jokes,

"Listen, guys, listen to her bleating. She asks God to save them. Nobody can save you, stupid bitch. We'll finish with you today. Do not waste your breath. For you, shitty bitch there is no mercy. You do not know, how to behave with the officers. We'll disembowel you and pull out your noble offspring."

Maria heard that the interpreter Novikov interrupted his tirade,

"Why do you need this clown show? Didn't they have enough?"

It was silence for a while, and then the chief demon ordered,

"Shut up! Take Kurbatovs to the servants' lodge."

Maria saw that nobody moved, and the older demon shouted,

"Are you deaf?! Clean the office from that noble trash! Do not forget to wash the walls and floors of his blood."

Maria saw how the group of military men moved into the vestibule. They surrounded the Kurbatovs, and the chief deputy hit Alexander's shoulder with his dirty boot. Alexander did not pronounce a sound. Maria looked at the rapacious faces of the tortures and recollected the words of nanny Ganja. She was right when mentioned that the nature of these species was not human. They represented satanic tools for interrogations, racking, torturing and extirpating the innocent people. They were born without souls or lost them, and the absence of God's essence made them atrocious and disgusting.

Maria sat on the floor near Alexander, waiting for her destiny. The deputy pulled her up by the hair, and the woman got up. He looked at her and said,

"Go on praying, bitch. Or maybe, countess, your god had made you smarter today, and you do not mind to continue f… with all of us?"

Maria did not want to look at him. Then he squeezed her face with his demonic strength, and the tears poured out of her eyes. He hit Alexander again with his heavy boot and looking in Maria's eyes continued,

"Look, Madam, you would never have this enjoyment with this corpse. Yesterday, we beat off all his desires. He made just one child, and we'll make you a lot. So, be smart and stop crying."

The Major and Captain Novikov entered the vestibule. Major looked at his deputy and shouted again,

"What did I order to do? Throw away this noble slut. Do not forget to throw her ugly husband from the NKVD office, as well. Wash the office! Move fast!"

They grabbed poor Alexander, pulled him to the servants' lodge and threw on the dirty bed. Maria saw that nobody cleaned the lodge or washed the linens for a long time, maybe starting from the time of soviet occupation. The interpreter Novikov brought both suitcases and Maria's purse. When Captain Novikov was about to leave, he stopped in the doorway and recommended,

"Keep the door locked at all times. Good luck."

Ganja was kind and came soon with full basket of healing herbs, goat milk, bread and some food. The Lord brought Maria to the window exactly at the moment when Ganja was approaching the main house. Maria opened the door and called her. Ganja entered the lodge, and Maria burst into tears. She wanted to tell her about everything that happened to them: disgrace, humiliation and destruction that Alexander and she underwent at night. Ganja tried to calm Maria down, but the young woman was inconsolable. Ganja was sitting for an hour near Maria, stroking her hair and telling her,

"Pannochka Maria, I was there early in the morning and saw Pan Alexander on the floor of the vestibule. That's why I have brought different herbs with me. We'll heal him. But now I want you to eat."

"No, Ganja. I don't want to eat. I feel nauseous all the time."

Ganja brought two buckets of water from the well and made some herbal tea. Maria was drinking tea and cried non-stop.

"Ganja, what will the monsters do to us? If I knew what to expect, I …"

"Only God knows what is going to be with all of us. You need to pray, and the Savior finds the resolution of the situation. Pray, Pannochka Maria. Crying without praying will never help. *Help us, save us, have mercy on us, and keep us, o Lord by Thy grace."*

Maria could not stand the dirt in the lodge, and it was dangerous to keep Alexander with his wounds in such unhealthy living conditions. Both women decided to change the bed linens and wash the floors in the lodge. Ganja left to bring her sheets and towels. They needed three beds to be ready by nighttime, because Ganja decided to stay with the young couple. And one extra bed they wanted to prepare for Alexander in case they made his bed wet after washing and soaking procedures.

While Ganja went home, Maria took her Prayer Book and started to pray,

"Save, O Lord, and have mercy on my husband and me and all those in sickness and sorrow, misfortune and tribulation, in difficult circumstances and in captivity, in prisons and dungeons and especially those of Thy servants that are persecuted by godless people, by apostates and by heretics; and remember us, visit, strengthen, comfort, and by Thy power quickly grant us relief, freedom, and deliverance."

On that day, Maria was not able to stand and bow down, so she was sitting near her husband and praying,

"Save, O Lord, and have mercy on them that hate and wrong us, and make temptation for us, and let them not perish because of us, sinners, but teach them righteousness in the way Thee can."

When Ganja returned, the women did the beds first. Maria could not move a lot and helped Ganja with Alexander's bed only. She did it professionally quickly, but any motion deteriorated his pain. Alexander groaned and bled more. Ganja washed the floors, covered one end of the long dining table with clean linen tablecloth with her beautiful embroidery and insisted in Maria having lunch.

"I can understand, Pannochka Maria that after everything that had happened to you, you've lost your appetite. You know better than me, your baby is disturbed and hungry. Look at you, Pannochka: you are so pale and weak. Please, sit and eat some cheese or potatoes. Drink some herbal tea. Later, we'll wash Pan Alexander and you need strength to do it."

By the dusk, Ganja suggested to start washing Alexander and soaking his wounds with the herbal remedies that she prepared in the stove after cooking dinner. She stayed with the young couple over the night. Alexander was still unconscious and talked deliriously. The fever was high, and his lips were constantly dry. His condition reminded Maria her own pain and fever after being tortured at the concentration camp. She was so grateful to Polish women who took a risk, brought her to their barrack and saved her. She was healed by Holy Spirit without medications and food.

By 3 a.m. Alexander fell asleep, but his difficult breathing wheezing and cough were Maria's biggest concern. She was not able to fall sleep. Every time she closed her eyes, she saw the ugly demonic faces of her abusers. Maria was cried and prayed nonstop, as she did it in the German concentration camp after unmerciful beatings of her. By the morning, the light appeared in their room and penetrated their bodies. She experienced warmth inside. That was the moment when she closed her eyes, praised the Lord and asked for forgiveness,

"Thank You, my Lord, for Your Holy light and warmth! Please, forgive my obsessive desire to come home, my constant complaints, non-equitable accusations, and inadequate cherishing of my happy life with Alexander. I repent for my stubborn insistence on our arrival to Ukraine, a country that is absolutely unrecognizable to me. Forgive me that I did not listen to my husband, my cousin from Poland and the Schulenburgs. Forgive me for exposing my family to danger, disgrace and suffering."

A new wave of light covered Maria. The light spread evenly all over the room. Maria again sensed the presence of her Guardian Angel, and she was afraid to move in order not to interrupt her connection with the Divinity. She whispered,

"Thank You, My Lord. I was not blessed for it for a long time and now, I can talk to my Angel again, as I used to do when I was at the Nazi camp or during my endless shifts in Linden Hospital. My Guardian Angel, please help Alexander to survive. Help me heal his wounds, fractures and sores. Please, do not leave me again without your Holy guidance and support. Ask Mother of God to protect our baby from the evil forces. *Help us, save us, have mercy on us, and keep us, O God by Thy grace.*"

Maria enjoyed the pleasant warmth in her sorrowful soul and anguished body. The Holy Spirit cleansed her, calmed her down and put her to sleep.

Glory to Thee, o Lord! Glory to Thee!

Chapter 6

It was the third day of their imprisonment, and the morning was unusually quiet. Ganja left early to milk her goats and bring more herbs for Alexander. She promised to cook something delicious for Maria; the mother-to-be could not wait for her food. Maria was not surprised with her fast recovery; the Holy Spirit restored her strength, appetite and inner spirit.

"For two days, I felt that I came close to passing away, and today, I feel strong enough to walk and to do something. My appetite is better than it was in Germany: I want to eat all the time. Thank You, Lord, for Thy miraculous healing. I am grateful to Thee for the restoration of the connection with the Divinity which I lost in vain of my postwar life. Glory to Thee, my Lord! Glory to Thee!"

Maria noticed that Alexander moved in his bed. The excruciating pain in his fractured hand woke him up. The pain was unbearable, and he moaned. Maria rushed to him and kneeled at his bed.

"Alex, can you hear me?"

He responded in a very weak and low voice,

"Yes."

Maria started to kiss his face.

"Alex, can you open your eyes? Look at me. Can you see me?"

The tears ran down her cheeks and dripped on Alexander's face. Maria continued talking to her husband, begging him to open his eyes, but he did not answer. He fell asleep again.

Maria's biggest concern was connected with his eyes and lungs. The swelling of the face had gone down a little bit more, and she could see that he had lost one eye.

Maria prayed,

"O Holy Father, Physician of souls and bodies, Who sent Your Only-begotten Son, our Lord Jesus Christ, to heal every sickness and to deliver from death: Heal your servant Alexander from the infirmities of body and soul which possess him and enliven him through the grace of Your Christ, through the prayers of our Most-holy Sovereign Lady Theotokos and Ever-virgin Mary, by the protection of the honorable and bodiless powers of the heaven... For You are the Fountain of healing, O our God, and to You we ascribe glory, together with your Only-begotten Son, and Your Holy Spirit, One in Essence, now and ever and unto ages of ages. Amen."

Ganja was back with "treats" and Maria told her about Alexander's awakening and pains. Maria shared her concerns with Ganja,

"Ganja, Alexander could hear me, but he could not open his eyes."

"It will take time, Pannochka Marie. The Lord will heal him. He is young, and with God's help, he will be all right."

Ganja took a piece of bread, poured a cup of milk and put these foods in front of Maria. The milk was very fresh. It was unusually tasty with the homemade bread. Then Ganja started the fire in the stove and began the simultaneous preparation of herbal remedies for Alexander and dinner for Maria. Ganja moved swiftly near a big stove, constantly repeating her favorite prayer,

"O Lord Jesus Christ, Son of God, for the sake of the prayers of Thy most pure Mother and all the Saints, have mercy on us. Amen."

Alexander again moved in his bed, and Maria sat next to him, asking,

"Are you hungry, mon amour?"

He answered,

"I am thirsty; give me some water, please."

His broken teeth and injured jaw impaired his speech. Both women were standing over Alexander's bed, looking at him with compassion. He tried to open his eyes and was unable to do so.

"Marie, I cannot see you. Why? Why cannot I open my eyes?"

Now there was an empty socket instead of the left eye. The right eye was not opened because of the swelling.

He asked repetitively:

"Why cannot I see you, mon amour?"

She lied, "Your eyes are still swollen, darling."

He tried to open his eyes wider.

"Everything is blurry," he said.

Ganja brought Alexander some water to drink and Maria lifted his head. He could not swallow it. He kept it in his mouth for a while until it began to leak out.

"I forgot how to drink, Marie." Alexander complained.

Maria put the cup on the table and turned to the window. Her eyes were full of tears. She realized that there was something wrong with Alexander's brain. Besides his eyes, which were obviously injured, there was a severe concussion or some other brain injury. The poor young lady could not imagine what those monsters did to her beloved husband. She came up to him again.

"Alex, Ganja has made some herbal remedies. I'll put the compresses on your face and body."

Alexander asked,

"What did they do to me? I cannot move or breathe."

He tried to move his right hand and screamed.

"Sorry, my dear, it's my wrist. What did they do to my wrist, the right one? It hurts terribly. I can't move it."

Maria examined it again and noticed that the swelling was not decreased in comparison to the previous day. What was obvious that the bones were misaligned and needed a professional alignment.

Maria shared her findings with Alexander. Alexander made the practical conclusion and asked Ganja,

"Do you know any bone specialist in the area who could come and fix the fractures without surgical intrusion?"

"Yes, I do, Pan Alexander. I know one good bone-setter who lives not far from here. I shall finish with cooking and go there. If she is at home, I'll bring her in the evening."

Alexander addressed the following questions to Maria in French:

"Marie, how are you? What did the monsters do to you?"

The delicate, beautiful lady looked at her unmercifully beaten husband with tears in her eyes and answered in Russian,

"They punched my cheek, and it is bruised; it's purple now."

Ganja looked at Maria and was pleased with her compassion toward Alexander. She had known her Pannochka since Maria was born and had never heard her telling untruths. But that was a white lie, and nobody, even God, could blame Maria for it. Alexander had enough suffering, and the knowledge that his beloved wife had been disgraced would greatly empower the suffering of her mutilated husband.

Maria tried to give Alexander some water again. This time, he successfully swallowed it. He drank from a teaspoon, like a baby. Alexander stretched out his left arm and touched Maria's belly. The baby had been quiet for the entire morning, but with his father's touch, started active moving, proving his existence to his father and expressing his happiness at having both of his parents around. Alexander smiled with his new distorted and ugly smile of a person with torn lips, fractured nose, empty eye and swelling of the face and ears. He whispered,

"I love you, Marie," and fell asleep again.

After lunch, Ganja left for the neighbor village to bring the bone-setter. She was not successful that time and returned alone.

"I was sorry, but bone-setter was not at home. Somebody took her to their place to help. We have to wait until tomorrow."

"Do we have any choice, Ganja? We'll wait. Did you leave the message for her?" Maria asked.

"Yes, I did. Her daughter-in-law promised to ask her to wait for me until I take her tomorrow. I mentioned that we have an urgent case."

"Good, Ganja. You did everything right. Thank you, dear."

Maria came up to Ganja and embraced the shoulders of the elderly woman. The tears filled Maria's eyes and were ready to pour.

"Ganja, why did this happen to me, to us?" the young woman asked.

"Only God knows, Pannochka. I want to feed you. Did you like barley soup we had for lunch? There is some more left."

"I'll eat it with pleasure."

They had their dinner and drank some herbal tea. Ganja was always a wonderful tea maker. She combined different herbs and her teas had pleasant aromas and taste.

After dinner they prayed together and read Akathists and Psalms. Maria changed the compresses with herbal remedies on her husband's face and body. Alexander tried to pray with women, but weakness put him asleep in the middle of a prayer. When Maria went to bed, she asked the Holy Spirit to heal her husband and prayed to Ever-virgin Mary to protect them from new attacks of the demons.

On the 4th of October, something happened in the area, and the NKVD detachment disappeared in their truck around 6 a.m. It was quiet at the estate after the monsters left. The women had washed Alexander, soaked him in herbs and changed his bed. They had their breakfast together. Ganja again brought fresh goat milk, chicken eggs and bread. Immediately after breakfast Alexander fell asleep. Ganja left to bring the bone-setter, and Maria washed the towels that they used for herbal applications and the sheets and pillowcases from Alexander's bed. She hung them to dry on the fence behind the servants' lodge.

Maria stood there for some time. The day was warm, and the sun was so pleasant that she flew back to her childhood. The children were allowed to be everywhere around the mansion. Her father did not want them to walk only along the alley, lined with linden trees or to run around the huge and magnificent fountain, being accompanied by nannies or governesses. He liked when they freely played their childish games and enjoyed the different weather. Only during freezing rains, the children were not permitted to go outside.

They enjoyed playing outside when it snowed. Sometimes they had to change their clothes several times per day, wearing two or three pairs of boots or fur coats and hats, as well as multiple pairs of muttons or gloves during one snowy day. Yet, how those small inconveniences be compared with their enjoyment?

The feeling of childhood was so vivid that it seemed to Maria that she could walk out of her hiding place and meet Papa with her brothers. When Maria was on her way back to the lodge, she noticed the NKVD truck, entering the gates of the estate. Maria rushed back to her hiding place behind the servants' lodge. She could see everything from there.

The truck drove up close to the main house. Two soldiers opened the back board of the truck and jumped onto the ground. Then somebody pushed out three men and a woman out of the truck. Their hands were tied with wires, and one of the men fell. Two other conveyers jumped after him onto the ground.

The older demon sat in the cab of the truck. He opened the door of the cab and shouted: "To the basement." The person-on-duty wanted to report him or inquire about something, but the demon pushed him back with both hands, jumped up to the woman and pulled the misfortunate one with the same strength, as he did it to Maria several days ago. Maria ran to the lodge, crying and praying: *"Help us, save us, have mercy on us, and keep us, o God, by Thy grace. Lord, have mercy! Lord, have mercy! Lord, have mercy!"*

Maria shook with fear. She heard the scream of the young woman from the room on the second floor of the main house. Maria felt nauseated and experienced sharp pain in her stomach. The door to the balcony of the bedroom was opened, and Maria heard how the poor woman begged them to let her go. She promised to tell all the truth that she knew about the officer and soldiers of General Vlasov's army, the captivity of their army, their imprisonment in the labor camp and escape from it. She tried to prove her innocence, saying,

"We did not do anything bad to you, people. I am from Belorussia, Edwin is from Lithuania and Vassily and Gregory are from Russia. It took long time for us to get here. We did not have food for days, while wondering in the forests. Three days ago, we were happy to reach the house of an old Ukrainian woman who let us in. She shared her food with us and found some cloths in order we can wash ourselves and change the torn clothing for the clean. We were glad to have rest after so many days of running away. Then you arrived and arrested us. You saw that we were not hiding; we wanted to stay for two-three more days there and to move forward to our homes. Why did you kill the hostess of the house? She was kind to us."

"Did I ask you, Nazi slut, about the hostess, food or rest? How did you cross the border? Who helped you? How come that the Ukrainian Nationalists did not kill you, Russian speaking people, in the woods? You must be their spies, or German spies and that was why you were not torn between two trees. How dare you come to the country that you betrayed?"

Maria had heard that he hit the woman and the woman screamed again:

"I did not betray anybody or anything. Please, trust me! I was a nurse assistant. Vassily was Lieutenant and Edwin and Gregory were soldiers. Nobody wanted us to betray anyone or anything. They did not want us to do anything against this country."

"Then why are you here?" shouted the demon. "I ask you, bitch, why are you here?"

"I don't know! We were returning home. You came and arrested us."

"Can you hear the voice of this innocent baby?" the demon asked sarcastically.

The squad answered with satanic neighing.

None of the tormentors paid attention to the screams of the young woman and her persistent complains:

"It hurts, stop it, please. I cannot stand it, it hurts."

The tortures on the second floor were lasting for two hours or so. For the last have an hour Maria heard just one monotonous word: "No, no, no..."

Maria was happy that her husband was asleep and did not hear anything. She could not move from the window; she just stood there, crying and praying for the poor people that the demons brought on that day:

"Help them, save them, have mercy on them, and keep them, O God, by Thy grace. Lord, have mercy. Lord, have mercy. Lord, have mercy."

Then the screams on the second floor stopped. All of a sudden, Maria heard the steps of several people, coming closer and closer to their lodge. Maria prepared an axe and stood behind the door. She blessed herself,

"Dear Lord, forgive me my sin. As a doctor, I was saving lives of people. I am not a killer but now, I have to protect my husband and myself from these demons."

Alexander moved in his bed and asked,

"Marie, darling, what did you say?"

"It's nothing, mon cher. Have some rest. Ganja is going to be here any minute, and we shall have our meal."

Next moment, she heard the voices of two women, one of which belonged to Ganja. Maria put the axe behind the curtain and opened the door. Ganja stepped in, and this time, was accompanied by another woman.

A new guest greeted Maria with the traditional Ukrainian greeting and introduced herself,

"Glory to Jesus! I am Pani Melina Bondar."

"Glory forever! It's nice to meet you, Pani Bondar," Maria replied and introduced herself,

"I am Maria Kurbatov."

"Ganja asked me to help your husband with bone alignments," continued Pani Bondar.

"Pani Melina is good with bones," Ganja confirmed.

They came up to Alexander's bed and found him sleeping again. After the tortures at the main house, he could hardly eat and was constantly exhausted. The bone-setter came up to Alexander, put his fractured arm on his chest and started to examine the injured area with her long, thin fingers. Maria watched her light and professional touches.

The woman turned to Maria and declared with deep sympathy in her voice,

"I am sorry, but he has fractures of both large bones above the wrist and joint misalignment. The worst thing is that one of the large bones, closer to the wrist joint, has been fractured with two chips. I can try to put them together, but I am not sure that his hand will heal fast and work as it did before."

Maria assisted the bone-setter. She smiled bitterly to herself, thinking, "I am destined to be an assistant forever."

It was her dream to assist Alexander in his future surgical work. She ruined that dream. Maria thought, "Nobody else could be blamed for it, except me. The demons did not come to our place in Germany or France. It was me who brought my husband to these tormentors, and it was me who ruined our lives and dreams."

Maria heard how the bone-setter moved something in Alexander's wrist, and he awoke from unbearable pain.

"Marie, are you there? What are you doing?" he asked.

She felt sorry for his pain and inability to see anything.

Maria replied,

"Alex, we have a bone-setter here. Pani Bondar is fixing the bones in your wrist. It won't last long. Please, be patient, darling."

It took some time for the healer to put the bones in the right position. Then she secured the wrist tightly between two wooden splints. Maria was surprised at how fast the talented woman defined the fracture through the swelling and set the bones in the right position. After the wrist and hand bones were aligned, Alex's hand was no longer turned 35 degrees upward with the rotation or turn to the right. Due to restored circulation, his hand became less purple in five minutes.

"It could be painful tonight, Pannochka Maria, but in a couple of days, he'll find that it feels much better," promised the gifted bone-setter.

"Do I need to do anything with his arm?" Maria asked.

"When the swelling is gone, he can start finger movements, and in three weeks, let him take the splints off for some time and exercise his hand. He should not lose his hand motions."

Pani Bondar examined Alexander's face. She saw better, than anyone else, what tormentors had done to a young man.

"Now let me see what we can do with the nose," the bone-setter said.

She examined Alexander's nose. The cartilage was crashed into pieces, and there was no way to fix it completely. She did what she could. It did not look a hundred percent straight, but the tip of the nose did not touch Alex's cheek anymore. Maria learned what an important part the nose plays in a person's appearance.

The bone-setter removed the ugliness of Alexander's face in fifteen minutes. Then she mentioned,

"His left cheek bone is fractured, as well. The blow of the boot was enormous. The cheek bones are strong, but the left one is chipped off. It is no wonder that he lost his eye. They are barbarians."

Then she looked at Maria and said,

"I know your father very well. Sometimes, he calls me to do this work, especially on children. Everyone misses his clinic. I have not seen another doctor who is as good in medicine, as he is."

"Thank you," Maria whispered.

Maria was pleased with high opinion of this extraordinary woman about her father. Her painful emotions exploded. She was unable to hide them deeply inside.

"I miss him, too. He was everything to me: a father, a mother, a doctor, a teacher and a very close friend. They shot him and did not even bury him. They told me that they threw him down in the ditch behind the garden, and somebody buried my father three days later near the old apple tree—his favorite one." Maria burst into tears.

The healer looked at Ganja inquiringly and asked,

"What does it mean?"

The old woman did not know what to answer. Maria caught the healer's glance at Ganja and clarified,

"It was you, Ganja, who buried my father. Am I right?"

"No, it wasn't me, Pannochka Maria. I did not bury him."

Maria was eager to find the answer, and she felt that these women knew it. Maria could not understand what kind of secret was behind the whole story with her poor Papa.

"Then who did it? Please, tell me the truth what happened to my father."

The healer looked at Maria with pity and said,

"As far as I know, he is alive, Pannochka Maria. He is in woods with those Ukrainians, who do their best to liberate us from Nazis and godless moscals (people sent by Moscow). We hated both invaders of our mother Ukraine. Moskals are not easier than Nazis. They killed my son in 1941, before the war started. They atrociously mock our people. They shot your father but, thank God, did not kill him. The NKVD banded shot into your father's big cross under the shirt, so everyone knew that the Lord saved the life of Dr. Kotyk. Now, your father is in the woods, saving the lives of wounded patriots."

Maria exclaimed,

"Is he alive?"

The news was too stunning for a weak Maria, and she fainted. Soon after, she heard the arguing of women in the lodge, but she was not able to open her eyes.

Ganja railed at Pani Bondar,

"It was better for her not to know anything in detail. She cannot meet or help him. Nobody knows what the demons are planning to do with them in a day or two. Look, Pan Alexander is so weak."

The healer had an opposite opinion:

"It is better for a daughter to learn that her wonderful father is alive, and he is our hero. You told me that she arrived here to take him to France. She is a good, considerate daughter. Why shouldn't she learn the truth about her wonderful father?"

Ganja attacked,

"Tell me this, can they meet or help each other? In a day or two, the young couple will be deported to Siberia, and it's better for Pannochka to think about herself and her future child. At the moment, everything else should not be of her concern. Look at her - it's too much for this delicate lady."

When Maria opened her eyes, both women were sitting on the bench across the room, watching her. When she opened the eyes, they jumped up and approached her bed quickly, holding a glass of cold water ready.

"Where is my Papa? Ganja, you said that they would deport us to Siberia. I want to see my father, hug and ask him to wait until we are back," Maria said in a weak voice.

"It's impossible, Pannochka. It's dangerous for all three of you." Ganja said.

The healer added with a smile, touching gently Maria's belly,

"It's dangerous for four of you, actually. Dr. Kotyk is in the woods. Our guys took him there. They guard very well him and the old Count."

Maria whispered,

"Who took my father there? Please, tell me!"

Pani Bondar answered with a smile,

"I don't think that you know them, Pannochka Maria. They worked for your father for only one season in fall of 1938. My son worked with them, and I met them later in the woods. They used to be the seasonal workers in our area, and I doubt that you have met them before. One of them found Dr. Kotyk alive in the ditch. Around 6 o'clock in the evening, they brought some vodka, home-made sausages, bread and salt to new NKVD authorities. While the demons were celebrating "welcome party", our fellows buried a huge log near the apple tree and put the cross there without anybody's name and dates."

Ganja added,

"Your father was taken to the woods, where your grandpa extracted a bullet together with a piece of a gold cross from Dr. Kotyk's chest and healed him. I saw him yesterday: he is fine. The herbs that I brought to Pan Alexander came from your grandpa's storage."

"Did you tell him about Alexander and me?"

"No, Pannochka. I was not sure that you wanted me to bring him such news. He is still in hiding and cannot come to help you. He cannot 'arise' from the dead and assist your husband and you in this situation. We pray the moscals will one day leave with their satanic communist ideas, and hundreds of Ukrainian people will return home from the woods."

"You are right. But he is arisen. What a miracle! Thank You, Lord for saving the life of my Papa!"

She sat in bed and looked with gratitude at both women who were devoted servants of God and people.

The bone-setter Pani Bondar said with a deep sympathy in her voice,

"I feel sorry, Pannochka Marie for everything those demons did to you and your husband. I will pray for you. I wish God bless you and your family with all the best."

Maria wanted to pay for her work. The woman refused to accept it, saying,

"I did this for your father. He was always good to me."

Glory to Thee, o Lord! Glory to Thee!

Chapter 7

Ganja cooked Ukrainian vegetable borscht for dinner, while Maria told her the horrible story about the woman on the second floor of the main house. Maria tried not to wake up her husband with loud sobbing, but she could not bring herself to come down. Poor woman repeated the same words,

"Ganja, how can they torture innocent people so easily? How can it be possible for a human being to become so coldhearted? The cruelty, brutality and mercilessness of those people are beyond all the borders of humanity."

"I have told you before, Pannochka Maria that they are not people, because they were not born from the regular women and were not created by God. Their seeds were planted by a demonic creature. *Dear God, be merciful to us, sinners.*"

Maria confessed,

"Ganja, today I was ready to kill the demon or his monsters, if they decided to come here."

Ganja exclaimed,

"Poor you! *Lord, have mercy*! Stop crying, Pannochka. You disturb your baby. The child had enough. Pray and try to forget everything that has happened to you. The child should not grow in outrage and hatred. If you feed him with these feelings now, he will grow on them and would never understand patience, forgiveness and kindness. Protect your child, Pannochka Maria."

Alexander woke up, and Maria was immediately near him. She could not keep silent and shared the wonderful news about her father.

Alexander answered, "I am happy to hear this, darling. The Lord was merciful to your father, and a miracle happened. I hope the Lord will save us too, and in future, your Papa will enjoy his grandson."

Alexander hugged his wife with his left arm and asked for her help,

"Marie, I am so tired of lying in bed for many days, and maybe, my headaches will be gone, if I sit for some time. Will you help me to sit up in bed?"

Staying in bed for several days was very unusual for Alexander who used to live an active life. Maria was happy to hear his request. She helped her husband with pleasure, but to their mutual apprehension, Alexander was unable to sit even for a couple of minutes. He became dizzy and nauseous immediately. The symptomatic picture proved that there was severe concussion. Some other symptoms frightened him: the sharp, shooting pain in his spine, and the enormous pressure in his head and the right eye. Alexander was very much distressed. He did not want to show Maria his disappointment, but the way he felt scared him a lot. Alexander asked,

"I think, it is good enough for the first time, mon amour. Let me lie down. Will you help me, darling?"

Maria noticed that every motion caused unbearable pain for her husband, but she did not know that the only parts of his body where he did not have pain were his feet – Alexander did not feel them at all.

"Marie, I feel like I have a pretty bad concussion, and there is something wrong with my legs, I cannot pull or push them. I feel pain in the spine but cannot move them. What do you think is wrong there? Is it my concussion or, God forbid, spine injury? Did I have any spine injury, Marie? When you washed me this morning, did you see any bruising or swelling on my back?"

Maria could not see Alexander clearly, because her eyes were filled with tears. She was choking with them. She tried to pull herself together but was not successful and let the tears flow. What should she answer? That his back is a mass of black and dark purple colors? Does he need to know that in two areas of the spine the swelling is immense? Does she need to mention that she had a suspicion from the very beginning regarding an extensive injury of his spine?

Alexander got nervous, stretched his left arm and waived with it in the air, trying to find his wife. She kneeled down at his bed, took his bruised hand and kissed it. She answered with the calmest voice she could manage, lying again. She hated to tell lies, but she did not want her husband to concentrate his attention on his multiple hurtful, sadistic injuries.

"I am here, mon amour. I am with you. There are no atrocious bruises on your back, just a couple of scratches. You can probably sense them in thoracic (chest) and sacral (lower back) areas of the spine."

Alexander experienced some relief and being a doctor, continued analyzing his injuries,

"I see. He hit me in my nose, and I fell on my back. The concussion can affect my motions and eyesight. Mon Chere, they knocked me down with the first blow. Can you see, Marie, how bad the blow in my nose was? And my eyes..., everything is blurry, and there is an annoying pressure in the right eye."

Alexander searched for trouble-free words to describe his condition without making it too scary. He spared Maria's feelings and asked again,

"What can you see on my face, Mon Chere?"

Maria tried to answer slowly,

"Darling, you were beaten by monsters until you bled. Your eyes are swollen, and it will take some time to heal."

Maria looked at his remaining right eye and asked the Divinity to restore his vision in it. She thought,

"Only a miracle could help him to see again. Black and dark blue bruises and swelling along his spine could also cause different problems now and later."

Alexander interrupted Maria's thoughts with his unexpected request:

"Marie, I am hungry. You said that two days have passed since that horrible night. Ganja is cooking something that smells unbelievably appetizing. What is it?"

"It's borscht, Alex. Borsht is our famous Ukrainian dish, full of flavor. It's like vegetable soup with lots of vegetables, beets and beans. You'll love it, I am more than sure."

She stopped for a second and gently stroked his hair. The emotions overwhelmed Maria. She signed bitterly and continued,

"It was my dream, Alex, to bring you here and introduce you to real Ukrainian dishes, like borscht with pampushka. Pampushka is our Ukrainian biscuit with a sauce made of freshly minced garlic and sunflower oil. The smell of the oil itself is so wonderful! It is freshly made, and the sunflower seeds that we use for it are of the best quality. My darling, who could imagine that my dream was the worst mistake of my life? Forgive me, mon amour."

"Marie, it is not your fault, darling. We lost the protection for some time, being involved in the vanity of our new busy post-war life. We paid for it. I ask the Lord to be merciful upon us. I hope that we'll survive. Our child needs to survive."

Alexander put his hand on Maria's belly and listened to the motion of his son. He tried to smile, but his torn lips dried up and did not allow him to smile. The lip wounds required several more days to fully heal.

When the food was ready, Ganja covered one side of the long table with a linen tablecloth and served the food. Alexander wanted to get up again, but Maria put another pillow under his head and did not take a risk to make him sit again. Maria mashed the vegetables in the borsht, as if she prepared it for a baby, and fed her husband with a teaspoon. He could barely chew. His injured jaws and broken teeth were very painful, but he did not want to cause additional suffering for his wife, so he pretended like nothing bothered him, except hunger. Maria was happy to see him eating. She knew it was a good sign of healing.

After the meal, Alexander fell asleep. Ganja left to feed her domestic animals, poultry, and milk her goats. Maria started her evening prayers. She thanked God for the survival of her father and husband, and for those people who helped them in their life-threatening situations.

She sensed warmth inside herself and wanted to share it with her poor husband, so she kneeled at his bed and hugged him gently with both arms. She loved him and was ready to share not only the warmth of the Holy Spirit, but with the years of her life.

The next day was Saturday. Maria and Alexander were awaked with the terrible noise around six o'clock in the morning. The noise was coming from the main house. They heard the screech of men in the office of the local NKVD. There were helpless shrieks of innocent people. The NKVD demons provided their satanic interrogation for several hours in a raw. They took several brakes to smoke on the porch and then continued their demonic torments of the poor captives. By four o'clock there was no more sounds heard from the main house.

Maria and Alexander could not stand the endless appalling torments. They did not touch the food Ganja prepared for them on the table. Alexander had a very bad headache on that day, and he felt nauseous for the most part. Maria cried and prayed constantly. She asked God to stop torturing the innocent people. For a while, they did not hear anything, and Alexander fell asleep.

Then Maria had heard the voices outside. She rushed to the window and saw how the soldiers pulled out three men in the yard in front of the building. The captives were dressed in their torn underwear that was soaked in blood. All three of them were unable to stand.

Maria exclaimed:

"O, my God!" and burst into tears.

She hugged her husband, questioning him:

"Alex, you cannot imagine what they did to them! Why do they have all the rights to anguish and harm the innocent people? Who gave them these rights, Alex? Why does the Lord allow them to continue committing crime?"

Alexander asked,

"What is it, Marie? Tell me, what do you see there? Who are the people that were tortured by the demons?"

Maria explained briefly the situation and rushed back to the window. She saw how the soldiers tried to force the captives to get up, beating them unmercifully with the butts of the machine carbines. The older demon came out holding a paper in his hand. Maria understood - it was their death sentence. One of the captives got up for a couple of seconds and collapsed.

The older demon did not even finish reading the verdict. He took out the pistol and shot in the chest and head of the misfortunate person. Then he gave the order to the soldiers, and they shot two other captives that were lying on the ground.

Maria was standing near the window and crying, watching how they pulled out nearly naked woman onto the porch. In the beginning, Maria could not recognize her. The young woman turned into an old, hardly walking person. She moved slowly, holding her abdomen with both arms, as if she was losing her internal organs. Maria saw how every step caused her an unbearable pain. The soldiers did not push her. They were enjoying the result of their violence.

The woman stopped near the bodies of the executed military men and looked at them for a while. Maria saw how her lips moved; she was talking to them. Maybe, she was saying her farewell words, or she wanted them to meet her there, behind the border of physical life.

The woman turned around and said something to the tormentors. Maria saw that the back of her torn underwear skirt was red with blood. The older demon moved forward toward the woman with the raised feast. She spat in his face. The demon grabbed the pistol, pressed to her chest and shot. The woman fell down dead. The demon hit her dead body with the boot, as if she could feel this last abuse. Thank God, the demon and his monsters could not cause any more harm to those four young people. Their suffering was over forever. The Lord would take care of their eternal souls.

Watching all this, Maria could not stop crying. Alexander asked her to move from the window, but she continued watching the bloody tragedy. The soldiers put the shot bodies together and covered them with tarpaulin. The older demon ordered something to the person-on-duty who called somewhere and prepared the shovels on the porch.

The deputy of the demon arrived with four militiamen. The demon ordered them to load the bodies of executed captives on the truck, and then somebody threw several shovels on the corpses. They took them somewhere to bury. Nobody would know what had happened to those four innocent people. Their mothers would never imagine how they were tortured and murdered not by Nazis or Ukrainian Nationalists, but by the co-citizens of their native country.

The soldiers were staying with the demon on the porch of the main house for some time, smocking, talking and neighing loudly. All of them were still discussing with pleasure the last event. They left together with the demon. Their Saturday mission was served to Satan.

Maria and Alexander prayed for the executed people,

"Remember, O Lord, the souls of those four young people who were tortured and murdered by demons and have departed this life less than an hour ago. Forgive them all transgressions, voluntary and involuntary, granting them the kingdom and the delight of Thine endless and blessed life. Amen."

Maria did not have enough air to breath and opened the door and both windows. On that day, the weather was sunny and warm. The fresh draft brought into the lodge a concentrated whiff of Ukrainian autumn. Usually the fall season in western Ukraine was rainy, but not that year. Nobody swept the fallen leaves on the territory of the manor, and they produced a pleasant bouquet of autumn aromas.

It reminded Maria of the smells in their forest during mushroom season, lasting from the beginning of August to the end of November. Maria liked gathering the mushrooms. During the mushroom season, her family and the workers got up early in the morning and loaded the horse wagons with hundreds of baskets. All the baskets were delivered to the forest and, every day, people collected mushrooms until 2 p.m. Then they delivered them to the Summer kitchen that was built, as a separate building, behind the main house.

The fall season was especially good for shiitake mushrooms. The Kotyks knew how to collect them in order not to ruin the roots of the mushroom families and the nature paid them exclusively. All the baskets were delivered to the mansion where the women took care of the fresh produce. They knew how to wash mushrooms correctly in order to make them clean, while at the same time, not letting them absorb extra water. Then they marinated, salted, sautéed or simply dried them.

Maria was fond of working with mushrooms in spacious summer kitchen. Only housekeeper Sofia knew Maria's secret, as to why the girl stayed there for hours, helping the women. Maria enjoyed the scent of mushrooms very much. She did not like any smell nearly as much, as she did mushrooms, even the scent of berries. Mushrooms were very popular in Europe, and the Kotyks had their continual contracts with the customers who purchased them every year for their European restaurants. Well-prepared mushrooms made a good portion of Count Kotyk's annual income.

Maria stood in the doorway, recollecting her previous life, and she did not hear at once that Alexander woke up and was calling for her,

"Marie, where are you?"

She rushed to him, asking,

"What is it, Alex? You do not feel well, do you?"

"I woke up and it's dark, and I cannot see anything. Darling, I was scared that something happened to you, and I did not even hear it."

Maria hugged him. Her touch caused some pain and he moaned.

"I am sorry that I touched your ribs, Alex. I promise to be careful next time. Are you hungry, mon amour? We did not eat today."

"Not really. What did you do there?"

Maria was not sure that it would be interesting for her husband to learn about her reminiscences. Alexander was persistent,

"Tell me, Mon Cherie, what did you do outside? Let me guess, Marie. You were day-dreaming, weren't you?"

"No, Alex. I was recalling something from my childhood. The smell of autumn took me back into my childhood. I liked collecting mushrooms in our forest. But most of all, I enjoyed preparation of mushrooms in accordance with different recipes."

Alexander found her with the left arm and pulled her closer.

"Marie, every time I learn something new about you, you surprise me. Why did you like the processing of mushrooms so much?"

"There was only one person who knew my secret, Alex. It was our housekeeper Sofia. Do you remember that I've told you about that devoted woman? She was like a mother to us. The Nazi colonel shot her here, near the fountain. My answer to your question is simple: I've enjoyed the concentrated aroma of mushrooms when they were sliced."

"What reminded you of mushroom gathering here in the lodge?" Alexander inquired.

"I opened the door and stood in the doorway for a while. I did not even notice, darling, how the smell of the fallen leaves took me back to my childhood. It is a marvelous smell of Ukrainian autumn."

Alexander was impressed with his wife. Today, Maria was stressed out with the execution of innocent captives, and then she managed to escape from the brutal world into peaceful memories of her childhood. He thought, "The Lord took her there. She needed to calm down for our child sake. Thank You, Lord, for giving my wife the opportunity to enjoy her memories."

Maria got up and went to close the door and windows. It became chilly after the sunset. She lit the candle and put it in the candle holder on the table. Maria thought about Ganja, "She promised to be here around this time and bring some herbs for Alexander. I miss her every time she leaves, as I missed her and Sofia in my childhood."

Alexander kept thinking about his extraordinary wife. Then he asked,

"Marie, gathering mushrooms is not an easy work to do, and, especially, cooking them afterwards."

"O no, Mon Cher, it was not so hard for us because we did it every year from five years of age. Our father taught us to work from childhood. We knew that during spring, summer and autumn we had to get up early in the morning and go to the forest. There he taught us how to gather the healing herbs, berries and mushrooms. It was our father who trained our sense of direction in the woods and we had never been lost or scared."

Alexander asked,

"How was your father so successful with organizing the children for work in the forest?"

Maria answered with her smile,

"Papa liked to repeat, 'I am grateful to my father for everything he taught me. But most of all I appreciated that he did not allow me to become lazy. As for me, laziness makes people bored, unhappy, envious and depressed. Laziness or sloth is the fourth Capital sin. Always stay away from such a sin. Diligence opens Heaven for people.'

I believe, he was right. If I grew, as a Countess only, could I survive the hardships of war? I doubt, my love. What do you think?"

"I agree with you, Marie. It's my sin that I do not work now and still want to eat. Will you check what Ganja left there on the stove?"

Maria went to the stove, when at that moment, Ganja knocked on the door and called Maria's name. She had two bags and a basket with her. She brought herbs and some food. In her basket, she brought Maria's delicacies – fresh eggs, milk and farmer's cheese.

"I knew that you were waiting for me. I went to your father's lodge today, and it took a long time. Then I milked and fed my animals at home. Somebody has to feed them so that they could feed us."

She was glad to see Maria and Alexander alive because on her way there, she had met her neighbor who told her about the executions at the Kotyks' mansion. Ganja did not want to start talking about this until Maria told Ganja the tragic story of the captives that she witnessed from the very beginning. She started to cry again, and Ganja reminded the mother-to-be,

"Pannochka Maria, you cannot cry so much. Please remember about your special condition. Feed your child with healthy food and not with your tears."

Maria pulled herself together and sat down at the table. Ganja served Maria's and Alexander's food and asked Maria to pray. Maria started,

"In the name of the Father, and of the Son, and of the Holy Spirit. Amen. The eyes of all look at You

with hope, and You give them their food in due season. Please, open Your hand and fill every living thing with Your favor. Amen."

The food for Alexander was the same but with one difference – Ganja had added some milk to the cottage cheese in order he could r chew it more easily.

When they finished supper, Alexander prayed without Ganja's reminding,

"We thank Thee, O Christ our God, that You has satisfied us with Your earthly gifts; deprive us not of Your heavenly kingdom, but as You came among Your disciples, O Savior, and gave them peace, come to us and save us. Amen."

Ganja did the dishes and accompanied Maria with praying the Evening prayers. Alexander tried not to fall asleep, but his weakness did not allow him to participate. The women had difficult day and tried to fall asleep. The light and warmth did not come to Maria immediately, as in previous days. Maria was lying with closed eyes, waiting for it. She needed to share the healing light and warmth with Alexander. Maria analyzed what wrong she did on that very day, and when she realized that she was not grateful enough for staying alive, she prayed,

"Lord, forgive us and have mercy on us; for we have hope in Thee. Be not angry with us greatly, neither remember our iniquities; but look upon us with compassion, and deliver us from our enemies, for Thou art our God, and we are Thy people; all are the works

of Thy hands, and we call upon Thy name now and ever, and unto the ages of ages. Amen."

Maria saw how the beams of light floated into the lodge. The light covered her, Ganja and reached Alexander. It stayed with her and Ganja and was melting on her husband's body. Maria whispered,

"Dear Lord, be merciful to my husband. If he needs more light, take mine but heal him, please. Lord, have mercy upon Alexander. He is good and loves You, our God."

Maria saw how a new wave of white light came into the lodge, filling every corner of their dwelling. It also penetrated into its exhausted inhabitants, restoring and rejuvenating them with pleasant warmth.

Maria praised the Lord from the bottom of her heart,

"Glory to Thee, O Lord! Glory to Thee!"

Chapter 8

When Alexander woke up early in the morning, Maria washed him and soaked his wounds with remedies. While she was taking care of her husband, the water was heated up for her bath. She felt fresh after taking a bath and put on her Sunday church dress. It was strange that Ganja had not yet been there. There were no church services any longer on Sundays. Religion was forbidden. The soviet regime had changed the regular life of Ukrainian people. Maria started her Sunday praying. When she had finished, Alexander asked her, like a child,

"Who will feed me? Who feels pity for a starving man? Nobody in this lodge feels sorry for me. Ganja refused to come and save me."

Maria laughed. She warmed up some soup from the previous day and fed her "starving" husband. Thank God, he had a good appetite and could sit a little bit longer. His only eye was opened, but it was blood red, and his vision was still blurry.

Maria could not look at her husband's face without tears in her eyes. The appearance of a man with the only one bloody eye, a twisted nose, torn lips and broken teeth did not look anything like the appearance of her handsome husband.

Maria tried to calm herself down,

"Thank God he is alive, and he is with me. Nothing else is more significant. I love him the way he looks. He is my brave, one-eyed Captain Nelson. My child is with his father, at least today. I am grateful to the Lord and His holy Mother for being merciful to my Alexander, our child and me. I witnessed what happened yesterday, and I am so much obliged to our Lord for keeping us alive."

Ganja appeared in the doorway with her arms full of food. She was happy to see Alexander sitting on his bed and eating soup voraciously.

She greeted,

"Glory to Jesus Christ."

Then she continued,

"Look what I have. I cooked pumpkin millet for you. It is tasty and highly beneficial. It will give strength to both of you, as well as your baby."

Ganja unwrapped the cast-iron pan and removed its lid. It was good that the pan was wrapped in linen towels. The towels did not allow the porridge to cool. The lodge was filled with sweet aroma of Ganja's pumpkin millet. Alexander was not sure that he had ever tried it before, but when he tried, he liked the taste of millet with sweet pumpkin. He drank a cup of goat milk at the end of his lunch. Tasty food made him feel better and he decided to try standing and walking. The women were ready to support him from both sides. He slowly walked outside and sat on the steps of the lodge. His bruised and swollen back made his sitting on the hard step very painful.

He joked,

"From now on Marie, you have to remember that I am a princess on a pea."

Maria brought a quilt, folded it, and Alexander sat on it.

"Thank you, darling. It's much better now."

The day was wonderful, and they did not want to think about danger, separation, death or torments. She sat next to him and snuggled up against his shoulder. He stretched his arm and put it on her belly. With active motions, his baby let him know that he was happy to feel his father close. Alexander smiled although his mutilated lips still hurt. It was an ugly smile of a stranger. The teeth and lips were not his at all. Everybody used to like Alexander's smile, but not this one. Maria's heart spoke,

"It has to be healed. Healing requires time."

However, her professional and clear mind was aware of the irreversible conditions when something in the human body was seriously injured, fractured, crashed, smashed, torn and twisted. She was sitting next to her beloved husband, crying quietly.

A thought that they had signed false '*confession*' bothered her constantly. She knew that the tragedy was not over. She continued to wish and pray for repatriation, returning them back to their previous lives, work and happiness. However, there was no way to be sent back, because in addition to taken away passports, travel documents and return tickets, Alexander and she were forced to sign the interrogation reports, in which they "pleaded guilty" to their "spy and terrorist mission against the communist country." Those signatures deprived the young couple of leaving the country without punishment.

The Kurbatovs sat outdoors for an hour or so. Maria thought they should go in, but Alexander enjoyed staying outside.

"Marie, we do not know what they are preparing for us. None of us know what to expect tomorrow. It is so pleasant to sit with you, feeling the motions of our baby and listening to the singing of the birds. Stay here with me, darling. When else we can experience such a peaceful moment?"

Alexander loved his wife and wanted to embrace her, but a shooting pain in his spine did not allow him to do it. Maria started to kiss gently his ugly face, saying,

"Sit still, darling. I will kiss and hug you gently."

She thought, "It seems to me that I am getting used to his new face because I love him so much." Alex tried to respond to her kisses, but his lips did not listen to him.

"O, Marie, you can bring any man to life. I love you. I want to be with you. I know that I am not able to be with you now, but my desire is back. Thank you, dear." Maria's face registered simulated surprise.

"What are you thanking me for? You are my husband. Don't mention it."

Ganja prepared the herbal remedy for Alexander and brought it outside. He continued coughing up a lot of blood, and the herbal decoction was intended on healing his lung damage and stop the bleeding.

Maria recognized her grandfather's handwriting on the bottle with extracts. She asked Ganja,

"You've been to my grandfather's lodge, haven't you? How are they?"

"They are fine. People found them and started to come for consultations and remedies. I worry for your father. If the demons find him, he will be in danger. I pray for him and ask God to return everything back to the way it was when we lived our quiet lives in our Blue Creeks."

It was getting cool to sit outside, and Maria worried about Alexander's injured lungs.

"If you do not want to go inside, let us walk a little bit, Alex. I do not want you to catch cold or, God forbid, get pneumonia."

Alexander could manage only a few steps. His dizziness and weakness in the legs forced him to sit down. His posture instability frightened Maria. She whispered in Ganja's ear,

"Alexander is in a very bad shape, Ganja. He cannot even manage standing and walking. A couple of steps had made him exhausted. Look, Ganja, how dizzy he is! He is losing his balance while walking. Every evening, the temperature still goes up. Every part of Alex's body is inflamed. Ganja, what should we do to expedite his healing? What else we need to do for Alex? Why didn't you ask my father?"

Ganja answered out load,

"Oh Lord, only few days have passed since demonic anguish. Why cannot you see the significant improvement in Pan Alexander's condition? He can see, talk, sit and walk outside. Alleluia."

Ganja came up and embraced Maria's shoulders,

"Pannochka Maria, I understand that you are concerned about Pan Alexander, but be grateful to our Savior for everything. To tell you the truth, I was not certain of his ability to survive. I am surprised with his fast healing."

Ganja's arguments did not calm Maria down, but her reasonable clarification extinguished Maria's anxiety. She embraced nanny and said,

"Ganja, I noticed only one obvious improvement: his appetite is back, and he enjoys our Ukrainian food."

All three laughed. The elderly woman gave additional reasonable answer to Maria's questions,

"Who can expedite the natural healing? The Lord and only the Lord can, but not us. We can pray, and God will heal Pan Alexander."

Maria knew that the nanny was right. She reminded herself: "He had a life-threatening combination of severe blood loss, contusions, concussion, multiple bone fractures and internal juries. It's a true miracle that my Alexander has survived without surgeries or strong medications. Thank God that he was able to take a few steps on the fifth day. Dear Lord, please forgive me my impatience." *Glory to Thee, o Lord! Glory to Thee!*

Chapter 9

Maria took Alexander into the lodge. They drank tea all together at the table, and it was the first time after that horrible night when he did not want to go to bed. Maria insisted in laying down earlier that night because she decided to tell her husband a story about Captain Alexander Stern, the wounded Russian pilot in Linden Hospital. He listened attentively without interruption. His face was tense. She asked him at the end,

"What was it, Alex? Definitely not love, but the attraction was very strong."

"You, Marie, were severely drained. You reached the highest level of physical, emotional and nervous exhaustion. You were completely lonely without any support. Your survival forces were used up, and you lost control over the situation. You needed human connection, reinforcement, collaboration, care and understanding in order to live."

Maria said,

"Alex, I was so cautious with my life and all of a sudden…"

Alexander interrupted her,

"That happened due to complete overtiredness, Marie."

Maria smiled bitterly,

"The Lord released the situation so quickly but painfully. Otherwise, who knows what could've happen, if we ever met each other again..."

Maria felt lightness after her "confession" and was grateful to Alexander for understanding. She said,

"I love you, darling. Do you know why? You are so intelligent and compassionate. You wisely explained the situation that has disturbed me this entire time. I thought about it again and again and could not find any reason for my unusually perilous behavior. Thank you, darling."

She kissed him gently in order not to cause him any pain. They prayed their Evening prayers when the person-on-duty appeared at the door. He did not greet them, just handed Alexander an envelope with an order and left. The message read:

"Tomorrow, October 7, 1946 you'll be moved to Lvov prison. It's the right place for political prisoners, spies and terrorists. Do not even think about taking your suitcases with you. In Lvov, you'll be given uniforms for prisoners and sent to Magadan for twelve years and six months of forceful labor."

Maria was frightened to death. The day was spoiled, the first day of hope for Alexander's healing. She exclaimed,

"Alex, why have they decided to send us to Magadan now? You are so weak!"

Ganja said,

"I need to find warm clothing for you—valyanky, foot-cloths, woolen shawls, and two pairs of boots. It's a very cold winter there."

Maria was in panic,

"Ganja, you have no time to find clothes. They'll take us to Lvov tomorrow." Maria burst into tears. The elderly woman was angry with the demons. They had to give poor Pannochka Maria a day or two to get ready for imprisonment.

Ganja suggested the young couple to lock the door and she rushed home. She couldn't let Pannochka Maria go without warm cloths. The poor nanny ran to the road, stopped a truck and rode to the place in the road that was closer to the Kotyks hunting lodge. It was completely dark when she entered the woods. She knew the path to the lodge, but it was difficult to stay on it in darkness. Ganja started to pray,

"Compass me about, O Lord, with the power of Thy precious and life-giving Cross and preserve me from all evil. Amen."

The woman repeated the prayer many times, and soon it was answered, as she saw a hunting lodge in a distance.

"Thank You, Lord. I am grateful to You, my Father, that I was not lost in the forest at night."

When Ganja came to the door, she heard dogs barking inside. A voice asked,

"Who is there?"

"It's me, Ganja. Please open the door."

The old count opened it, and let Ganja in. He was surprised to see her so late.

"What happened, Ganja?"

"I need your help. My relatives arrived from France to see me and were arrested. The NKVD beat them unmercifully, and tomorrow they want to transport the young couple to Lvov and from there to Magadan. They are sending them there for twelve and a half years."

The old count was confused even more.

"I did not know, Ganja, that you had relatives in France. Why were they sentenced for such a long term? What did they do?"

"Do people need to do anything to be sent to Siberia? They came here from France. It was enough."

The old count listened to Ganja attentively and could not understand, how the problem with her relatives was related to her night visit. He asked her,

"In what way can I help you, Ganja?"

"My niece is six months pregnant, and she doesn't have warm clothing. Her husband has a concussion, fractured ribs and a broken wrist. I've been taking your medicine and herbs to him. He can hardly walk due to the traumas and wounds. He doesn't have anything warm to wear either."

The old count listened carefully and could not understand where Ganja found her relatives or how the relatives found Ganja and why NKVD arrested them and sentenced them to twelve years of imprisonment. However, it was late evening, and the elderly woman was waiting for his help. He went to another room and asked from there,

"How big is your niece?"

Ganja replied,

"She is small, like Pannochka Maria."

He found something for her and brought it to the kitchen. It was Maria's rather new fur coat. Ganja shook her head.

"No, Pan Kotyk. That won't be good for her. They will take it away."

The old count said,

"We do not have anything else, Ganja."

Losing hope, she asked,

"Do you have Pannochka Maria's valyanky?"

"Yes, we do," he answered.

He brought them to her together with foot-cloths. Ganja asked,

"Do you have any warm boots for my niece? She arrived in light shoes."

The old count asked Ganja to go with him and look at Maria's old things.

"Take anything that you'll find helpful for your niece."

Ganja dove into a huge chest full of Maria's clothing and found a pair of boots with fur lining, two pairs of woolen high stockings, two warm pajamas that she could wear like underwear, two sweaters and two downy shawls. From the other side of the chest, she found Maria's old fur coat. Ganja packed everything in a tablecloth and tied it up. The elderly woman thanked God and the old count for this treasure.

The old count saw something strange in Ganja's behavior, and he tried to find the explanation for it, but could not. Usually, she was a very shy person, and, at that moment, she was different. She asked him,

"Can you find anything for her husband?"

The old count asked Ganja how big he was. She described,

"He is a little bit taller than Dr. Kotyk."

At that moment, Dr. Kotyk appeared in the room with the words,

"What a surprise! We have a guest here. What happened, Ganja?"

She burst into tears, repeating the story about her close relatives from France. She complained through sobbing,

"The NKVD arrested them on the very first day of their arrival and sentenced to more than 12 years of forceful labor in Siberia. My niece is six-months pregnant and her husband was brutally mutilated by the monsters. Please, give some clothing to my niece's husband."

The gentlemen were ready to share with her anything they had. It was easier to collect warm clothing for a man.

When the second sack was collected, Dr. Kotyk asked a logical question:

"Ganja, it is completely dark outside. How can you walk through the woods with two sacks?"

The old count suggested staying until morning, and early in the morning, he would take her to the Creeks in the horse wagon. Ganja continued crying and insisted on leaving right away. Dr. Kotyk said,

"You could be killed on the road just for those sacks of clothing."

Ganja replied,

"But they could take my niece and her husband tonight. You know that better than I do. The demons practice arresting people at night. Nighttime belongs to Satan."

It was difficult to disprove such an argument. The old count went outside, talked to the guards and returned in five minutes. He entered the room with the words:

"Let's go. You cannot go alone at night. The horse is ready."

They arrived at Creeks in fifty minutes. The old count asked,

"Where is your house, Ganja?"

She showed him the one closer to the mansion. Ganja jumped down from the wagon and pulled the sacks. She thanked the old count, and he went back to his lodge in the woods, thinking about Ganja's very strange behavior.

It took five minutes to get to the servants' lodge. Ganja knocked on the door, but nobody answered. Ganja called,

"Pannochka Marie. It's me, Ganja."

Maria opened the door.

"What happened, Ganja? We did not expect to see you tonight."

"I was afraid that tomorrow would be too late. I've brought some warm clothing for you. We need to try some things for Pan Alexander, especially boots and valyanky. All the rest of the clothing I've brought will fit you both."

Maria opened one of the sacks and was astonished with what was inside.

"Where did you get my clothing, Ganja?"

Alexander sat up in bed without anybody's assistance. Ganja answered,

"I was at your grandfather's hunting lodge. A long time ago, your father took a chest with your clothes there. I had packed it for him, and I knew exactly what was there. When the demon said that you would be transported to Lvov, I went to your grandfather's lodge and brought back everything you'll need for icy cold Magadan."

The young couple was speechless. Maria hugged nanny Ganja and kissed her on both cheeks. Alexander said,

"We appreciate your help, Ganja. Let God bless you with everything you dream about."

She asked,

"Do you know my dream?"

The young people said in unison,

"Tell us, please."

Ganja kissed Maria's shoulder and told them,

"I want you to be free, and I want my Jennie to come back."

Alexander suddenly asked:

"Does anybody want to eat?"

Maria moved to the table and answered,

"I do."

Ganja added,

"I also want some tea. I am thirsty after my ride to the lodge."

It was eleven at night when they sat at the table and ate their late supper. Ganja made fresh herbal tea and put a jar of preserved strawberries on the table. Nobody wanted to talk about the next morning. They thanked the Lord for tonight.

"*Glory to Thee, o Lord! Glory to Thee!*"

Chapter 10

On Monday morning October 7, 1946, Maria decided to go to the committee. She told Alexander,

"I have to ask them to postpone our departure until you feel better. I hope, they will understand it."

The intonation in her last sentence did not contain any confidence. She was not sure that the demons in the main house could understand anything human. She had not been raped in the concentration camp by Nazi in Germany. It was the truth. She knew that it was dangerous to go there, but at the same time, she realized that Alexander was not able to meet all the rules and requirements of inmate life. She felt like she had to go and talk. Maria ran away before Alexander could protest. She knocked on the door of the chief demon and opened it without waiting for permission to come in. There were three officers in the room, sitting around a table. Maria had not met two of them before. Maria thought, "Do I care who they are? Let them listen to my request and decide what to do."

Maria did not want to greet them. Instead, she started with the reason of her visit:

"I came here to ask for your permission to keep us at the servants' lodge for another week, until my husband can walk and become able to see. He is very weak due to blood loss and severe injuries. After your torments, he lost one eye completely and can barely see with the other one. His right wrist and arm are fractured. He expectorates a lot of blood due to lung damage, and he has two broken ribs. Everything is inflamed, and he continues to run a high fever."

One of the officers was obviously a physician. He asked a couple of professional questions regarding Alexander's traumas and injuries. Maria provided him the information in details. Both visitors decided to verify Maria's information about her husband's condition. They asked her to wait for them in the office, while they went to the servants' lodge. They left Maria with the chief demon. It was strange, but at that time, she was not afraid of him, and it looked like he was confused with her visit. Maria thought, "Maybe, Captain Novikov initiated the visit of these officers. One is definitely a physician."

The examiners came back very quickly. The doctor was agitated with what he found. They arrived at their conclusions regarding the events that took place six days ago in this local office of NKVD. Maria thought, "They definitely learned something from the interpreter. I am quite sure that Novikov does not belong to the demonic group. May God bless him for his human kindness."

The older examiner told Maria in a loud voice of a commander, "You may go to the lodge, and we'll let you know of our decision regarding your future transfers."

Then he noticed her belly, which was moving in different directions. Her child could not stand mother's stress easily.

"Go to the lodge and wait there." This sentence was pronounced in a gentler tone.

When Maria returned to the lodge, Alexander was in bed. The stressful situation had provoked a severe headache and vomiting. His voice was weak again.

"Marie, I do not want you to ask the monsters for any favors. I'll be all right in half an hour, and we'll go."

Maria decided to change the topic and asked,

"Alex, where is Magadan?"

Maria hadn't heard of that city before. Both of them were constantly thinking about their new place of destination and their stay there for twelve and a half years. Maria thought they would stay there together, as the Decembrists' couples had.

The doctor came back to the lodge with some pills and eye drops. He explained how to use them and was about to leave.

"What have you decided about us, doctor?" Alexander asked.

"You are right, I am just a doctor. My opinion is that you need to be hospitalized before you go to the camp. What the committee in Lvov decides is out of my hands. The only thing I can promise you is submitting the factual report of my personal evaluation."

Maria looked at him and asked,

"Can you tell us where Magadan is? I'm embarrassed to admit that I am not familiar with the name of this city. Is it far from here?"

There was frank pity in the eyes of the military doctor. He thought,

"Poor beauty, you cannot imagine how far it is from here. I doubt both of you will survive your stay there."

Then he answered,

"It is very far away."

Maria continued asking,

"Is that where Tsar Alexander sent the Decembrists?"

"Farther," answered the doctor and left.

She cuddled up to Alexander, kissed him and said,

"Alex, we'll survive, and our baby will be with us. The important thing is that we'll be there together. We shall pray, and they'll release us sooner. I believe that a new miracle can happen again just like they happened to me so many times during the war."

Alexander looked at his wife with admiration. He thought,

"This tiny, delicate bird has such strong faith and willpower. All I have to do is be as strong as my wife in everything I am destined to undergo."

He looked at Maria and realized an interesting thing: when his headache was lighter, he could see her face better.

"Marie, now I can see your bruised cheekbone. You look like a small boy after a fight. You are my brave fighter. We do not have a way out. We'll be new Decembrists or Octobrists or Novembrists."

Alexander was tired again and fell asleep. Maria looked out of the window and saw the old demon, staying on the porch. He was watching how both inspectors from Lvov were taking their jeep. The driver started the engine. Maria heard the noise of the engine and ran out of the lodge to find out what to expect. The older officer noticed her running to their car. He opened the door and said,

"We decided to give you three more days. Then the transport will pick you up and deliver to Lvov prison. From the prison you'll be deported to Magadan Gulag."

"Thank you."

The officer was surprised with her politeness. Then Maria asked the question that had been on her mind constantly:

"My husband and I are staying together in Magadan, aren't we?"

She saw how her question choked the officer. He coughed for a couple of minutes and when he took a breath, he decided to ask,

"What do you mean to 'stay together'?"

"You want us to stay in exile, as the Decembrists did."

The officer looked at her in surprise.

"Definitely not, Madam Kurbatov. We have not arranged yet the families' camps."

Another thought suddenly came into his mind: "She cannot be a spy agent if she is so naïve. They must have used her, or our officers here forced the couple to sign the 'confession'."

Maria looked at him with eyes opened wide and asked,

"What about our child? I do not want him to become an orphan. I want to see him every day, hug him, nurse him and play with him. I want him to have a real mother."

"If you work well, they will allow you to see and nurse your child, Madam Kurbatova. If not..."

Maria did not hear the end of the sentence. She turned and ran to the lodge, sobbing loudly.

The officer closed the door of the car with a heavy feeling, thinking, "This case is not a regular one, and whatever the couple had signed does not look, as a true conformation of guilt." He commended to the driver, "Go." Both officers could not stop thinking: "She was born here. The Nazis deported her to Germany. She arrived back home and brought her husband to meet her family. Could it be true? Why not?"

The inspecting officers tried to stop thinking about the naïve pregnant woman, but they continue talking about her and her husband. The doctor asked,

"The only reason to view this couple as the enemies is their nobility. Are they so stupid to insist in returning the properties?"

The older officer replied without hesitation,

"I don't think so. Being a surgeon in France, I doubt that he needed any property here in the Ukraine or to come here, as a spy. They mentioned in the interrogation report that he arrived here 'to find the contact with the Ukrainian nationalists and to take vengeance on the Soviets for his parents, who were deprived of their civil rights as nobility in 1917, for dispossession and disinheritance.' It sounds false and stupid. He doesn't look like a person who gave such a deposition."

There travelled in silence for some time. Then the inspector's thoughts were interrupted by his companion, an experienced doctor from the Lvov military hospital, who was sent to examine Alexander and Maria due to somebody's call from the headquarters.

"I must say that your major is a tormentor from the time of inquisition. He sees an enemy in every person. I do not belong to NKVD, but I am positive that those people are innocent, and we'll send them to the camp only because they are Count and Countess Kurbatov, who were scared to death, humiliated, tortured and mutilated. If the same tools of interrogation were used for you or me, we would sign any paper in order to stop the torments of the inquisitors."

The lieutenant colonel did not answer. He thought, "We definitely need to change the head of this local committee because he is too aggressive. If somebody sent a doctor here to see the 'work' of the major's detachment, it means that all of us and our opinions are under somebody's investigation." He wanted to find out who sent the doctor to the local committee to examine that particular case, but he was afraid to ask. He thought, "Tomorrow, I'll write the report, and they will send somebody else to replace the 'tormentor from the time of inquisition,' as the doctor referred to him." After reaching this decision, he fell asleep and snored loudly.

The chief of the local committee was surprised and furious about the inspection from Lvov. He suspected that the interpreter might be the reason for the unexpected visit. The major demon could not let it go, as his deputy had suggested. He sent the person on duty to the local store to buy four bottles of vodka and a couple of rings of homemade Ukrainian sausage. They drank at the office until the middle of the night. When they had finished vodka and sausages, they decided to visit Maria and to force "that pregnant bitch" to serve them a good supper or breakfast with all the rest of services included. The person on duty was left drunk by the phone, and two other demons went to the servants' lodge.

The door was closed, and the demons started to knock loudly. Maria and her husband were sleeping in their clothes. They had not discussed it, but they were ready for a visit of uninvited guests any night. Maria kept a small but heavy axe under her pillow. She knew that the demons would not stop hurting them, as long as they lived on the same property. She was ready to kill them if they again decided to become violent with her or her poor husband.

Maria jumped out of bed and said to her husband quietly,

"Sit in the corner, darling."

She helped Alexander to move and rushed to the door with the axe ready.

"Marie, what are you doing? Sit next to me, please. I did not protect you last time; I was not ready for their aggression. This time, I shall not wait."

Maria answered in a firm but calm voice:

"Me, too. Stay silent. You cannot be nervous. Don't forget that you get terrible headaches and nausea after each stressful situation. It is my fault that we are in danger. It is easier to die than to go through all this again."

The demons commanded:

"Open the door! You, bitch, open it now!"

Maria was silent. They started to shoot at the door, cursing Maria and Alexander with horrible words. Then the monsters decided that they should blow up the lodge by tossing grenades through the windows. With that plan in mind, the older demon promised,

"We'll send you to heaven in five minutes. We'll bring 'sweets' for you, and then goodbye, frog-eaters. We cannot be loyal to the enemies of the Soviet power. We'll write one more report saying that you burned the lodge and yourselves by using the stove incorrectly. Everyone will believe us, because everyone understands that Count and Countess did not learn in their childhood how to use the stove. They will send another person to perform an inspection, but there will be nobody and nothing left to inspect."

They expected Maria to be scared and open the door for them after threatening to blow up the lodge, but she did not. The demons went back to the main house to get the grenades. Maria sat near her husband. It was quiet, and the young couple started to pray: *"Our Father, Who art in heaven, hallowed be Thy name. Thy kingdom come, Thy will be done, on earth as it is in heaven. Give us this day our daily bread, and forgive us our transgressions, as we forgive our transgressors; and lead us not into temptation but deliver us from the evil.*

For Thine is the Kingdom and the Power and the Glory, now and ever and onto ages of ages. Amen."

They were repeating the prayer for the third time, when they heard an explosion in the main house. In five to six seconds, there was another one, then again and again. Maria saw how the tongues of flames were jumping from the windows of the first floor. The fire was in the left wing of the main house. The team of local firefighters arrived at the property in seven minutes with their loud sirens blaring. By that time, everyone heard an endless chain of explosions. There was not a single intact window left in the house, and the explosions continued.

The fire fighters tried to prevent the fire from spreading to the rest of the building. They realized that something had happened in the basement, as they heard inhuman screams from the lower level of the building. The fire officer found the person-on-duty sleeping near the telephone; he was completely drunk and could not answer a single question. The person-on-duty was so drunk that he was unaware of the fire and explosions in the house.

The fire fighters tried to reach the basement as fast as possible because they heard again and again somebody's screams from there. When they were close to their destination, the roof of the left wing and the external wall started collapsing, covering the fire fighters with wreckage. The detachment rushed back, and the wall collapsed completely, pulling the roof down. No other explosions or voices were heard, and the fire team continued to work until morning, extinguishing the rest of the fire and clearing the way to the basement.

Maria looked out of the lodge window, telling Alexander about everything that took place at the main house. It was strange, the house—the house of her childhood and youth —was destroyed completely, but Maria did not feel any regret about it. From the first hours of their arrival, this house was not hers, it was the house of humiliation and abuse. She thought that the fire could have grave consequences for her and her husband.

"Alex, do you think they will blame us for starting the fire?"

Alexander was sure that they certainly would, since they were already labeled, as "spies and terrorists." The arson of the NKVD office would be one more uncommitted crime to be convicted for. However, he did not want his poor wife to become upset, so he answered,

"I don't think so, Mon Chere. We were under their arrest from the very first day of our arrival, and they kept their huge beasty person-on-duty there to watch us all the time."

"Alex, do you think the demon and his deputy are dead?"

"I don't know, darling. Why do you ask?"

"I am afraid, Alex that they can be back again," Maria answered.

"I doubt, Mon Amour. Don't stay there. You are tired already, Marie."

She came closer to her husband, but in complete darkness, he was not able to see, as Maria kneeled at his bed and kissed him gently.

"Good night, dear. Or to be more accurate, Alex: 'Good morning'. Have wonderful dreams."

Glory to Thee, O Lord! Glory forever!

Chapter 11

Maria returned to the window and could not pull herself away. At a quarter to eight on Tuesday, October 8, Maria noticed a car from Lvov—the same one that had brought the inspectors to the committee on the previous day. A group of military men got out of the car and went to the main house. The fire fighters had finished their work, and their commander had completed his report. The person-on-duty was still drunk and could not give any answers to the senior officers. Two soldiers took him inside the right wing.

One of the inspectors said something to another one, and they moved together to the servants' lodge.

"They are coming. Alex, they are coming!"

Maria exclaimed and sat down next to her husband. Then she ran back to the door and opened the lock.

The officers entered the lodge with a normal greeting:

"Good morning."

They sat at the table and prepared the map-case with a notebook to write the protocol.

"You have to tell us the truth about everything you did or saw last night," one of the officers said.

Maria looked at her husband and answered in a surprisingly calm tone,

“They came here to the lodge last night and insisted that we open the door. We sat quietly and did not answer.”

“Did they require anything from you?” the senior officer asked.

“Yes, to open the door.” Alexander answered.

“Why didn’t you open the door?” the younger officer asked.

“They were too drunk and were cursing and harassing us,” Maria complained.

The younger officer inquired:

“And what was their primary request? What did they want from you?”

Maria answered:

“They wanted me ‘to cook supper or breakfast with the rest of the services included.’ I’m sorry, but I’m just repeating their exact words.”

The senior officer continued questioning:

“What happened after you refused to open the door?”

“They began shooting in the door,” Alexander said.

The younger officer looked surprised.

“Oh, really?”

The inspectors went to the door, opened it and checked for bullet holes; two bullets were still in the door.

“What happened later?”

“They decided to blow up the lodge,” Alexander answered.

"Why did they decide to blow up the lodge?" the younger officer asked.

Alexander described the scene:

"When they realized that shooting in the door did not persuade us to open it, they threatened to throw grenades into the windows."

The younger officer was persistent:

"Did they have grenades with them?"

"No. They went to the main house to get them. They promised to bring 'the sweets' and to send us to heaven in five minutes," Maria added.

She was not sure whether the officers believed her and Alexander or not. She was not certain of anything with those people. It would be strange, if the inspectors did not blame her and her husband for arson. She and Alexander were already sentenced to twelve and a half years of imprisonment for nothing. After the night event, they could be condemned to death.

The baby was "jumping" in Maria's abdomen. The officers tried not to pay attention to it. Maria put a hand on her noticeably large belly and smiled. She said:

"I beg your pardon, or we beg your pardon."

She was absolutely startled when both of officers smiled. The officers got up and left without saying goodbye. Maria watched them leaving without saying a word and thought, "They probably found something suspicious in either Alexander's or my answers? I wonder, what it could be?"

Alexander pulled Maria closer and looking straight into her face, he asked, as if he was a small boy,

"They might be back soon, Mon Amour, but I am hungry now. Do we have anything to eat? Please, feed me."

Ganja was on time, as usual. This time, she brought some cooked food. Everything was hot and smelled appetizing. Alexander got out of bed and walked slowly to the table. Maria was wonderstruck.

"Look at him! Ganja, he is walking without our support!"

"Hunger could force any man to do anything," Ganja concluded.

The three of them prayed together:

"The eyes of all look to Thee with hope, and Thou give them their food in due season. Thou open Thy hand and fill every living thing with Thy favor. Amen."

They sat at the table, ate potato pancakes and thanked God for keeping them alive and together. Ganja watched Maria and Alexander eat with a hearty appetite, and it reminded her of a peaceful life in Count Kotyk's family with feeding the children after playing outdoors and watching their good appetites.

Every day, the young couple drank Ganja's herbal therapeutic teas. Alexander and Maria had different teas for different health reasons. The teas created a mixture of smells in the room, and it reminded Maria of the bouquet of smells at her grandpa's herbal storage. What a pleasant memory! Her grandfather used a lot of herbal remedies in his medical practice. Usually, his season for gathering the herbs started in early spring and ended in November. He knew perfectly well, how to use herbs for different health disorders. Maria recollected, how patiently he explained to her father, what part of the plant can be more beneficial for every particular case. Old Count separated flowerets, leaves, stems and roots. His knowledge could not be compared with the uninformative lectures of her professor in medical school. Maria took classes in herbology, and she hoped to enrich her knowledge through practical work with her father and grandfather. They knew hundreds of herbal recipes that healed different disorders.

Maria was far away in her thoughts and did not notice when Ganja took two buckets and left to get some well water. When the nanny returned, she brought stunning news. Ganja's goddaughter worked for the local NKVD committee, as a genitor. She told Ganja that at night, the chairman of the local NKVD was burned in the basement together with his deputy. In the morning, the firefighters found their remains.

Maria looked at her husband and saw that he was frozen. He got up without saying a word and went back into his bed. Maria followed him, embraced him and covered his mutilated face with gentle kisses. She asked, "What's wrong, Alex? Calm down, please. You cannot get nervous, darling. You know, you get terrible headaches every time when you are stressed."

Alexander explained in French, "Marie, yesterday I asked God to stop those people. I asked Him to stop them in any possible way. When we were sitting here on the bed and they left to get grenades, we started to pray to Our Father. Do you remember? I prayed for a miracle so that nobody would see those monsters again."

Maria replied, "Thank God, it happened. People had had enough of them. I am positive that those two tortured and raped to death many innocent people. Nobody will see them again. God has finished their demonic existence, Alex. God's punishment is the most just."

Maria look at an old icon of Jesus in the corner of the lodge, blessed herself with the cross and said, "*Glory to Thee, o Lord! Glory to Thee!*"

Chapter 12

Alexander and Maria expected the officers to return, but no one came back. Maria decided to put Alexander to bed so that he could rest after another long and stressful night and day. She asked him to go to sleep earlier, but the inner tension after Ganja's news did not allow him to fall asleep.

Maria packed her necessities and Alexander's separately, in case the people from the Lvov committee would separate them. Ganja brought Maria another pair of valyanky (warm woolen high boots) and a quilted coat in case the guards took away her fur coat. Maria examined the elegant clothing that Alexander and she had brought from Germany. They arrived in light woolen mackintoshes, elegant hats and fairly warm shoes. They planned to be here one week or ten days, the longest.

Maria thought, "Living in civilized European world, who could imagine that NKVD had the right to imprison innocent people, torture, rape, execute or depart them to the coldest part of Russia? As for us, we were sentenced to mortification, mutilation and slavery work in Siberia just because we arrived into this godless land to find my family. What an absurdity! There is no logic or justice in their sentence. There was no court. We did not see a judge, attorney or prosecutor. It is

1946, but this country does not have civilized laws. There is no possibility to protect ourselves. There is no way to prove our innocence."

Maria gave a deep sigh. She appreciated everything that Ganja had done for them during this difficult time. Ganja was called "an old nanny" in the family although she was only four years older than Maria's mother. It seemed absolutely natural to Maria that the "nanny" would know so many things, such as how cold the climate in Siberia was and what clothing was required there. Ganja said that it was already winter there with plenty of snow and severe frost. She had found a man's quilted jacket and a pair of quilted warm pants for Alexander. She also brought a pair of man's valyanky, but they were too big for Alex. Ganja promised to exchange them for another pair by tomorrow. Maria reminded her about them when Ganja was leaving.

"Ganja, I hope you'll find us here tomorrow," Maria said.

There were tears in the eyes of both women. They loved each other. Maria admired Ganja's bravery in assisting Alexander and her during their arrest. How could they survive without Ganja?

"Pannochka Maria, remember, I am here, waiting for you. Every day, I will pray to God and ask for His protection for all three of you, for easy birth of your child and defense of the baby from evil people. One day, I'll go to your father, and when he is strong enough, I'll tell him that I was blessed to see and help you for a short while."

Ganja looked at both Kurbatovs and blessed them with her cross, saying,

"God bless you, children, for survival and happiness. Lord, have mercy!"

Alexander got up, moved slowly forward and embraced a small woman.

"We'll be back, Ganja. Do not cry, dear. I hope, we'll return quickly, maybe even before the birth of our son."

Maria asked her,

"Ganja, do not tell Papa anything about our arrival. We'll see him next time, when they liberate us. I do not want to add new sufferings to my Dad. I love him so much," Maria said, crying sorrowfully.

Ganja left in tears. She had never wished to lose pregnant Pannochka Maria and her husband forever. On her way home, the woman repeated, *"Help them, save them, have mercy on them, and keep them, O God by Thy grace!"*

Alexander could not fall asleep, and Maria stayed in bed quietly, pretending to be asleep. She was so grateful to God that He took care of the demons. Holy God showed them hell on earth for all their demonic deeds. He burned them. Maria realized that God wanted Alexander and her to stay in the lodge at the time when He sent the righteous chastisement to the demons. She thought, "The Lord showed us that there was nothing stronger in the world than the power of God and never would be."

“Marie, are you asleep?” Alexander asked in a low voice so that, if his wife was asleep, the question would not awake her.

“No, mon amour, I am not. I am thinking about God’s punishment of those monsters. Alex, maybe we were destined to come here, suffer, be among the last victims of their cruelty and see God’s punishment?”

“I want to believe so, darling. Otherwise, it is so stupid. We survived the war, found each other, and came here to meet your family. Instead, we went through brutal torture and imprisonment for nothing. I’d prefer to stay away from all of this and not to become the victim of any demonic outrage.”

Maria had never seen such a strong emotional explosion in her husband before. She was trembling with feelings that overwhelmed her.

Alexander continued,

“Their state system does not have civilized public laws. Somebody has hurled an accusation, and there is no civilized defense mechanism that could protect us. They have ruined us physically, and they’ve planned to ruin our love and lives. They want to kill our child in cold Siberia.”

Alexander stood up in a fit of anger. He came over and sat down on Maria’s bed. He put his hands on her belly and felt the slow, “sleepy” motions of his child. Alexander’s hot tears ran down his face and dripped on Maria’s quilt. Maria tried to wipe his tears from his face, but then she burst into sobbing. Maria could not stop blaming herself.

"I am a sinner, Alex. I brought you here. I did not listen to my beloved husband and sincere friends. I was selfish, stubborn and stupid. I love you all—you, my tiny baby, my father, my brothers, my little sister Jenny, and grandpa."

She hugged him and said,

"I understand, there is no excuse for what I have done. Alex, I beg you, please be merciful and forgive me. Otherwise, I will not survive in that accursed Magadan."

He covered her face, neck, body and legs with kisses. He kneeled and, crossing himself with a wide cross, repeated many times:

"O Lord Jesus Christ, Son of God, for the sake of the prayers of Thy most pure Mother and all saints, have mercy on us. Amen."

His fractured hand still bothered him a lot, but he crossed himself again and again, as if there was no pain. Maria admired her husband. All of a sudden, she felt that warmth inside. She closed her eyes in order to sense it better, and she saw, how the white light touched her child inside, covering him with a gentle, puffy coverlet.

Maria whispered, "Thank you, Father, for sending down the grace of Thy Holy Spirit upon us, sinners." Alexander looked at his wife and noticed that she was smiling.

She said,

"Thank you, my dear husband, for your sincere prayer. Our Father blessed us with His Holy Spirit. We'll survive, and our son will be born."

Alexander did not want to be alone on that night. He made love with Maria, as passionately, as he could with all his traumas and pains.

Maria cried and repeated persistently,

"Please, be careful. Be careful with all of us, my love. All of us are injured and stressed."

Alexander could not understand, why Maria became so tense and hysterical.

"Did I hurt you, Marie?" he asked.

"Not you, my dear, not you. You are always gentle with me. I love you, Alex, and I want to belong to you," she replied.

The tension was released. That night, they did not want to pay attention at their emotional and physical pains. The misfortune was separating them for twelve years of impending imprisonment in freezing Magadan. That night, they were again one body, one mind and one soul.

Glory to Thee, o Lord! Glory to Thee!

Chapter 13

Wednesday, October 9, was the first morning when Ganja found the young couple sleeping together. Maria opened the door for Ganja and went back to bed to sleep. The old nanny looked at them and understood - God healed them to the point that they could love each other again. Something painful pricked in Ganja's heart. She looked at them and thought, "What are you doing here, Count and Countess Kurbatov? Why did you come to this God-forsaken land?"

Ganja unpacked valenki for Alexander and compared them with his shoes. This time, she was satisfied with the size. She cleaned the stove as quietly as possible, then brought in some wood and kindled the fire. It was warm in the lodge when Maria opened her eyes. Strong hunger interrupted her sleep. Maria got up and started the day with her usual words: *"Glory to Thee, o Lord. Glory to Thee!"*

Then Maria looked at Ganja who was setting the table, and said in Ukrainian with her beautiful smile,

"Glory to Jesus and Good morning, Ganja. I am so hungry. I will die, if I do not eat anything right this minute."

Maria kissed her husband and gently bit his chin. He screamed theatrically and asked,

"Oh, my darling, you want to eat me, don't you?"

The young woman had already disappeared, washing herself behind the curtain.

Everyone could hear her ringing voice.

"Darling, ask Ganja to give me a bite of something immediately or I can start with eating you." Ganja took some food to Maria with the words, "Here it is."

Maria washed herself and her hair. She combed, braided and fixed it around her head, like a beautiful crown. She put on her elegant dark blue dress with white lace color and cuffs and looked charming again.

Alexander took part in her game with joy.

"Ganja, please give my wife some food to bite. Otherwise, she will eat up the father of her baby, just like a black widow spider."

The elderly woman crossed herself with the words,

"God forbid!"

They all laughed, as if there was no more danger. Maria sat at the table, eating homemade farmer's cheese and drinking her favorite goat milk. She continued joking,

"Alex, wash up quickly. If you stay there five minutes longer, you'll find nothing on the table. Do not forget that two of us are 'working' hard here, a baby and I. Ganja made a delicious breakfast for us."

Ganja could not stop laughing. Maria remembered Ganja's clear voice when she sang, as well as her rumbling laughter that could be heard in every corner of the house when she played with children. It was a real pleasure to see her playing with kids in the playroom.

After breakfast, Maria put on her shoes, mackintosh and a hat and invited Alexander for a walk around the property. Her joy disappeared when she came up to the main house. The explosions and fire ruined the house completely. Only one wing reminded them the beauty of a magnificent blue-and-white mansion with marvelous colons, statues and balconies.

It was the house of Maria's childhood, where she was born, lived happily with her mother and father for ten years. It was a house of her first misfortune, where their mother left Marie, their father, brothers and a little Jenny and departed to Canada, following her new love. It was a distressing place, where the Nazi colonel shot poor housekeeper Sofia and ordered the soldiers to take Maria and Rosa for endless suffering.

It was a horrific house in which her handsome husband was mutilated and tortured by monsters, and where she was sadistically abused by the monsters' authorities. It was a place where NKVD interrogated, humiliated, extorted and extirpated innocent people. Those inquisitors had been born without or lost long time ago anything benevolent and enjoyed only rapacious harshness. The terror, blood and anguish of the agonized people brought them to ecstasy and reinforcement of their evil nature. Maria was looking at the ruins of the house without sorrowfulness in her heart.

Alexander interrupted Maria's thoughts,

"Marie, you feel sorry for the house, don't you?"

"Not at all, darling. Thank God, one of the dreadful satanic places was destroyed. I wish the Lord would destroy all their places together with those who serve the dark forces. Maybe, I sound naïve, Alex, but I am sincere in this desire."

The person-on-duty saw the Kurbatovs outside and walked out to meet them. Without saying a word, he handed Alexander an envelope. The paper stated that they were "sentenced, as *people's enemies*, in accordance with *Article 58 – High Treason* to twelve years and six months of imprisonment in Magadan camps of GULAG. The sentence should be executed October 15, 1946. The sentence is final and without right of appeal." It was signed by the chairman of the court martial.

On that time, the Kurbatovs did not know anything about the court martial. Military courts consisted of three people, and the review of the case and passing the sentence did not require the presence of a defendant. All the civilized laws of jurisdiction were destroyed from the very first days of the proletarian revolution and new depraved laws were created in order to protect the dictatorship of the evil structure.

The paper had destroyed Alexander's hope to prove in Lvov court the absence of any other mission except meeting his wife's family. He thought that the court could compare his mutilated appearance with the photos on his entrance documents and passport. The court would take into consideration that his wife and he were forced to sign the documents. As for his signature on demons' paper, Alexander was not sure that he signed it. If he did, he had to be half-conscious. The differences in signatures could be easily defined, when compared to the one in his passport.

He had dreamed about repatriation, relying on his mutilations and the testimony of Captain Novikov, the interpreter. Maria mentioned that the interpreter was the only civilized human being among all those monsters. They returned to the lodge and sat silently for a while. Ganja left home to take care of her domestic animals.

"Alex, how many days do we have?" Maria asked.

"I'm afraid we don't have any, Mon Chere. If I understand it correctly, on October 15, 1946, we must be in prison in Magadan," Alex replied.

Maria still tried to understand, how military court could pass sentence without seeing them and questioning.

"Alex, we are sentenced on more than twelve years of imprisonment, aren't we? How can we appeal against a sentence?"

Alexander looked at his wife with love and pity.

"Marie, the paper has declared that the sentence is final, and we have no right for appeal. Darling, they'll arrest and separate us today or tomorrow. Please let us live peacefully for another few hours that we have. I want to write a couple of letters, and Ganja will take them to your father. He'll know what to do with them. One letter is in German to the Schulenburgs. It's regarding our investment in the hospitality business in Germany. Do you mind, if I ask them to transfer part of the income to my mother? The rest of the money they will put on our account."

Maria shook her head,

"How could I be against the support of your mother? I took her son from her and never returned. Alex, I feel guilty for everything that I did to you and your mother. My imprudent idea killed all our dreams, plans and hopes. Instead of happiness and success, we'll meet hardships and our child will be born in slavery. To my mind, we can ask the Schulenburgs to send all our money to your mother. As for us, Alex, twelve years is a very long term. In case we survive with God's support out imprisonment, we'll find how to make our living."

"Thank you, Marie," Alex replied.

"Who do you want to write the second letter? Maria asked.

Alexander explained, "I will write another one in French; it's to my mother. I understand that your father is trapped in this country. But if he finds the possibility to contact her, he'll let her know that I am alive. She'll pray and wait for me—I mean, for us. Mother's prayers will help us for sure."

The thought of his mother made Alexander sad and very emotional. He felt the beginnings of a pressure headache and wanted to squeeze his head with both hands, but the pain in the right arm and wrist did not allow him to do this. Maria helped him with her hand and the pain recoiled.

He continued in a low voice.

“I shall write a small note to my child. I believe, we’ll survive all the hardships, and twelve years will not be the last years of our lives. We are young, my darling, we love each other, and we expect our child to be born. These three factors will help us pass another test in our life together. I want my child to know that his father loves him very much.”

Alexander wanted to tell Maria something else, but the pressure headache hit him again with another strong blow. Squeezing his head did not help. He went to the door, opened it and inhaled the cold air. He walked out and closed the door behind him. In a minute, Maria heard him sobbing behind the lodge. Maria’s first instinct was to run to him, but then she stopped herself, thinking,

“He needs to release the pain of his soul. I should not interfere. He’ll feel better afterwards.”

When Ganja came, Maria was sitting and crying quietly. She showed her the order. Ganja and Maria sat at the table, when Alexander came back. He finished writing the last letter, and his only eye was full of tears. The letter was short. He handed it to Maria and said,

“Keep the note with you, Mon Chere. Read it to our child when you have a chance.”

He looked at two women, sitting quietly across the table and asked in a loud and teasing voice,

“Are we going to have lunch today? What do we have to eat? And where is my favorite herbal tea?”

The women “woke up” and simultaneously moved to the stove. All of them laughed. Maria asked,

"Ganja, what do you have here? Let me guess."

Maria slightly opened the lids and inhaled. She jumped up, as if she was a small girl. Maria exclaimed to her husband,

"Dear Alex, it's my favorite—potato and zucchini pancakes with sour cream,"

Ganja smiled with tears in her eyes.

"Yes, my dearest Pannochka Marie. I remember how you enjoy them when you were a small girl."

Ganja brought a jar of sour cream to the table and stuck a spoon in it. Then she put two large bowls with potato and zucchini pancakes on the table and opened the lids. The smell of the hot pancakes was so good, and they looked so delicious that the young couple was ready to start their lunch right away. Maria placed forks and plates on the table and couldn't wait to eat.

Alexander smiled, watching his wife; she was in a hurry. He teased her.

"Marie, with this food, you can gain a few extra pounds and lose the beauty of your figure."

Maria parried fast:

"That's all right, mon amour. In our betrothal, you promised to love me and to be with me always, no matter of what... And another thing is important: one or two extra pounds would never be noticeable with my present shape, trust me."

Ganja's heart was aching, she felt sorry for them. She suggested quietly,

"Let us pray and start our lunch."

The tears rolled down her cheeks and, as long as she did not want the young couple to see them, Ganja turned away and went to the stove to make and bring their teas.

Alexander said,

"By the way, Marie, in my letter to your father, I thanked your father for you, my dearest wife, and I expressed my appreciation to your grandfather for the miraculous therapeutic herbal teas and compresses. When we come back, we will learn beyond doubt the art of herbal remedies, and we'll use the herbal medicine in our practice."

Maria looked at Alexander with interest.

"Do you think they can reduce the term of our imprisonment, Mon Cher?"

Alexander answered with firmness in his voice.

"Everything is possible with God's will. During the war, you learned it better than me. And you know well, what we need to do."

"The only thing we must do is pray. Alex, during the war, I prayed all the time, and I was saved."

Alexander hugged Maria gently and kissed her hand. The eyesight in his right eye had not recovered completely, but he could see Maria's beauty, and he said,

"Darling, if you only knew, how much I love you…"

He could not finish the sentence because a huge spasm tightened his chest and interrupted his breathing. Alexander became pale. Maria screamed,

"Alex, please…"

The chest pain slowly released, and he was able to inhale.

Alexander apologized,

"Marie, I did not mean to scare you. Pardon me, Mon Amour."

Maria interrupted him:

"Please, calm down, Alex and let me take you to bed. You are too emotional today."

Maria turned back to Ganja and asked her to drop Alexander some valerian drops. He did not like valerian drops and usually refused to take them, but this time, he took mixture without arguing and lay down. Maria sat next to her husband, stroking his hair until he dozed. She prayed: *"Help us, save us, have mercy on us, and keep us, O God by Thy grace."*

"*Lord, have mercy! Lord have mercy! Lord have mercy!*"

Chapter 14

Maria learned from Ganja that NKVD used to arrest people at night. She thought, "One more proof that they are demonic, and nighttime is their time." The NKVD followed their own rules and arrived at the estate at a quarter to three in the morning. Maria heard the sound of car engine, peeked out of the window and saw the light beams. She awoke Alexander.

"Alex, they are here. They have arrived. I do not want to be separated from you. Let's ask them again not to separate us."

Alexander was calm; he did not want to ask the enemies for any favors.

"It will not work, my love."

Two military men knocked on the door. Alexander opened it widely, and they entered the lodge. They handed him the order for arrest. Alexander read it carefully and asked for a couple of minutes to say goodbye to his wife.

"You'll have about two hours together. The lieutenant colonel ordered us to transport you in one car. He sent warm clothes for you, Madam Kurbatov."

He handed a heavy pack to Alexander, but Maria was the first to pick it up because of Alexander's fractured arm.

"Thank you. We appreciate it very much."

"Are you ready?"

Alexander answered,

"Yes, sir."

He took the heavy package sent to Maria with his good hand, and Maria took two others prepared by Ganja. The officer looked at them and asked,

"What do you have there?"

"Valenki and quilted jackets," Maria answered.

"You probably do not need them. We supply all political prisoners with some clothing and valenki, when they are transported to prison. You can have a change of underwear and a couple of shirts or sweaters."

"What about mittens?"

She showed him two pairs of her colorful mittens that Ganja brought her yesterday. The officer looked at them, smiled and answered,

"You may have them, as well."

The Kurbatovs sat down for a minute in accordance with their national tradition and prayed. They were about to leave when Maria looked at the stove and saw potato and zucchini pancakes left from yesterday. She stopped and looked at the officer.

"May I have them for later?" Maria asked in a pleading voice.

The officer was more than surprised.

"How could she be hungry at such a moment?"

When she moved to the stove, he noticed her belly and understood, why his commander said,

"Don't be too zealous with them. They've had enough hardship from the local committee."

The bags with their belongings were packed, and the young couple took the rear seat of the car next to the armed soldier. Maria looked out of the window at her former home estate and could not keep quiet, she burst into sobbing. Alexander squeezed her hand and tried to joke, suggesting to eat some pancakes. Maria did not hear his words and sat frozen for a while.

In ten minutes, to Alexander's surprise, Maria fell asleep. Alexander put his hand on Maria's belly and was in touch with his baby. He had "a gentlemen conversation" with his child about the tragic circumstances of their life and adversity they all had to undergo. Alexander asked his son to be nice to his mother, and to remember that one day, they would see and hug each other again and feel, as if they had never been separated.

The voice of the officer awoke Maria.

"I want you to know that as soon as we arrive to Lvov prison, you'll be separated."

It sounded like thunder in the near distance. Maria caught Alexander's hand and whispered, looking straight into his face,

"They cannot do it, Alex. It is not fair. We did not do any harm to them, to this land, to anybody in this world. We could not betray them because we did not live in this country, I mean in the USSR."

Alexander kissed her crying eyes and reminded her in a low but firm voice,

"You, Countess Kurbatov must behave and pray. Try to remember, darling: you are an example of human dignity and patience for our son. Trust in God only, mon amour and be strong."

The high metal gate opened slowly, and the guard came up to check the documents of the passengers. Then the transport vehicle entered the backyard of the prison and parked near the building entrance. The officer ordered the soldier to unload the Kurbatovs' belongings and asked them to get out of the car. Alexander got out rather fast and offered his hand to his wife. Maria could barely move. She hugged her husband and did not want to let him go. Alexander repeated the same words,

"Mon amour, take care of yourself. Darling, I beg you to take care of our baby and yourself. Marie, please stop crying. You know, I cannot stand it. God is merciful, Marie. Soon, He will help us out."

A strict woman in uniform appeared in front of Maria. The severe tone of her voice revealed an absence of mercy. She ordered,

"Prisoner Maria Kurbatov follow me! Now!"

Maria moved after the prison guard, then turned around, looked back at the disfigured posture of her pale and deface husband and screamed,

"Alex!"

Maria did not remember what happened after she rushed to her husband. She fainted. They put her on a couch in the nurse's office. After a while, Maria regained consciousness, but she was very weak and couldn't open her eyes. She heard different voices in the medical office and recognized the voice of the officer who had transported them from the estate. He shared some information with a jailor. What Maria overheard surprised her a lot.

"They arrived to find her family. There is no more family, as a family. Her father was executed by the local NKVD in 1944. He was a physician who operated on the high-ranking Nazi during the war, so he saved the life of the future burgomaster. We tried to find her siblings but had no luck. They exist somewhere in the orphanages or colonies - depending on their age, but they were given different last names, as most of the kids from the landowners' families. With time, they'll forget about their nobility and become normal kids. You know, the ideological propaganda in orphanages brings successful results and with time, all the kids hate their parents for the exploitation of the working people."

A woman who sounded reasonable, asked,

"Why weren't they repatriated right away? Wasn't it easier to tell them that the family was executed by Nazis and that nobody was left alive?"

"There was no way to do this. What the former chairman of the local NKVD did to this couple, the lieutenant colonel considered 'mockery.' Using rape and torture, he persuaded them to sign their '*open-hearted confession of a spy and terrorist mission*.' They left her husband without an eye, missing teeth and with multiple bone fractures. Five or six men from NKVD beat him up and raped her, so you can imagine what those people did to them."

The jailor asked,

"How did you learn everything about the couple?"

"Our chief received a report about the facts describing how the head of local NKVD exceeded his authority. The colonel went to dismiss him. When they arrived in Blue Creeks, the building of NKVD had been blown up and burned. A drunken head of the local committee was burned in the fire together with his deputy, and the person-on-duty was so drunk that being in the same house, he did not hear the explosions in the basement. He was surprised to see the fire fighters, working on a scene. Can you imagine?"

They laughed. The story seemed funny to them.

"How did the Kurbatovs get to Blue Creeks?" the jailor asked.

"By the way, she is from landowners, and the estate in Blue Creeks belonged to her family. They arrived home and found warm, even hot reception."

They laughed again. The jailer asked:

"What should we do with her?"

"As the colonel ordered, 'Don't be overzealous. They had enough.' Follow the protocol and send her to the camp, as fast as possible. Let them have a headache of her and her child delivery."

The jailer came up to Maria and asked her to open her eyes. Maria could not do it. She tried her best but there was not a trace of strength in her entire body.

The jailer said to a nurse,

"Let her stay here for an hour. Then we'll see."

She left to prepare all the necessary papers for Maria's departure to the camp. The jailer was back exactly in one hour. Maria was sitting on the couch, eating her pancakes. She was hungry again but did not have the strength to chew.

The woman said,

"This time, you are more alive. Come with me. You can bring your food and whatever you have with you."

Maria followed her. She could not believe that any of this was happening to her. She felt so, as if she was just an observer there, or had watched it in a movie. The jailer ordered Maria to take off her clothes and examined her body and vaginal area. Then she took her naked into the room next door and cut Maria's beautiful hair, as had been done in the Nazi camp.

After cutting Maria's hair, the jailer gave Maria soap and a towel and took her to the shower room. There were about twenty shower stalls there, and at that time, eight women were taking showers. As if in a trance, Maria showered, not paying any attention to the women who looked at her big belly with surprise and pity.

After Maria showered, the jailer ordered to put on prisoner clothes. Maria did it without hesitation or resistance. She looked ugly in the oversized prison dress. Presently, she did not care about her appearance and left the shower room without even a glance in a mirror.

All the paperwork was prepared. The jailor gave Maria two documents to sign. She signed without reading them. If it was her death sentence, she signed it easily.

Lord, have mercy!

Chapter 15

After signing the papers, the jailer took Maria to a large prison cell that accommodated thirty people. All the tenants turned their heads toward a new prisoner. The jailer pushed Maria in and locked a heavy door behind her. Maria stood at the door, staring at the opposite wall. She was ready to collapse again. Somebody of the inmates called her, but she did not hear the woman's voice. Another inmate helpfully pulled her bag with Maria's belongings, and the third prisoner took her hand and brought shocked woman to a narrow bed in the middle of the room.

Maria sat down on the edge of the bed and closed her eyes. She was exhausted, sleepy and hungry. Maria smiled at her first thought: "Thank God, I must be still alive, if I can experience so many feelings at the same time."

She opened her bag and took out the last two of Ganja's pancakes. Maria was chewing the cold pancakes, and the tears were running from her closed eyes. She had become again a person without a name, just a number. History repeated itself with one difference: her new number was much longer than in the Nazi camp.

Maria finished her snack and decided to lie down. In a minute, she was asleep. The women woke her up because she sobbed loudly and called her husband's name. In her dream, she was lost in the woods; she heard Alex's voice somewhere not far from her but was unable to find him. Maria opened her eyes and looked up in terror at the group of women, standing around her. She started to cry, being helpless to understand right away what they wanted from her. The elderly one stroked Maria's short hair and sent all the women back to their plank-beds.

"When is your transport?" the elderly woman asked in a soft voice.

Maria looked at her in wide-eyed astonishment. She knew nothing about any transport, date or time.

"I don't know anything about my transport," Maria answered in a perfect Ukrainian language.

"I am Sister Olga, a nun. What is your name?"

"Maria Kurbatov."

Sister Olga introduced the younger nuns to Maria. There were eight of them from one convent. Maria visited that convent twice with her godmother when she was seven and thirteen.

"What have the nuns done that they were also imprisoned?" Maria thought, looking at Sister Olga suspiciously.

Sister Olga read Maria's thought and explained, "We are not criminals, Maria. We are ***people's enemies,***".

Maria noticed that Sister Olga's smile and voice were very sad when she declared the reason of their staying here.

"Have you heard anything about such a caste?" asked the nun.

Maria was not aware about the existing of *people's enemies'* caste and shook her head.

She was curious about it and asked,

"Why did you need to join such a caste, if you are nuns?"

The elderly woman looked at Maria kindheartedly and could not understand, how it was possible that this poor girl did not know anything about the "people's enemies."

Sister Olga was afraid that something outlandish had happened to Maria that she lost the comprehension of current life. Everyone in the cell listened to their conversation with interest. It seemed to them that this pregnant woman fell down from the sky and did not know anything about the terrible world and what was going on in it.

Sister Olga asked,

"Maria, why did you join '*people's enemies'* society? How could you become a traitor and perform something harmful against your native land and people?"

"Who? My husband and I?" Maria whispered in shock.

She did not have enough air to breath and was about to faint again. She thought, "How dare they pronounce such an accusation against Alex and me?! They do not know us, and they know nothing about us."

Then she pulled herself together and explained,

"We arrived home from Germany a week ago to visit my family in Blue Creeks. Sister Olga, believe me, we did not join any caste and had never in our minds to cause any crime. They punished us brutally just for coming home. We did not do any unruliness. Nobody was harmed, but us."

"Have you read the Judgment? Same sentence, same clause with all of us. Our "crime" was categorized with the same ***'Article 58: High Treason***'. Do you know, Maria, what it denotes? In accordance with this article, we all betrayed and instigated harm to our communist Motherland and Soviet people," Sister Olga explained.

Maria became pale, and she heard the ringing in her head again, as it happened when they brought Alexander and her in the early morning. She joined all her inner forces in order not to lose her consciousness.

"Sister Olga, what did my husband and I have in common with this regime? We are citizens of France."

"However, you arrived in godless and unlegislated country, Maria. The Soviet occupants took away our lands, churches, monasteries, laws and lives of our Ukrainian people. They brought the pictures and statutes of their demonic idols Lenin and Stalin. They have one desire: to kill the faith of the people in God and to implant the ideas of communism. They want people to believe in their 'communist democracy and in justice of their evil proletariat dictatorship'. Their mechanism is rather powerful, but completely demonic, Maria. They do not take into consideration the most important thing – their victory in our land is temporary. The Almighty God will restore the justice, because there is nobody more powerful than God. 'Blessed are those who are persecuted for righteousness' sake, for theirs is the Kingdom of Heaven.' We are blessed, dear Maria, because we had never bowed and would never bow to their satanic idols and ideas."

At that moment, Maria completely realized the horror of Alexander's and her situation. She burst into tears.

"Maria, do you know what can help you and us?"

"Yes, Sister, I do."

Sister Olga did not expect to hear a positive answer.

"What is it, darling?"

Answering the question, Maria felt herself again, as if she was a student of the convent school.

"It's a prayer, Sister. God has always been merciful to me."

She turned back and looked at the sisters in the cell. They watched Maria with pity, but at the same time, they were happy to find one more of God's souls in that chaotic world.

Sister Olga promised,

"Maria, our transport is tomorrow morning. If they plan to transport you with us, we'll help you during the long trip to Siberia."

Maria specified,

"They're deporting my husband and me to Magadan."

"All of us are sent to Magadan region. They developed the long chain of labor camps there for political prisoners - GULAG. It is impossible to run away and survive in the white desert of snow and frost."

Sister Olga explained to Maria the itinerary and destination of their journey. The voice of the nun was calm and firm. She sounded like Maria's husband: not hysterical or frightened. Maria could sense a person's dignity through her voice.

The young woman admired Sister Olga's behavior, "What a person! She looks absolutely calm, as if tomorrow she is going to Paris to see her friends there in a Christian convent, and these impertinent events do not trouble her life."

Maria promised herself, "I have to learn her heavenly manners. I am too frenetic. It's not good for a baby."

Maria started her evening prayers with a phrase: "Thank you, God, for sending me Sister Olga. Now she is my best support."

Glory to Thee, o Lord! Glory forever!"

Chapter 16

It was six o'clock in the morning on October 16, 1946 when the prisoners were given their breakfast. The kitchen personnel brought some sticky porridge and tea without sugar for breakfast. Then they supplied every prisoner with ten slices of dry rye bread, as their journey allowance. Sister Olga asked for some more bread for Maria,

"Look, she is pregnant. Give her another norm, please."

"No, it was not ordered. If you are so generous, share with her your supply," answered a huge jailor.

Maria wanted to be sure that she was scheduled to leave together with the nuns. She came up to receive her dry bread and asked the delivery man about it. The people who delivered the breakfast and bread did not know anything about the schedule of Maria's transport. At 7 a.m. sharp, the door of the cell was widely opened. Two jailers started to call the names of the inmates and ordered them to line up in the corridor by the wall. Maria's name was called among the nuns, and the young woman was happy. She caught herself with the thought,

"O my Lord, what am I happy about?"

She had to admit that the evening and night with the nuns had filled her with peace. It was not as if she linked her destiny with life in prison. It could not be like this due to absence of any knowledge about prison life. However, she learned one very important lesson from Sister Olga,

"People should not waste their strength, spirit and health for the things that they are not able to change. *'A sacrifice unto God is a broken spirit; a heart that is broken and humbled God will not despise..."*

Maria agreed,

"I have no strength to fight the malicious circumstances or to struggle against the completely demonic system. I must preserve my child and me. We ought to survive. We should not leave Alex alone."

The guards with carbines and dogs pushed women into the truck, and two armed soldiers sat with them. They transported the prisoners to the Lvov freight railway station. The train waited for them on the platform. The women were forced to run to the carriage in the middle of the train. Several carriages had heavy metal doors opened and there were thick metal bars on the windows. There were other prisoners in the carriage, which had been picked up and delivered earlier from another prison. The nuns and Maria were lucky to find two compartments side by side at the end of the carriage for the nine of them to sit in.

The train was about to start, when Maria noticed through the bars on the windows that another transport had arrived. There was a group of men running to the train. Guards with dogs surrounded them. She saw her husband, who was not able to move fast. He fell on the platform, and three dogs were near him. Maria screamed and bit her lip. Two other prisoners helped Alexander to get up and the third picked up his bag. The train made a move and stopped again, waiting for them. They caught the train. In a minute, it pulled away, taking a new group of "people's enemies" to the GULAG. The demonic system arranged this terrible journey to Magadan for millions of people. For millions of them, it was departure forever.

Maria was sitting near the window, trying to see the scenery as it changed, but the iron bars limited her observation. She prayed her Morning prayers in a quiet voice, since she had no possibility to do it in prison due to early transport:

"Having risen from sleep, I hasten to Thee, O Master, Lover of mankind, and by Thy loving kindness, I strive to do Thy work, and I pray to Thee: Help me at all times, in everything, and deliver me from every worldly, evil thing and every impulse of the devil, and save me, and lead me into Thine eternal kingdom. For Thou art my Creator, and the Giver and Provider of everything good, and in Thee is all my hope, and onto Thee do I send up glory, now and ever, and unto the ages of ages. Amen."

Some of the nuns reclined the upper berths and fell asleep. Maria wanted to do the same, but it was very risky to climb up there with her belly. The jailers and four armed guards occupied the two front compartments. From time to time, they walked along the carriage, watching the prisoners.

Maria was hungry. She opened her bag and took out a piece of dry bread that they gave them in the morning. The jailer noticed Maria eating dry bread and brought an aluminum cup of hot water. Maria thanked the jailer sincerely and warmed her hands with the hot cup. Her snack was set.

The jailer found a lower berth for Maria in another compartment and transferred her there. Maria put her bag under her head to use as a pillow and fell asleep. She slept for a few hours until hunger awoke her. The dry bread was the only food she had with her. Maria went to the jailer and asked for another cup of hot water.

Persistent hunger and poor meal arrangements reminded her of the wonderful schedule for a mother-to-be that she had followed during the five months of her pregnancy. She left that schedule on her working desk—the beautiful desk of an executive director—or, to be more precise, she left it in her fairyland, where she was "a princess" and Alexander was her "prince charming."

God rewarded Maria for her suffering during the war in multiple ways. She was grateful to her Savior and Mother of God. Nobody could blame her for the absence of appreciation. Nonetheless, she wanted more and very fast. She had been so happy with Alexander that she decided to make everyone in her family, as happy, as they were.

"What was wrong with my initial intent that brought me to such a punishment?" That thought was the most repetitive and disturbing one.

Maria tried to analyze and understand what had happened in her life. Different thoughts and questions flashed into her mind,

"Why did we come to this wild country? Why was it initially permitted for us by God to come here? Why did He allow the brutal violence against us? Why is it so that, instead of our return home, we are going in the opposite direction to Siberia? Why didn't He give us a way out of this?"

Maria closed her eyes, but the disturbing thoughts continued to hunt her,

"We committed a mistake by His assumption, didn't we? To be imprisoned for the mistake that was permitted from Above is not fair. Was it from Above? Wait a second. Where did the intrusive idea come from?"

Maria asked God to help her get rid of the disquieting thoughts, but her Holy Father wanted her to discover the correct answer. She presumed,

"Maybe, I had compromised my relationship with the Divinity by insisting on something that was not meant to be at that time."

She recollected the words of her husband:

"Marie, you have to be sure that this is the right time to go there. The political system of that country is unpredictable. They will always consider us their social enemies. To visit the Ukraine right after the war is dangerous."

. The Lord showed it to Maria in different ways, but she was close-minded and stubborn. She insisted on having her way, refusing to read the stop signals. Even

God's blessed pregnancy did not stop her. Now, Maria realized clearly: she was not supposed to arrive to the Ukraine, when everyone had asked her to postpone the visit.

Maria exclaimed,

"O, my God! Here is the answer. I had a feeling that it was me, who caused all the problems. I have blamed myself from the very beginning, and I was right. It was my fault. I followed the evil suggestion that made me crazy. When everything after WWII turned out to be great, I lost Lord's guidance. I stopped feeling warmth and seeing light while meditating. I did not pick up the Angel's voice. I became blind and multiple signs did not stop me. My nice intent was twisted by evil force and became corrupted."

Her regrettable life experience proved the truth of a prayer that Maria learned in childhood at her convent school: *"You have said with Your most pure lips: for without Me, you can do nothing... Help me, a sinner, to complete through You this work, which I am about to begin, in the name of the Father, and of the Son, and of the Holy Spirit. Amen."*

Maria understood,

"I began 'the work' definitely without God's blessing; that was why it was not successfully finished by Him."

The sounds of the train were monotonous, and nobody interrupted Maria's analysis of true reasons that caused her tragedy. She recollected her grandfather's explanation,

"Satan always wants people to live a miserable life. He makes them self-centered, confused, disturbed, scared and unhappy. He drags them into darkness— to depression or feeling of personal superiority. When they are lost in darkness, he interrupts their connection with the Divinity. At that point, people make their mistakes and start blaming not only their loved ones but even the Father Almighty for misfortunate events in their human lives."

The words of Maria's grandfather were ringing in her head,

"Children, I want you to remember, our Lord wants us to live a wonderful life. The only requirement people have to admit is that without God's blessing, we are unable to do or achieve anything desirable in this life. The people who sold their souls to Satan can also attain something with his evil support. However, they pay for it with the loss of their eternal life."

Maria turned to the window, crying. "*Forgive me, Father Almighty. Do not punish my child and my husband for my sins. Save them, please.*" Maria was unable to stop sobbing. "*The Most Holy Theotokos, forgive me and cover my child with your protective patronage. O Lord, cleanse me, a sinner, have mercy on me and help me.*"

The train was moving further and further from Lvov. It was cold in the carriage and Maria woke up in the middle of the night. She tried to walk and exercise to warm herself, but it did not help significantly. She had to put on a quilted jacket to feel more comfortable, and only then she was able to fall asleep again.

Maria had a very strange dream: she saw a blue sky without a single cloud on it and a green meadow filled with yellow and white flowers. There was a birch tree in the middle of the meadow, and a small boy was with his mother under the tree. Then a strong wind, like a tornado, appeared out of nowhere. The wind picked up the small boy and took him away. Maria saw again the beautiful blue sky, the sun shining brightly, and a pleasant landscape, as though nothing had happened. Only the young mother had turned old; she looked like Alexander's mother, who was looking for her son.

Sister Olga woke Maria up. They were ready to say their Morning prayers and wanted Maria to join them. The nuns saw Maria's agony yesterday and her strong desire to open up and release something through praying. The nuns did not interfere.

Sister Olga asked,

"Did you clarify yesterday everything that you accumulated inside, my child?"

"Yes, Sister Olga, a lot," Maria answered, being surprised with Sister Olga's observation.

"It was between Him and you. Am I right?" the nun asked.

Maria was amazed that the nun, who seemed not to pay much attention to her yesterday, still knew and felt what was going on with Maria.

"Now you can live in harmony with Him again. Poor child, it was so difficult for you to lose His guidance and protection. Let us pray and thank our Father in Heaven for everything He blesses us with."

It was nice to pray with the sisters. The light appeared faster in comparison to when Maria worshipped alone. Again, she experienced her favorite feeling within - the white light and warmth. Sister Olga whispered in Maria's ear,

"Holy Spirit is within. Feel Him."

After praying, she whispered again,

"You are blessed, my child. Stay always blessed!"

Maria told the sisters about her strange dream. Sister Irena was sure that Alexander's mother had started looking for her son. The last time they contacted her was a week before their departure to the Ukraine, and Countess Kurbatova was preparing to meet many guests in two weeks—the whole Kotyk family. She dreamed of seeing Maria and taking care of her during her pregnancy. Madam Kurbatova had said, "The mother-to-be needs the right supervision and thoughtful assistance. Otherwise she'll never have a strong child."

The journey seemed to last forever. It was the tenth day, and they were somewhere in Russia. Maria could pick up different accents of the people on the platforms. She was pronounced their enemy, but she was not even familiar with their life, culture, traditions and customs. She had been sentenced, as a political prisoner.

The thought of 150-months-term in the Magadan camp made her stressed every time. Their child was destined to be born in a country that was not his parents' homeland. His destiny was not to be surrounded by comfort and love of his family but among inmates of a political forced labor camp in frosty, far-off Siberia.

Maria asked every day,

"Lord, have mercy on my child and help him! Help us, save us, have mercy on us and keep us, O God, by Thy grace."

It was difficult to sit all the time, so Maria was allowed to walk along the carriage. However, it was not easy because the train reeled. Once, Maria lost her balance and fell. She did not sustain a serious injury, but her hip was bruised for a week. Every time the train stopped for more than ten minutes, they allowed Maria to stay on the platform of the carriage and to breathe the fresh air. Maria knew that her jailer told the team of guards the true story about Madam Kurbatov and her husband, the nobility from France.

It was the fourteenth day of their journey. The train was about to stop at one of the railway stations in Siberia. The jailer allowed Maria to leave the carriage under her supervision and to walk on the platform for forty minutes. Maria was very happy. They walked along the train and came to the other carriages containing prisoners. She sensed that Alexander was in one of them. She looked in the windows, but the bars did not allow her to see much.

Maria continued passing the carriages, when she saw her husband standing on the platform of a carriage behind a guard and jailer. She stopped and looked at him. He greeted her by winking with his only eye and smiling. The jailer said to Maria,

"Do not stop!"

They continued walking. Maria turned to her jailer and said sincerely,

"Thank you."

The last week of the trip was the most difficult. There was not a single railway station with a platform to walk on. It snowed constantly. In the snow desert, the train moved much slower. The train stopped four times, waiting for the teams of railway workers to arrive and clear the rail tracks and switches from snow in order not to be derailed.

Sometimes they opened the carriage door, and Maria was allowed to stay for five minutes in front of the door. She looked at the endless white snow fields and prayed. The guards got used to her, and it seemed as if nobody paid attention to Maria. The snow in Siberia differed from Ukrainian snow, that she used to play with during her childhood. This snow was frosty and dry, as quicksand.

During long stops, the jailers and guards used to jump into the snow. Maria did not take that risk with her belly. For some time, she stayed on the carriage platform, supplying her baby with fresh, frosty air. When she got cold, she came back in. Persistent hunger bothered her a lot. Maria was hungry most of the time. The dry bread did not help. She lost weight, and there were days when she felt weak, dizzy and was not able to stay in front of the opened door.

The nuns tried to support Maria, sharing their portions with her. The other women prisoners watched her and thought that she belonged to the group of nuns—that she was just a "pregnant nun"—and they did not like the idea of sharing their food with her. Maria learned not to expect anything extra due to her special condition, but she was very grateful to the sisters. "Thank You, Father for sending me Your wonderful sisters. I doubt that I could survive this journey without their support."

Glory to Thee, o Lord! Glory to Thee!

Chapter 17

At night, the train arrived in Magadan. The carriages with the prisoners were taken to the dead end of the railway station. It was very cold, and all the windows were covered with hoar-frosting, the natural "painting" or "engraving" of severe frost. The prisoners in the carriages were completely out of firewood and food, and it seemed that the frost was getting inside their bodies, "introducing" itself to their bones and testing, who of the newcomers was able to stand such a low temperature.

The guard supervisor ran to the station master to make a call to the local camp authority about their arrival. They promised to send the transports to the railway station to pick up the prisoners and deliver them to final points of destination.

His question was,

"When? There is no food and wood. All the guard and jailor teams are hungry and frozen, as well."

"The transports will be sent, as soon as possible, but not earlier than noon," the authority answered.

The nuns let Maria sit in the middle and tried to keep her warm. Maria fell asleep for a while, but a hungry child in her womb did not allow her to be in the same position longer than half an hour. She walked to the jailers' compartment to ask, if she could have some hot water.

The guard supervisor had just returned and brought the news that the camp authority would send the transports to pick them up around noon. Until that time, they had to keep the prisoners in the carriages without warmth or food.

He tried to jest,

"After all this, they will find camp soup delicious."

One of the jailers asked,

"Who cares about them? What about us? We are freezing and hungry, as well."

"You will go and eat at a buffet at the railway station. Thirty minutes is enough time to run there and get some food. The buffet opens at 7 a.m. You'll go two at a time: a jailer and a guard."

Maria knocked on the opened door. They looked up at her, and she asked for some hot water. Her jailer answered,

"No, Maria, we do not have any hot water because we are out of wood."

Maria was about to leave, but then she said,

"I am hungry. I'm sorry, but I am very hungry. Can you possibly give me some dry bread?"

They stared at her and did not say a single word. The poor woman wandered back to her compartment. She heard her jailer was saying something about her to the guard supervisor in a low voice. He shouted at her,

"I don't care. She'll wait for her camp soup, big-bellied bitch."

It was a quarter to seven in the morning. The nuns and Maria were about to finish their morning prayers, when her jailer appeared in their compartment. She commanded strictly,

"Maria Kurbatov, follow me."

Maria got up and moved fast behind the jailer, but she was not able to catch up with her. They left the carriage and walked quickly toward the railway station. Maria was passing by the long line of carriages containing prisoners. All the doors were closed, and the windows looked beautiful with a variety of fairy paintings made by the frost.

Maria was dizzy, but the thought that she might get some food, filled her with new strength. In five minutes, they were at the station buffet. The jailer brought to Maria some soup, bread and hot boiled sausages with mustard. Maria blessed the food and prayed. She must have been starved for a long time, because after soup, she was not able to eat the sausages. She wanted them enormously, but a spasm in her throat did not allow her to swallow another bite. Maria had not eaten anything normal for many weeks.

The jailer brought a glass of hot tea and ordered,

"Sip some, and it will help you."

"Thank you. You are very kind to me."

Maria looked at the face of her jailer and finished,

"I do not know what God has prepared for me at a camp, but I shall always remember you in my prayers."

"It's nonsense. I did what I had to do. Stop talking. Finish your food. Your time is up."

Maria noticed that she frightened the jailer with her appreciation. The communist women tried to look strict, strong and non-sentimental. But this one was not rude or torturous toward her young prisoner. She was just afraid to be a sincere woman.

Swallowing the sausage was much easier with hot tea. Maria was full. She thanked the jailer again. The jailer replied in her usual manner,

"Take your and my bread with you for later. Anyway, it has been already paid for."

Maria was happy and thanked God and the jailer for a wonderful breakfast. The woman smiled for the first time, saying,

"Oh, Maria, I was mentioned together with your God."

Then she shifted her facial expression, assuming her usual one, and looked at her watch. She commanded Maria,

"March ahead!"

Maria was happy because she had fed her baby and her with real food. She got up and prayed,

"*More honorable than the Cherubim, and more glorious, beyond compare, than the Seraphim, without defilement you gave birth to God the Word. True Theotokos, we magnify you. Glory to the Father, and to the Son, and to the Holy Spirit, now and ever and unto ages of ages. Amen.*"

They ran to the carriage. After three minutes, Maria could not stand that speed. She begged the jailer to slow down. They were passing again the carriages with prisoners. At that time, the doors of some of them were opened. The guards were smoking on the platform of the railway station.

Maria ran faster to look inside of Alexander's carriage. Yes. Her Alexander was there on the steps of his carriage. He asked the guards for permission to tell his wife two words. The answer was,

"No. Absolutely no. Forget it!"

Maria and Alexander looked at each other for a couple of seconds, and Alexander demonstrated his wrist without splints, and how he could move with his hand and fingers. The hand was facing a little bit upward, but all the fingers were moving. One of his guards roared at Maria,

"Move fast. Follow your jailer…" he cursed her at the end, but she did not want to pay attention at him.

Maria moved backward, waving her delicate hand at Alexander and smiling her unforgettable smile. She tried to catch her jailer, whispering on the run,

"Thank You, my Lord, for an unexpected 'rendezvous' with my husband. Thank you for the healing of his arm and wrist. Thank you for my miraculous breakfast. With Your blessing, we shall survive in this endless snow land. I do believe that one day we'll be together again, happier than ever. *Glory to Thee, O Lord! Glory to Thee!*"

The transports appeared at 2 p.m. The chain of big trucks lined up on the platform, picking up new groups of "people's enemies." The prisoners were assigned to different camps depending on gender and "severity of crime." The misfortunate people were ready to make their first steps into the horrible new life. The hunger and cold were merciless and pushed them quickly out.

The guards with huge dogs arranged two long corridors from the train carriages to the trucks. The prisoners were forced to run quickly along the "corridors." The dogs jumped and barked furiously. The guards of the carriages roared and pushed people, like crazy. They were simply throwing the prisoners out. Maria looked at the whole picture, and the closest comparison that came to her mind was satanic hell.

Somebody shouted in her ear,

"Jump! Now!"

That "somebody" threw her bag on the platform. Maria could not move quickly in valenki; her big belly did not allow her to see the narrow steps of the carriage. She snatched at the railing with her right hand, and somebody pushed her out with demonic force. Maria lost her balance but did not lose her grip on the railing. She slipped off the steps on her right side. At that very moment, she heard her husband's voice, shouting,

"Marie!"

"I am fine. I sledded down. Nothing hurts. Just my wrist a little bit. I pulled the ligaments there."

That was her mental message to Alexander. Later, Maria would send her messages every day, keeping hope that her Angel could deliver at least half of them to her dearest Alex. Maria picked up her bag and ran, as fast as she could, along the "corridor" and was sure that she heard the word "Schnell!" and the crack of the whips. At that moment, Maria was aware of the similarity of events in her life: the present in Russia and previously – with German Nazis. Her heart was tearing apart: "Another camp! O Lord, not again!"

Somebody pulled her into a truck. She sat down on a bench, recovering her breath and crying resentfully. Sister Olga caringly pulled Maria's shawl over the head of a disturbed woman. While running to the truck, Maria nearly lost the warm woolen shawl that Ganja had given her. Sister Olga realized that Maria did not know how to wear the large shawls on her head, and she taught her how to fix it comfortably without losing it.

The armed guards got into the trucks, and the trucks were ready to move. The dogs continued barking. In a couple of minutes, all the trucks started, taking a new group of convicts to their final destinations. The final trip took more than an hour. Everyone was freezing. The transport stopped at the gate of a camp, and the women were glad that they survived the trip. They hoped that soon they would get into the warmth of the barracks. Maria could not pronounce a word; she was trembling from the cold. The gate was opened in five minutes, and the people were commanded to get out of the trucks.

Once Maria was out, she noticed that only two trucks had come to that camp. The new inmates were lined up near the administrative building. Two officers came out and took them inside for registration. After registration, they were sent to take showers and change their clothes. Maria felt better after she washed herself and warmed in the shower room. The new inmates changed the prison clothing, and this time, Maria looked in the mirror. She was skinny and pale but the only feeling that disturbed her constantly was intolerable hunger.

The jailers subdivided the new prisoners into their cells in the barracks. There were thirty women in Maria's cell. Two nuns were settled with her. The jailer put Maria's bag on one of the beds in the middle of the room. The two nuns found beds near the door.

It was not as warm in the cell, as it was in the administrative building. But the worst thing about the cell was the odor; it was very bad—pungent and concentrated.

"I will get used to it with time," Maria thought.

She felt nauseous.

"Where is the restroom?" Maria asked.

The neighbor pointed at the door. Maria jumped up and ran. Near the door, she found a bucket and vomited. Afterward, she knocked on the door, and when the jailer opened a small window in the door, Maria asked to change the bucket because she had vomited, and it stank. The jailer answered in a loud and rude voice,

"Not authorized!"

Maria could not understand, why it was not authorized, and why the changing of the bucket required anybody's authorization. She knocked and asked again, explaining that she can go and wash it by herself. The jailer repeated the same answer using different words:

"Not permitted, you stupid woman."

It was very difficult for Maria to understand, why they wanted people to stay in such a stinking room. She overheard, how the jailer told somebody in the corridor,

"The pregnant bitch vomited and wanted me to change the bucket 'because it stinks.' Let them all enjoy it!"

They laughed loudly and went in different directions. Maria covered the bucket with a lid and washed her hands. She looked at the women in her cell and said,

"I'm sorry."

Then she introduced herself.

"I am Maria Kurbatov."

Nobody answered, and Maria went to her bed. Everyone was sitting quietly. Maria's neighbor looked at the young woman with surprise and said,

"Natasha."

Maria wanted to know, when they were scheduled to eat, but she found it impolite to start a conversation with such a trivial question. Instead she asked,

"When did you get to the camp?"

Maria expected the answer to be "in the morning," or "in the first half of the day," or at least "yesterday."

Natasha looked at the young woman with interest and answered,

"In 1940."

"What? Six years ago!"

Maria could not catch her breath. The moment she started to breath, she asked,

"How old were you when you were imprisoned?"

Natasha replied emotionlessly,

"Twenty-one."

Maria counted and thought,

"Now, Natasha is twenty-seven, but she looks older, much older, than a twenty-seven-year-old woman."

Maria's thoughts were mixed up again. She knew that her husband and she were sentenced for twelve years by mistake. She hoped that somebody had to correct the fated mistake, and in a month or two, they would be released. She could not wait for their return home.

She looked at Natasha, trying to understand, why she was still in the camp.

"Were you sentenced for a long term?"

"Fifteen years."

Maria counted again. She thought,

"She must have been sentenced for something really serious. That's why they did not release her earlier. But what serious crime could she commit at the age of twenty-one?"

Natasha read Maria's mind and said,

"What do you try to understand? Do not try to figure out what I have done. Think instead about what you did."

Maria had no answer. How could she prove to Natasha, Olga, Masha and the whole world that she and her husband were innocent people? Everyone could have doubts because they were sentenced to over twelve years in prison.

The door of the cell was opened, and they saw two jailers and a person with two buckets of food. Maria jumped up and rushed to the door.

"Sit down! You are the last. Learn our rules!"

Maria went back to her bed. The jailer said something to the person who brought the food. They giggled, and Maria was certain that they were laughing at her. Everyone in the cell had been given their food and then Maria came up. They showed her empty buckets. The jailor came up to Maria, poked a finger in Maria's belly and pronounced with sarcasm in her voice,

"Look at your fatty belly. You are too big, that's why you do not need any food. You wasted it by vomiting today. From now on, we'll arrange a special diet for you."

They left demonically satisfied. Maria went to her bed, lay down and turned to the wall. She was crying and praying for her enemies, so that God would help them realize the good and bad things that they did to people during their lives,

"O Lord, Lover of mankind, forgive them that hate and wrong us. Do good to them that do good... To them that have charged us, the unworthy, to pray for them, have mercy according to Thy great mercy. Amen."

In five minutes, the door was opened again. The jailer was back with two bowls of food for Maria and a thick slice of dark bread. She could not find Maria among the women.

"Where is the pregnant one?"

Maria turned around and smiled. Her smile was not addressed to that nasty woman. She was grateful to

Almighty Father, who answered her prayer so quickly, knowing better than anybody else, how hungry the baby and his mother-to-be were. The young woman was filled with appreciation.

"Thank you, Lord. Thank you."

She accepted her food, and on the way back to her bed, Maria noticed that all the women in the cell looked happy for her. Unexpectedly, as always, light and warmth filled her body and spread out all over the room, touching gently the souls of other God's children.

Glory to Thee, o Lord! Glory to Thee!

Chapter 18

The alarm siren awoke inmates at 5 a.m. The twelve-hour work shift was scheduled from 6 a.m. to 6 p.m. The women prisoners worked in mines, mining golden ore. Maria, like most of the prisoners, had zero knowledge of mining, and the first day was very important. They had breakfast at 5:15, and at 5:30, they were lined up in front of the barrack. During the first morning hour, Maria realized that there were not only Russian women in her cell. She heard at least three more languages there.

One was the Polish language, which she already knew, as her native Ukrainian. She got acquainted with a group of four Polish inmates during breakfast. Maria considered them the Poles from Western Ukraine, but she was wrong. Those women were arrested in 1940 in Poland together with their husbands. The NKVD executed their men and deported the women to GULAG. At the beginning, there were five couples arrested and delivered to the USSR. The Poles mentioned that one of their friends got in mine collapse two years ago. Maria felt sorry about her, but Barbara concluded,

"Bozena was the luckiest among us. She stays in Heaven with the Lord and her husband Stanislaw for two years, and we are still here."

"Poor Barbara," Maria thought. "She is envious for the death of her friend. She is obviously depressed."

The siren let them know that it was time to line up and go to work. It was a freezing morning. The women covered their faces with shawls, leaving only their eyes opened. Most of them knew, if they left mouths or noses opened, the severe frost would not allow them to breathe and in ten-fifteen minutes the skin, exposed to the wind and frost, would become colorless and insensitive, the initial signs of freezing that led to the skin wounds.

The mine was twenty minutes away. The overseers forced the inmates to run. Maria tried her best, but after five minutes, she realized that it was impossible for her to keep up with the others. She slowed down. Two huge overseers approached her and pulled her under her arms so fast that Maria's feet barely touched the snow.

When they reached the mine entrance, she noticed Sister Olga there, watching her running, and Maria burst into tears.

"Sister Olga, how can I survive here? There is no way for me and a baby to survive."

"Do not cry, Maria. I know that it's difficult for you. In a couple of months, you'll be free from your pregnancy, and then you'll run like the rest of us."

An elderly man with a hoarse voice gave all the necessary instructions to the group of new miners. He warned,

"Remember, the major danger for you is in the frequent collapses of mines. It has always been the main cause of prisoners' mortality. Your intensive work will prevent you from being frozen. Be sure, the watchers will assist you in it."

Maria thought,

"Since those miners were 'people's enemies,' nobody paid much attention to their high death rate. The solution to this problem was in ordering a new group of condemned women."

The elderly man repeated several times the daily norm of gold that every miner was supposed to mine during a shift and to hand him at 6 p.m. He did not look friendly at all, and at the end, he reminded the new women in his spiteful manner,

"You have to learn one more rule of our camp mining: *No gold, no food*."

The new group of women went into the mine. Sister Olga warned Maria,

"Stay close to us. Watch the shifts of the ore and listen to the noise. We have to watch over one another. They do not support the top and walls of the mine. We have to follow the golden row lodes and move farther and farther inside the hill. If there is no support of the walls and the top in the corridor, it will definitely collapse, just a matter of time – earlier or later."

Maria remembered only the last warning of that ugly man: "No gold, no food." She thought, "They feed us twice a day, and if they cut out the second meal, I won't be able to bear it." Maria kneeled and started to work simultaneously with her Morning prayers. She repeated maybe fifty times or more: *"O Lord Jesus Christ, Son of God, for the sake of the prayers of Thy most pure Mother and all the saints, have mercy on us. Amen."* It helped her to calm down and release the fear of not getting the evening meal.

While she prayed, her pick hit something firm. She tried to find the edges of the stone and dig it out. She succeeded, and to her big surprise, she found that she had mined a huge piece of gold, a virgin that contained not less than twenty or even thirty norms. Maria was ready to get up from the knees, run out of that dangerous place and hand her huge virgin of gold to the ugly man. Something stopped her. She again sensed the connection with her Angel, as she used to feel it during the war. He did not want her to run and deliver the treasure.

Maria waved to Sister Olga. Sister moved slowly in Maria's direction so that overseers would not notice that she crawled there just because Maria wanted her. Maria continued working. She found a couple of more golden pieces, the exact weight needed to have supper that night and put them in the basket. She kept the big godsend hidden under the tail of her dress. It was difficult for Maria to kneel for 12-hour shift. The baby moved all the time, being compressed in his mother. When his motions were painful for Maria, she talked to him, and it seemed that the baby understood her requests, became quiet, feeling sorry for his poor mother.

The overseer came up to Maria. He looked in her basket and saw several small pieces there. Then he checked the baskets of some others and left. Sister Olga was close enough to see what Maria mined. The miners were not allowed to talk. Sister Olga continued digging for a couple of minutes, and then she suggested, while not looking at Maria,

"We have to hide it here in the mine, and in case you are not able to find anything or to work hard, we'll chip off a piece, and you'll be saved."

"How can we find it later?" Maria asked.

"We'll bury it under the rails," the nun answered.

As soon as nobody was watching them, the women dug a hole under the rails where the mine trolley ran and marked the place that only they could see it. On that day, they were lucky to find some more pieces.

During the second half of her shift, Maria was not able to kneel. She did not have enough air to breathe. Her legs were cramping, and the weight of her belly felt like fifty pounds and not an ounce less. She sat down on the ground, being unable to continue digging. She was so exhausted that she did not notice the overseer who appeared behind her from time to time. The overseer was checking the results of the mining. Maria had already mined the norm, but nobody was permitted to sit, waiting for the end of the shift. He jumped over to her and pulled her shawl and hair down.

"Keep working, big-bellied woman, if you do not want me to kick you in the stomach and help you get rid of your ugly belly."

Maria began digging and sifting again. She was not able to see what she was mining because of her tears, which were pouring down her dirty face. Maria started to pray: *"O, Lord, Lover of mankind, forgive them that hate and wrong us...*" Then she stopped crying, looked at the overseer and prayed three times:

"Compass me about, o Lord, with power of Thy precious and life-giving Cross and preserve me from every evil. Amen."

Thank God, the shift was finally over. It was her first shift in hell. Maria hardly moved in line *to* turn in her gains. She prayed, *"All my hope I place in you, Mother of God: keep me under your woman's protection. Lord, have mercy. Lord, have mercy. Lord, have mercy."*

The nuns helped Maria run back to the barrack. She took a shower and felt numbness throughout her whole body. She was so exhausted that lost her appetite completely. Maria thought, "I have to eat just because I have to feed my child." She put on her clean dress, washed the dirty clothing and wandered to her cell. The food was handed out at the next-door cell. She had gotten back at the right time.

While having a supper, Maria noticed that there were two other groups of women who spoke the languages different from Russian, Polish and Ukrainian. Natasha mentioned in a low voice,

"They are from Latvia and Estonia. Some of them were here a year after my imprisonment. They were deported in spring of 1941. At the next-door cell, there are women from Lithuania."

"What did they do that NKVD deported them here?" Maria asked.

Natasha smiled,

"You are still so naïve, Maria. Do people need to cause any harm in reality in order to get here?"

Maria answered honestly,

"I cannot get used to injustice and tyranny. Why did they arrest, execute or imprison people from the neighboring countries?"

"They belong to the USSR," Natasha explained.

"You mean Poland belongs to the USSR? I haven't heard anything about it," Maria contradicted.

"No, I was talking about Baltic countries," Natasha specified quietly.

"This means, they were forcefully occupied by the USSR. Otherwise, why have they deported people from the sovereign countries to GULAG? These countries were not happy with a new soviet regime, am I right?" Maria asked.

Natasha did not answer anything. She did not trust anybody. She thought, "Maria is not familiar yet with the system of informers in each cell."

The siren in the corridor of the barrack reminded them that it was time to sleep. In two minutes, the light was off. The first day in the mine was over. Maria prayed Evening prayers and fall asleep at the final sentence. *Lord, have mercy!*

Chapter 19

The long shifts in hell were exhausting for Maria. There were three days that they dug and sifted with nearly no results. The poor prisoners did not get any hot food in the evenings. They were given just an aluminum cup of water and a slice of dry bread. Sister Olga was absolutely right regarding Maria's chunk of gold. They chipped it daily and got it dirty from all sides, as to make it look freshly dog-up. Maria had her hot soup regularly.

The New Year of 1947 came. There was no celebration for prisoners, and nobody allowed them to have a day off. Maria was at her shift in hell, when she felt nauseous and fainted. The overseer ordered Sister Olga and another prisoner, working in the closest distance to Maria, to take her out. The guard ordered them to deliver the poor woman to the camp hospital. The hospital was far away from the mine, and it took more than an hour for two women to deliver unconscious Maria there. When she regained consciousness, her first words were:

"What did I do? I did not bring my norm, and I interrupted the mining of both of you. Please, forgive me."

The women were older and joked. Biruta said,

"In our opinion, you are about to deliver a real treasure. Your treasure could be more than four kilograms, Maria. Be prepared to work hard."

There were many times that Maria wanted her child to be born, as soon as possible. However, the moment she went into labor, she was frightened. Sister Olga sensed Maria's fear and asked,

"If you have a boy, what will you name him?"

Maria answered without hesitation,

"Alexander, Jr., and for me, he'll be Sasha. I shall name him after my wonderful husband. Alexander Sr. is Alex for his mother and me, because he was born in France. Alexander Jr. will be called Sasha within the family–its Russian version."

Sister Olga surprised Maria with her reply:

"My son's name was Alexander, too. We called him Sashko. It's Ukrainian version. He was killed in 1939 together with my husband, who was a priest, and who was against closing the church. The soviets wanted him to stop church services, however, my husband did not follow their demands. One evening, my husband and Sashko went to the church to prepare everything for Sunday service and were murdered there. The demons did their dirty job. Our son was seven at that time. I left for convent to pray for them and many others who were tormented by soviet demons for their faith in the Divine."

At that moment, they were at the door of the camp hospital, when Maria felt something warm leaking from inside of her and getting her legs wet. The first contraction was so painful and strong that she kneeled at the door. Sister Olga and the other woman took Maria in, and a nurse appeared in front of them, as tall and shapeless, as a sleeper in a railway. Her voice was hoarse and unfriendly.

"Why are you here? The doctor is not here today. Come tomorrow."

Maria was shocked.

"There is no way that I can come tomorrow. I am in labor."

A new severe contraction forced her to scream. At that moment, the nurse "Sleeper" bent over Maria and whispered with all the hatred she had accumulated inside her long and shapeless body,

"If you, trash, make a single sound, I'll kill you and your baby with my own hands."

In order to proof her intension, she shook her fists in front of Maria's face. Sleeper commanded:

"Take her clothes off and do it fast! I am not going to help her."

The contractions became frequent, one after another. Maria tried not to scream; and bit her lips. Thin streams of blood ran from her lips. Sister Olga noticed that and gave the young woman the edge of a towel to bite. The nurse coated the area between the legs with iodine. It burned, but it was nothing, in comparison to the inner rending pain and pressure that seemed wanted to tear Maria from the inside.

The baby was coming out. Maria could feel it; her baby was coming. A nurse passed by. She stopped for a second and screamed with her terrible voice that sounded like a funnel,

"Push stronger! Do not stop now. Push, you bitch!"

Maria concentrated all her strength and pushed. The baby came out. The nurse gave Sister Olga a towel and ordered her to hold the baby. Sister Olga came up to Maria and said,

"You are a good girl, Maria. Look at this Hercules that has been born!"

Maria looked at her son, smiled and fainted again. The nurse brought Sal-ammoniac. The smelling salts did not work; Maria was in a dead faint. The nurse hit Maria's ear. Maria tried to open her eyes but did not have the strength. The nurse hit her again and screamed,

"Wake up, bitch."

Then she checked Maria's blood pressure and left. In a minute, she came back with a syringe filled with medication. Three minutes after the injection, Maria was up.

Sister Olga looked at her and said in a quiet, angelic voice,

"Maria, you made it. What can be more important for you now?"

Sister Olga was touching Maria's face, stroking her hair and whispering in Maria's ear.

"In order to survive, your son needs a strong mother with plenty of milk. Gain your strength back, Maria. Please, get well as soon as possible. Stay calm, girl. Otherwise you'll lose milk. Be strong, Maria!"

Maria listened to sister Olga. She tried to smile with her bitten lips but was unable to open her eyes. The weakness conquered her body and occupied her mind. She was about to faint again. She heard Sister Olga saying,

"Maria, stay with us! Maria, don't go away! Your son will never survive without you. You are a mother from this moment on, and you cannot betray your son! Maria, you cannot betray Alexander!"

The second prisoner was watching Maria passing away and turned to the window, praying and weeping bitterly. The nurse entered and said,

"The doctor is coming. You, bitch, don't be in a hurry to die. Who wants to take care of your stinky offspring? If you die, he'll go after you in a day or two."

Maria cried. She whispered,

"I cannot die because of Sasha. My boy is still attached to me with feeding. Sister Olga, I have to do my best..."

She fainted again.

The camp doctor entered the procedure room. The nurse reported how critically low Maria's blood pressure was. He concluded quickly,

"She needs blood transfusion. Prepare everything quickly."

Then he asked the women to leave. He noticed Sister Olga's hesitation and added in a polite and calm voice,

"Don't worry, everything is under control. I'll do my best to help your friend. You may leave now."

Maria was conscious again, but she was extremely exhausted. It was nothing like the tiredness after work or a long journey. It was a complete absence of strength to the point of being unable to inhale. She had experienced that condition twice in her life during the war. The moment she fell asleep, she was on the borderline between sleep and death. Her blood pressure was critical. A physician examined Maria and wrote several diagnoses on her file:

1. Malnutrition. 2. Emaciation. 3. Anemia. 4. Hypotension.

It was the fifth month that Maria had been living a hectic life with extreme emotional and physical stresses, pregnancy, an exhausting transportation for more than one month to Magadan, 12-hour working shifts in the mine and two poor meals daily. The doctor did not know what this delicate woman underwent during the WWII and in her family estate before the Magadan camp.

Maria was in bed for six days. Her condition was so poor that nobody could send her back to work. It was strange, but from the very first moment, the camp physician felt sorry for the young prisoner. Her blood test showed severe anemia. It looked like she had given her healthy son all the nutrients and strength of her body, withdrawing even her life energy.

As soon as the child was born, her body collapsed, and she was nearly in coma. The big and strong baby was a surprise to the doctor, who had many years of experience. How could this fetus have such a healthy development, coming from such a malnourished and drained mother? He thought, "It must be a miracle!"

Maria knew how, but she was not going to share her knowledge with the enemies. She was blessed by God to carry under her heart a child of her love, a child of the only man in the whole world, who she dreamed to belong to.

Nurse Sleeper did not "discriminate" Maria with her hatred. She hated Maria and baby Sasha, as she hated the whole world. One day, during her shift, she "forgot" several times to bring the baby for breast-feeding, and the child was crying for hours until he was exhausted and fell asleep for short intervals. At night, a nasty person who wanted to sleep used to bring the baby for nursing and "forgot" to take him back to the nursery.

Maria was more than happy to keep Sasha with her. She was weak, and she had bleeding, but the happiest time for Maria was when her son stayed with her. She did not sleep for hours, watching her son asleep. A new mother was gently touching his tiny legs and hands. It seemed to her that he was smiling at her. "He smiles because he knows that I am his mother," she thought.

Maria was proud of herself for giving birth to such a boy. The only thought that made her sad was the absence of the possibility to show baby Sasha to his father. She kissed Sasha, thinking,

"Alex can hardly imagine what a boy he has. Sasha is Alexander's copy."

After a week, Maria was sent back to work. The doctor was against it, but he was afraid to insist on his opinion. He looked at Maria guiltily and said,

"I know that you are not ready for mining. I suggested the commandant to keep you for another week in the hospital under my supervision and on medications. You'll be working in the hospital this week, and then we'll see."

Maria looked at him with gratitude. For one more week, she could see her baby and nurse him as frequently as they allowed. While she worked in the hospital, Maria never mentioned that she was a physician. She was performing multiple tasks: washing the floors, cleaning the rooms and bathrooms, washing and feeding the patients, doing laundry and taking the dead bodies of the "people's enemies" to the crematory.

Maria was good at all of her tasks, but she was not able to please the nurse Sleeper. The witchy woman hated Maria and her baby. Sasha was gaining weight well. Maria washed him late at night, and he was always clean. She was given old sheets to wrap the baby in. Maria cut them in half and whitened in bleach; they looked crispy white again. The young woman slept for few hours, but her baby was always well cared by his concerned mother.

The nurse Sleeper insisted on sending Maria back to the mine. The doctor tried to argue with the impudent nurse, pointing to the results of Maria's work: a clean operating room, unusually clean patients' rooms and restrooms, and really white towels and linens. The nurse complained that Maria spent too much time with her child.

"If she is strong enough to work hard here, she can mine again."

The doctor looked at her and understood,

"She is taking revenge on the poor young woman because of her audacity to become a mother in prison."

The doctor kept Maria in the hospital for one more week, and then afterwards, he had to send her back to mining.

The prison law for breast-feeding mothers was savage and completely inhuman toward the newborn babies. A mother had to mine ***two norms*** in order to be allowed to nurse her child. If she was unlucky and mined less than two norms, that day her baby was not given anything except water. Usually within a couple of days, the child became weak and was not able to suck. In five days to a week at the longest, those babies died. Nobody was interested in saving the lives of the babies whose mothers were "peoples' enemies."

Maria could not understand, why they were sending her back to the mine and bringing another woman to work in the hospital. She had done her best. Everybody noticed it. In the evening, she looked at the happy face of Sleeper and understood that she was the initiator of Maria's return to her prison cell and mining. The poor mother begged,

"Please, let me stay here until Sasha is one month old, only for one more week."

The doctor looked at Maria with pity and said,

"I cannot do it."

Maria wanted to scream, "Why?" The moment the doctor left, nurse Sleeper threw Maria's clothes in her face, growling,

"Change and go away!"

Maria went to her room, crying and praying. She had changed her clothes and looked in the mirror. What a change! Her dress looked two or three sizes too big. She was pale and skinny again; only her breasts were big, filled with milk. Maria saw the doctor at the end of the corridor. She ran up to him and asked,

"Doctor, what should I do with Sasha's feeding?"

"Collect the milk and bring it to the hospital before your morning shift. Do the same in the evening after your shift. We shall feed your son with your milk. If you have enough strength, stay with him in the evening, wash him and feed him at bedtime. Here we will arrange your third meal. The third meal is the only thing I can prescribe for you to help with your severe anemia."

"May I take a look at Sasha?"

The doctor looked at Maria with respect.

"Yes, of course. You created not a child but a miracle. Prisoner Kurbatov, in your severely compromised physical condition, you were lucky to give birth to an absolutely healthy and strong boy.

Maria smiled. Dr. Leskov continued,

"You are a wonderful mother, Maria. In spite of your weakness, you took very good care of your son for three weeks in the hospital."

He called for the nurse. When Sleeper appeared in the doorway, the doctor ordered her (this time he did not ask),

"This mother should be given the third meal and allowed to see, feed and take care of her son anytime she is here. Do you understand my instructions?"

The nurse Sleeper looked at the doctor with surprise and answered,

"Yes, Doctor."

Maria thanked God and Virgin Mary for the miracle they created: A "voiceless" physician demonstrated his temper toward the impudent nurse. Maria was about to leave, when she mentioned,

"Doctor, I am a physician, and I've had three years of practice, as a surgeon assistant. If you ever need me, and I am allowed to help, I am here for you."

The doctor was surprised.

"Where did you graduate from?"

Maria answered,

"In France. From Sorbonne University."

He was happy that the nurse had been offended by his tone and left. She should not be present during their conversation. The doctor asked,

"How did you get there?"

Maria answered,

"I am from western Ukraine. We belonged to Poland before WWII."

They entered the babies' room. Three babies were there. Maria's was the youngest. The oldest (seven months old) lost his mother two months ago; she perished in a mine. Natasha said that the woman was alive for three days after the mine collapsed and called for help and tried to dig her out. Nobody helped her, and she died there due to suffocation. The third child in the room, a skinny and bluish baby girl, was coughing, and Maria was afraid of contamination. The doctor promised to examine the baby girl and to take care of her cough. He felt awkward,

"Nobody reported to me earlier about this child's illness. You saw our nurse."

Maria took Sasha out of the crib, sat on a stool and nursed him before she left. The boy was already hungry and very happy to eat. Maria looked at the doctor and said,

"I wish I could baptize him so that he could get his Guardian Angel."

The doctor smiled, and Maria understood exactly what her father and this doctor had in common: a smile. It was the smile of a kind and intelligent person. Maria thought, "How can he stand his work for monsters? He does not look like one of them."

Maria kissed Sasha, blessed him with a cross, put him in the crib and was about to leave. The doctor stopped her.

"I do not know why I've decided to tell you this, but I was a prisoner for ten years in one of the Magadan camps. Now I am on settling for an additional five years."

The doctor's puzzle was completed.

"Do you have your family with you, Doctor?"

His eyes grew dim. He said,

"Yes, my wife is with me. Both of our daughters had been sent to orphanages, and for many years, we were not successful in finding them."

Maria said,

"Doctor, you could not find them because they were given different last names.

I know this for a fact. They did it to my brothers and a sister."

Maria wanted to help the doctor in any way she could.

"Maybe you are right. That's why we were not able to trace our children."

"How old were they when you were imprisoned?"

"One was thirteen and another girl was ten."

"Your daughters will find you because they remember their real last name."

Maria did not have any hesitation about it. She thanked the doctor and expressed her fear regarding the nurse Sleeper.

The doctor whispered,

"She is leaving next week. I know that she is a monster. She is not one of us, and she will never understand us."

Maria left. She was running to the barrack cell with a good feeling in her heart. The doctor was supportive. The Divinity placed her child in the hands of a nice person.

"Thank You, Lord for everything that has happened to me. You made me a mother of a healthy child. Now,

I ask for the patronage of Your Holy Mother. I ask her and Your Holy Spirit to be with my boy, to protect and save him."

Glory to Thee, o Lord! Glory to Thee!

Chapter 20

Maria returned to her prison cell, and her cell inmates congratulated a young mother with her child being born. The following day, she had to get up at 4 a.m. and run to the hospital to nurse Sasha and to leave some milk for his later meals. She had to be back to barrack at 5:15 a.m. in order to have her breakfast. At 5:30 a.m., she ran to the mine with other prisoners. She worked hard for 12 hours, mining two norms of gold, so that she would have permission to nurse her son.

Maria noticed that without being pregnant, it was much easier to work the 12-hour shifts, kneeling, digging and sifting the ore. She enjoyed praying while working, and she was blessed to find another big piece of golden virgin. It was not less than one kilogram. Maria thought,

"It's so unfair that they do not give me at least one day a week free to be with Sasha, if I bring in so much golden ore."

Maria continued digging. Her first day in the mine after Sasha's birth was the luckiest. She mined another large chunk of gold in the second half of the shift. Maria showed Sister Olga both her findings, and when the overseer left for his fifteen-minute break, they hid the bigger one, as a whole piece, and chipped the second into smaller pieces. Three women, including Natasha, did not find anything, so Maria shared with them.

It was so natural for Maria to share. She never expected anything in return. Maria had always shared just because she felt the necessity to do it. On that day, she shared with her inmates because she comprehended well, as a physician, that after a long, exhausting winter working shift, people could not go to sleep without hot food. They would not be able to get up in the morning and work another twelve-hour shift. She joked, when the women were refusing to accept it and suggesting Maria to preserve it for "empty" days:

"You are human, not saints. You need food to function. Our Father will bless me with another finding, believe me."

After work, Maria ran through her routine quickly: shower, meal and run to the hospital to nurse her baby, wash him, do his and her laundry and get back to the barrack. It was helpful that the doctor gave her a written order signed by the commandant of the camp allowing her to be in the hospital at 4:20 a.m. and then until 10 p.m. every evening. Otherwise, nobody would allow her to leave the barrack.

Every evening, when Maria returned to her cell, she was so tired that she fell asleep on top of her quilt, fully clothed. The chilly temperature woke her in the middle of the night, and every time, she was greatly surprised to see herself dressed and not covered. She had the same excuse,

"I must have been very sleepy yesterday."

Then she lay down under the quilt and when 4 o'clock came, she could barely open her eyes to greet the morning.

The nasty nurse was gone, and they hired another woman. Her name was Masha. Masha was a Russian version of the name Maria. The new nurse was older than the previous one, with a good-looking face and a thick blond braid that was styled into a crown around her head. She was about fifty and differed greatly from the predecessor. She was not *one of them*, not a prisoner, but she had been through a lot of hardships in her life. Maria could read the signs of a difficult life in Masha's eyes.

Endless working days turned into weeks, and weeks turned into months. Sasha was already eight months old. Everyone in the hospital liked the boy. It did not matter that he had been born in Magadan camp; he was a happy child and smiled at everyone who passed by. He did not want to sit in his crib any longer. He was attracting people with his baby screams and stretching his arms, asking them to release him from his crib and give him half an hour of freedom to crawl around the nursery. Nobody noticed, how it happened, but he started to walk around the furniture and pulled everything he could reach, dropping it on the floor in the process. It looked funny, and Maria did not stop him because there was not much to drop. She taught him to put everything back in its place, and every day, they "worked hard" on it.

The nurse Masha fed him on time during Maria's working shifts, and Sasha did not cry of hunger. Maria still had enough milk to feed two children: her son and a weak girl, who lost her mother. The doctor concluded that since Maria began nursing the girl regularly, she became stronger and forgot about persistent colds.

The doctor stayed long hours in the hospital. He performed all the surgeries by himself because nobody wanted to be bothered with the lives of "people's enemies" and keep for them a surgeon assistant on staff. His patients were on the other side of human existence; they were outcasts and lived as long as they were able to mine the norms. Inability to get the norms meant absence of food and death; it was as simple as that.

Every day, Maria prayed for the "people's enemies" while she was mining. She asked the Savior to be merciful to all of them, especially her husband Alexander and liberate them as soon as possible, so that they could return to their families and enjoy freedom, as she had enjoyed it for a year and a half after the WWII. She also asked the Lord to bless the people with one more thing - their understanding and appreciation of God's mercy. Long hours in mine gave Maria the opportunity to think, analyze and draw conclusions about human life.

She thought,

"When everything goes smoothly, we forget to thank God for our peaceful lives. We take good times for granted, or even worse, we consider ourselves, as if we are so smart, talented, educated, creative and fortunate that we do not want to admit the presence of Divinity in all these things. We do not want to admit the necessity of having God's blessing for whatever we have discovered, learned, created, fulfilled and achieved in our lives. People separate themselves from the Universal Goodness. It was my biggest mistake in the post-war life."

Maria learned this law of the Universe the hard way. She compared,

"During the war, I knew that there was nobody but God who could protect and save me from peril. After the war, I believed in "I" and allowed the destruction of the unity within myself. The sound of my appreciation to Divinity became monotone and did not contain the beautiful harmony of *heart, mind* and *soul* trio. Now I understand that when a person is not a solid creation with the presence of Divinity in it, the density of the human structure is low, and it could be easily influenced and crashed by the demonic forces."

Maria stopped digging. She was shocked with the results of her discovery. She bowed and prayed,

"I confess to Thee, my Lord God and Creator, all my sins that I have committed in all the days of my life... Sorrowing for these, I stand guilty before Thee, my God, but I have the will to repent. Only help me, o Lord my God, with tears I humbly entreat Thee. Forgive my past sins through Thy compassion and absolve from all these which I have said in Thy presence, for Thou art good and the Lover of mankind."

Maria continued working, appreciating the discovery that the Creator allowed her to make.

Maria tried to be good in everything: motherhood, work and friendship. There was no friendship in the camps from the point of view of regular human relationship. You did not visit your friends, celebrate their birthdays, exchange family news, or share joyful or sad events that they or you had experienced during the regular family life.

The inmates were separated from their parents, spouses, children, grandchildren, siblings and close friends. It was outlawed to hear anything from them or let them know that you were still alive. The prisoners existed in the same physical world with their beloved and friends, but it felt as though they were relocated to another horrendous planet with the name of Magadan, with its outrageous, atrocious Magadan camp laws, rules and regulations. Any connection with their previous regular life was prohibited. The price for trespassing was death.

Maria continued to take care of her friends. She was not afraid to share her mining and food from her third meal that she received in the hospital, as a breast-feeding and anemic mother. Every night after supper, the nuns and some other women would pray "The Agreement prayer" for Maria and her child. How could she be indifferent to them who sincerely prayed?

"Dear Lord, You told us with your pure lips that if two or three people on Earth agree to ask for anything in Your name, they'll receive it from the Father Almighty.

Where two or three people gathered in Your name, You are among them. Your words are unalterable, Your mercy is incomparable, Your love of mankind is endless. In agreement with God's servants (they named every co-prayer), we dare to ask you: Dear Lord Jesus Christ, accept our mutual prayer and bless Maria and her child Alexander with health and happiness, but not in the way we want, only as You wish. Amen."

A tragedy occurred in the middle of September 1947, when Maria was returning to work from her five-minute break. She heard a horrible noise in the mine: the mine was caving in. Maria saw the walls of the cave, where they had been working for ten months, collapsing like a house of cards. The people tried to escape. The worst thing that happened on that day was in initial collapse of the front part of the cave. The huge boulders quickly blocked the only exit. The alive women were trapped. They screamed of fear and initiated a new wave of destruction with the resonance of their voices.

The overseers and guards did not even try to go inside to help their colleagues and prisoners; they knew the danger of being buried under the boulders. Maria was shocked. She had heard about the mine collapses from her very first day in the camp, but she did not know, how scary they were in reality. Her friends were in there, and nobody could help them. Three people got out: one of the guards and two nuns. They were bruised, scratched and scared.

The noise of the ore shifts was loud, but the groans of the suffering people was also heard at the entrance to the mine. Maria noticed two women wandering toward the entrance: Natasha and one of the nuns. Maria realized that she was waiting impatiently for Sister Olga to return. The elderly nun had become Maria's second mother with her wise advices, spiritual support and constant assistance. To lose such a person was impossible.

Maria had never lost her faith in God's mercy. She started to pray out loud, not paying attention to the guards, although she knew that it was forbidden to worship the Divinity. She asked the Savior to help Sister Olga and return her alive so that the elderly nun could continue praising Him and His Virgin Mother in her everyday prayers.

One of the guards wanted to interrupt Maria's praying by shoving her in the back with his foot. He yelled,

"Stop it! Now stop your crazy praying!"

The push was strong, and Maria fell on her knees. What happened later nobody could understand, and everyone explained it in different ways. A severe cramp twisted the guard's leg. He fell down, rolling on the ground and screaming of unbearable pain.

Maria did not want to look at him and continued praying. She looked fixedly into the darkness of the tunnel where two more contours of human figures were moving slowly. Maria rushed inside. She saw Sister Olga helping another woman to come to the entrance. Their cloths were torn. They were scratched, bruised, and bled. The Creator had helped them to find the way through boulders and a wall of dust.

Maria praised God – Sister Olga, Maria's mother in Christ was with her again. The guards lined up seven women and sent them back to the barrack. They did not guard them that day; they had some other work to do. The shower room was unusually empty because most of the prisoners did not come back. Many poor women were killed there. Some of the inmates were trapped in the mine to be buried alive. It was the worst that could happen to the miners.

The nuns did not touch their food before they had prayed for the departed: *"Remember, o Lord, those who have departed this life today and have mercy on them. Dear Lord, forgive them all transgressions, voluntary and involuntary, and settle them where the light of Thy countenance shall visit them. Make their memory eternal. Amen."*

After praying and having supper, Maria ran to the hospital. She hugged Sasha and covered his head, face and body with kisses. Nurse Masha had heard about the collapse in the mine, where Sasha's mother worked and was not sure that the boy would ever see his mother again. She liked Sasha's mother and felt pity not only for the boy but for the young woman as well. She was sincerely glad to see Maria safe and sound.

Maria sat down on her small stool, nursing Sasha, when the doctor opened the door. He was also pleasantly surprised to see Maria.

"We heard about the collapse of your mine …"

He smiled with her father's smile and left, in order not to interfere with mother's and son's moment together.

"God bless these nice people!" Maria cried and smiled at the same time. Sasha stopped sucking and looked at his mother with interest. Maria burst into laughter.

"What a boy! You notice everything, just like your father. Nothing could be hidden from you."

Maria's face became sad. She had not heard anything about her husband since she saw him running to the camp transport. She recollected her thought: "The long journey worked for him in a positive way. He had time to heal and exercise his fractured hand, as well as rejuvenate in general."

Doctor Leskov opened the door again and whispered,

"I have wonderful news for you, Marie."

Maria clearly heard that he named her Marie, not Maria. "It's strange."

Somebody called him and he disappeared again. The nurse delivered Maria's food and also left. Maria could not keep waiting. She wanted to hear about the news. She thought,

"What can it be? What wonderful news the doctor has for Marie?"

The doctor seemed was not in a hurry to be back. Maria was anxious and could not wait,

"What could it be? The doctor mentioned not 'good' but 'wonderful' news. What is this wonderful news about?"

In five minutes, Dr. Leskov returned to the room and said in a low voice,

"Maria, I saw your husband yesterday. His camp is twenty minutes from here. I have assisted him in surgery. I have told him everything about you and Sasha, who was born in January, and what a miraculous boy he is now. One more thing I mentioned to your husband that made me have special respect for you – you are a very devoted mother."

Maria wanted to interrupt him with hundreds of questions, but the doctor whispered again,

"I will see Alexander again on Wednesday next week. Write a very short letter for him, and tomorrow, I'll take your picture with Sasha. I have a camera here. From time to time, they require us to take pictures of the dead but very important prisoners for archive documentation."

The doctor smiled again.

"I prefer to take pictures of live people, particularly the wonderful boy Sasha with his beautiful mother."

The child took a slice of bread from Maria's plate and bit a big piece. Maria took it out of his mouth, and the boy looked upset. The doctor laughed. Then he became serious again and said with bitterness in his voice,

"What a pity that his father cannot see these precious moments! They will not last for a long time. Right, Sasha?"

Sasha looked at the doctor and gave him his inimitable baby smile. Then he again pulled his mother's bread from the tray. Maria nipped off a small piece and put it in Sasha's mouth. He had only four teeth and it looked funny; he tried to chew properly. Then the boy tried a piece of boiled beets and made a face indicating that he did not like it. Maria gave him some boiled carrots. The boy enjoyed them. He pulled some more from the plate. Maria wanted him to try the beets again. He closed his mouth tightly and refused to put them in his mouth. They laughed. The doctor said,

"You are so picky, Count Kurbatov."

Maria was frightened that somebody in the camp had learned about her and Sasha's nobility. She looked at the doctor and asked him,

"Who told you this?"

"Don't be afraid, Maria. Who could tell me your sad story? Only your husband,

Count Kurbatov. He works full time in the camp hospital."

Maria was surprised,

"How is it possible? It's hard to believe that they placed him, as a doctor at the hospital."

"One day, they could not deliver a surgeon due to nasty snowstorm. The weather was unpassable, and the snowstorm did not stop for several days. They had an emergency - the camp commandant's appendix had nearly burst. He was afraid to die, and they had no choice but to bring your husband to the operating room. Alexander demonstrated good skills, even with his damaged wrist."

Maria's eyes were full of tears, ready to spill onto her cheeks at any moment.

"How is his hand now?"

"Still a little bit dislocated, turned up and limited in motion. But he learned to operate with it."

"How is the commandant after surgery?"

"The commandant is a monster, but they want to keep reliable specialists on hand, who can help them at any moment. That's why we are here."

In one day, Maria had so many things happened. When she got back to her half-empty cell, she was so overwhelmed with exhaustion and emotions. She was not able to say all her Evening prayers. After praying "Our Father," she thanked God for being alive after the mine collapse. She thanked the Divinity for the possibility of seeing her son and learning something good about her husband. She thanked the Savior for those people who understood, sympathized and, in a way, reunited her family.

Maria was sleepy and could not keep her eyes opened. She whispered with already closed eyes,

"*Into Thy hands, O Lord Jesus Christ my God, I commit my spirit. Please bless me, do Thou have mercy on me, and grant me eternal life. Amen.*"

Maria fell immediately asleep. She saw a dream, in which Alexander and she were again students, and after classes, enjoyed walking in their favorite Parisian park. Everything looked so real, as if it happened with them in veracity of their pre-war life. There was just one detail that made her dream a true dream – their son Sasha was with them in Paris, playing in the park. Maria smiled and woke up. It was 4 a.m., her time to get up. A new day started.

Glory to Thee, O Lord! Glory forever!

Chapter 21

September was the last month of Maria's breast-feeding. In October 1947, they insisted on weaning the child. Nobody knew, why the commandant of the camp made this decision. Sasha learned to eat some regular food but still waited for his Mama and Mama's "dessert." From the middle of October, Maria was allowed to see her son only on Sundays. It was difficult for both of them.

Sasha could not understand with the mind of a ten-months-old baby, why his mother stopped coming every day. He could not learn to wait without daily crying due to her infrequent visits. He was so happy every evening, when he was with his mother, "helping" her to wash him and do his laundry. He missed Maria very much and talked to her all the time in his childish and hardly understandable language.

The nurse Masha liked children and spent her free time in their room. The doctor had never minded it, and every day, he personally found time to visit the nursery room. Masha was a very responsible person and fed them three times daily. Every time, they delivered carrots and cabbages to the camp, she brought some fresh for the children. The salad of those raw vegetables was the best delicacy for the camp kids.

When they did not have complicated cases in the hospital, she played with the children and taught them to speak, sing and dance. She was the age of a grandmother and had rich life experiences with her own children and grandchildren. Masha's three children had given her seven grandchildren, and the whole family lived with her in one big house not far from the camp.

Maria had always expressed her appreciation to Universe for the replacement of the nasty nurse for a kind grandmother to the camp children. Maria asked the Lord to bless nurse Masha with health and happiness.

The years in prison, like the working shifts, went by slowly. The people lost their hope for amnesty and earlier release. With time, most of them became robots. Some of them were in a deep depression, and many of them moved into another world. Maria worked hard in order they allow her to see Sasha every Sundays. The pestering rule for mothers forced them to work harder in order to get the permission to see their kids weekly.

There were two more mine collapses, but the Divinity protected Maria both times. The last mine collapse killed ninety-three prisoners. It was a real miracle from God that she escaped. The other woman, who was working next to Maria, was killed by the stone fall at the very beginning of the cave-in.

Maria noticed the shaking of the walls, and it seemed to her that Sasha called her. Everything started to move, and Maria was picked up from her knees and pulled out by invisible force. When she was out of mine and looked back, she saw the cave closed completely with the huge boulders. Only seventeen people had escaped. That time, nobody could hear the voices of the prisoners buried in the mine. Maria looked at the faces of survivors. Nobody looked panic-stricken or on the contrary – uproarious due to survival. Sister Olga prayed quietly, asking the Lord to admit the souls of those who perished some minutes ago. Maria thought, "We are robots. They killed our emotions with dangerous overwork every single day, constant fear of being buried under the huge boulders, worries of staying without food and dying from hunger."

The winter of 1954 was the severest since Maria's imprisonment in 1946. Every day, there were snowstorms with strong winds and enormous frost. It was impossible to be in the mine for twelve hours. They lost thirty-seven prisoners due to pneumonia in January. The administration of the camp sent sick people to work, and in five to six days, their high fevers and coughs made it impossible for them to get out of bed. By the time the doctor was allowed to visit them in the cells and hospitalize them, it was too late. They usually died in a day or two after the hospitalization. Some of them died in their cells. The commandant of the camp did not care about his prisoners. The usual process for restoration of the number of the working inmates was to bring in a new group of "people's enemies" for replacing those who had died or were buried in the mines.

During working days Maria lived in her praying. When it was too cold, she would pray with low bows. The overseers did not interfere since they had witnessed or had heard of what had happened to one of their co-workers when Maria was praying on the day of the first mine collapse in September 1947. Five minutes of praying with prostrations was enough for Maria to feel again hot and energized. Then she was able to continue her mining for another hour.

In February, the severity of the winter and the constant temperature 45 degrees below zero had changed the routine life of the prisoners; their working shifts were shortened to ten hours—not because of the numerous deaths of the inmates, but because seven of the overseers had developed pneumonia and died.

The women were happy to be back from work two hours earlier. They took care of their clothing because it was torn fast due to working on their knees; their limited free time had not allowed them to mend it. Two hours made a huge difference in the lives of the prisoners. They looked tidy in their fixed dresses. Maria asked for permission to knit Sasha some sweaters and pants. She was surprised, but they allowed her to do it. She overheard how one jailer explained to another one,

"She prays like crazy. I don't want to be the one who forbids her."

She added some curses about Maria but allowed her to knit. The nurse Masha brought Maria raw wool for knitting. Every evening, the young mother worked for several hours and then by Sunday, Sasha could enjoy a new sweater or pants, a hat or just another pair of socks.

After that Maria started to knit for Sasha's friends. The children did not look alike, even though the yarn was the same. She knew how to make a dress and a sweater for a girl, and how to make hats of different styles. The kids looked nice. They enjoyed their beautiful clothing very much.

That winter took away lives of hundreds of inmates. Everyone was happy to survive that murderous season. Maria received two secret letters from Alexander. She read them two to three times in the hospital and the doctor burned them. Nobody wanted to take the risk of saving the letters, as a keepsake. She wrote replies and sent them with doctor Leskov. In one of her letters, Maria complained that his letter to Sasha, that was written in servants' lodge in Blue Creeks, they took away from her in Lvov prison.

Maria learned from doctor Leskov that Alexander coughed frequently. Once, he mentioned that it was the result of a lung injury caused by demonic massacre. The doctor was afraid that if they decided to send Alexander for mining, it could cause serious complications. He prepared him some herbal teas and tincture to reduce the cough.

Maria was grateful to the doctor, saying,

"Thank you for treating all three of us in such a special way! I appreciate your support, doctor. I am sure, Alexander is happy to meet such a person, as you, in this wild land."

Then she added, "I'll pray and ask Holy Mother of God to protect Alex and heal him. He'll be all right, doctor."

Doctor Leskov smiled. He was not a religious person. He saw his wife praying every night but did not participate in it. At that time, he still belonged to the "lost generation" who did not know anything about the

Divinity. His wife tirelessly asked the Lord in her own words to guide them in the search of their daughters.

He looked at Maria and asked,

"May I ask you for one favor?"

"Certainly, doctor."

Maria noticed that he looked awkward, touching the soft sleeve of Sasha's new sweater. She smiled, thinking that he wanted her to knit something for him or his wife. Looking at three children in nursery, Dr. Leskov asked her,

"Would you pray for my girls? Ask your God to find them and to bring them to us, their parents. We missed them so much."

Maria did not expect to hear such a request from an atheistic person, but she did not show it, saying,

"I promise to pray for them every day until you find them. It won't be long." Maria was surprised with her own conclusion. She thought,

"Why did I say that? Only God knows how long it will take to find their children."

Maria had prayed for two weeks for doctor's daughters. When she visited Sasha on the following Sunday, she met a woman playing with the children on the floor of the children's room. The woman got up and said,

"You must be Sasha's mother. Your name is Maria."

Maria picked up Sasha and answered,

"You are right. And you are ...?"

"My name is Sofia; I am your doctor's wife. I came today to meet you and to thank you for your prayers about our girls. We found them. No, to tell you the truth, they found us."

The woman's face was shining with happiness. The woman kissed Maria on both cheeks. She continued,

"They are coming next month. You understand, how long it takes to get all the papers and permission to come to our area."

"I was praying for months, and nothing happened. You started to pray, and they found us. You mentioned that it wouldn't take long. You are blessed to know."

Maria tried to explain that she and her prayers were just the addition to a mother's multiple requests. The woman did not want to accept that explanation.

"Every person in the camp knows, how you pray. You are the only one who hasn't been forbidden to pray in the camp, since that incident with the overseer. Do you remember? It happened near the mine entrance on the day of the mine collapse in 1947."

"People always like to make stories, exaggerate or embellish," Maria replied. Then she added with her special smile, "Thank God for everything. With Him everything is possible."

Glory to Thee, o Lord! Glory to Thee!

Chapter 22

The summers in Magadan were always short. The twelve-hour shift was restored in April 1955. The administration of the camp tried to find other jobs for the prisoners to do on Sundays, so Maria could not see her son every week. It was an additional torture for a mother. She asked twice for permission to see Sasha weekly, but her requests were refused. The commandant of the camp threatened Maria, roaring in her face,

"If you insist on seeing your son weekly, we will give your boy a different name, like Ivan Ivanov, and send him to the worst orphanage, where you would never find him."

The doctor and nurse Masha took good care of Sasha, but the boy waited for his mother. He missed her a lot. There were days, when Sasha did not want to play, listen to Masha's reading or communicate with two other kids. Sometimes, he refused to take off the hat knitted by his mommy. They allowed him to fall asleep in his hat, and once he was asleep, the nurse took it off gently, but left it near his pillow, so that he could find it easily.

One Sunday, they took women from Maria's cell to break tree branches for making brooms to clean the territory after the snow thawed. Maria had a bad feeling that morning. They lined up the campers in front of the barrack. The women waited for about half an hour for somebody to escort and guard them to the area where they were assigned to work.

Maria looked at Natasha. The woman turned gray after the mine collapse. It was the last year of her imprisonment, and she was expecting her release in a month or two. Natasha left a two-year-old daughter with her mother years ago and couldn't wait to see her again. Natasha's only "crime" was her marriage to a well-known engineer who worked for a military industry. They killed him during the first interrogation and sent her to Magadan. Nearly fifteen years had passed. Natasha was not sure that it would be easy for a seventeen-year-old girl to accept her as a mother.

One day Natasha shared her worries with Maria,

"She is seventeen now. She was educated and brought up in a different manner. She was stuffed with hatred for us, the '*people's enemies*.' They inspired our children with the only 'truth': 'cleansing of the country from its enemies.'"

Maria saw how these persistent thoughts daily disturbed Natasha, and the woman was depressed most of the time. Maria suggested her to pray together every evening in order to ease the inner tension and release the deep emotional pain.

"Ask the Divinity to help you. Who else can support us here? Who can help your daughter to understand her own mother and to awake sympathy in her heart?"

Natasha refused to pray, bringing up arguments,

"Where was your God, when they killed my husband, a talented and kind man?

Where was He when my child became an orphan at two years of age? Why didn't He help me to be released earlier and support my daughter and old mother?"

Maria understood that Natasha had closed her heart to God. She was not born and grown with God, because her parents had not worshipped in her childhood and youth; it was difficult for her to start worshipping at the age of thirty-six. Maria felt sorry for the soul that was caged inside the misfortunate and depressed woman.

The soul suffered, being neglected, restrained and drained. Natasha did not learn to feel her soul's wishes, advices, joys and peace. Misery, suffering, and pain overwhelmed her. The misfortune and lack of spirituality made Natasha numb. In a way, it was rather comfortable not to feel anything. However, it was totally inhuman. She did not acknowledge her human essence and denied taking into consideration the appeals of her heart and soul to be connected with the Divinity.

Four guards came up to the lined-up inmates. Maria sensed a strange mood in those men. They were looking for fun, like those demons in Maria's mansion. They took the prisoners to the hills at the very end of the camp territory. The hills were covered with short one-sided Magadan trees. The women were given all the instructions and began to work. For years of imprisonment, they were familiar with this type of work and the heap of branches was gathered quickly.

Two guards sent three women, including Sister Olga, back to the tree area to gather some more branches. The rest of the inmates were ordered to fasten the branches into the brooms. Maria started to pray repetitively, asking the Lord and His Holy Mother to protect them,

"*Help us, save us, have mercy on us, and keep us, O God, by Thy grace. O most holy Theotokos, save us.*"

Maria's team was making brooms rather quickly, but Maria's tension did not disappear. She saw Sister Olga's faded gray shawl in a distance. The nun was working near the front line of the trees. Two other women were somewhere farther.

The overseer ordered Maria's group to finish with the tying of the brooms and loading them into wheelbarrows. He motioned toward three women near the hill and said,

"Finish fast. They are bringing more branches."

When three women had finished with breaking the branches, another guard commanded,

"Pick up the gathered stuff and add it to the previous heap."

Three women just moved forward from the line of the trees, with armful of the branches, when somebody fired two shots, one after another. All the women of Maria's team rushed to the tree area and saw only Sister Olga running back towards them, dropping the branches from her arms.

"Stop there! Don't run here! They killed them," she warned in a distance. "They shot them there."

Maria understood that her Angel had protected her and sent the warning about Natasha. One guard was coming back. He approached the group of frightened women and said,

"The inmates were shot, while attempting to run away. We'll do it to you too, if you just think to do the same."

Maria was ready to shout,

"Why did you kill them? Where could they run? Why did you kill the innocent women?"

Instead of that, she turned away and began to cry, praying for Natasha's soul. They were not close friends with Natasha, but their plank-beds were side by side for so many years. Maria did not know well the second woman that was shot with Natasha, because she was new at their camp. Something happened to her at the previous camp, so they transferred her recently, and poor young woman found her death here.

The women saw, how the second guard was staying for a while between the shot women. Then he dropped his carbine there and ran. He did not even slow down near the group of inmates and guards. Paying no attention to them, he went on with a petrified expression on his young and pale face. That night, the young guard was examined by the doctor and sent to a psychiatric unit of the Magadan hospital.

The doctor told Maria, that being under the stress, the young guard was saying repeatedly,

"She (Natasha) turned around, looked at me and asked, 'Why did you kill me? My daughter has been waiting for me for fifteen years. She has nobody in this world, but me.'"

He repeated the last sentence of the poor woman again and again, "She has nobody in this world, but me."

The commandant of the camp rewarded both guards with watches and extra vocation for "the excellent fulfillment of their duties." Afterwards, nobody saw Natasha's killer in the camp. The doctor mentioned that he was discharged from the military service and left for a central part of Russia accompanied by his mother.

Lord, have mercy!

Chapter 23

Maria learned that the days in prison passed slower in comparison to a regular life. It seemed that the working shifts were endless. Maria tried to keep her mind busy with prayers, pleasant memories and Sasha's life. She was grateful to God that she did not lose track of goodness and hope, and did not sink into depression, as it happened to many innocent political prisoners. Most of them lost their belief in human justice and goodness.

Those, who tried to fight the harshness of the system or humiliation of political inmates used to disappear forever. Nobody knew exactly what happened to them, but everyone was sure that they were not in this world any longer. The system of demonic monstrosity destroyed them not only in moral and political ways, but also physically, grinding them to powder or burning them to ashes. All the prisoners of Maria's camp learned the favorite expression of the camp commandant: "No person, no case."

The daughters of doctor Leskov received the permission to stay with their parents only for one month, and Maria noticed that the family reunion was not going smoothly. The girls had been brought up in an orphanage for the children of the "people's enemies." The orphanage had one purpose: the following generations - children and grandchildren had to repudiate their parents and grandparents.

The propaganda in the educational system successfully promoted the idea that their loved ones betrayed the communist Motherland and the dictatorship of workers and peasants, who made life so "beautiful and complete for correct development of the democratic human society." The children were the easiest material for "brainwashing."

The girls missed their parents, as parents. But the educators planted and grew the hatred toward the closest people. The children blamed the parents for a double crime -against the Motherland and their own kids. It took about two weeks for the parents to explain patiently that their father and mother had not committed any crime. The system persecuted the talented and educated people in order to leave the country without good specialists, or to be precise, to get rid of thinking individuals who could retaliate against the dictatorship. Somebody from the top rulers of the country did this intentionally.

The doctor and Sofia explained to their girls that every prison is full of talented, sometimes one-of-a-kind scientists, engineers, military commanders, and physicians, as well as their spouses, who had nothing to do with the "guilt" of their husbands or wives. What crime could be committed by the poor women, who were just married to the talented specialists? The girls had the example of their mother in front of them. She was imprisoned for six years because she was the wife of their father. After her six and his ten years of imprisonment, both parents were released from the camps, but they did not have permission to reside in the area of their former settlement.

Maria asked herself the same question:

"Why? If even they committed a crime and served their sentence, why weren't they allowed go home and stay with their children and elderly parents?"

They had to live in Siberia until the end of their lives. Maria felt sorry for doctor's family that was destroyed by soviet regime.

"Is it fair to keep innocent people in this wild land? Was it fair that NKVD gave their daughters two different last names? Nobody can believe that they have one mother and one father. Their parents have the last name that now is different from both girls'. According to their passports, they were not even sisters."

"Doctor, where is the truth?" Maria asked.

Doctor answered in his calm manner,

"Somebody was interested in creating chaos before and after the war. That "somebody" wanted to keep the nation in fear. The frightened people preferred to be first in writing anonymous denunciations against their innocent neighbors or relatives, so that their relatives and neighbors could not use the chance and blame them earlier for a crime that was not committed. The first false accusation won."

Maria continued,

"I can see that it's difficult to explain everything to your children. And this is even more difficult for them to understand."

"Sofia tries to explain this to our daughters."

"What does she say?"

"Sofia found an important argument, 'They would never keep your father, as a camp physician, if they knew that he was really guilty."

"Do they believe in it?"

Doctor confirmed with sadness,

"Maria, this conclusion was so logical to both girls that they started to see us not as the social and political enemies, but as victims of the political system. Now, they feel sorry for us and hate those who separated us and lied them for such a long time. Nevertheless, we try to be careful and do not want to seed hatred towards the system in the minds and hearts of our girls. They have to live in it because presently, nobody is going to change the system."

"Maybe you are right. With age, they will understand it better."

The doctor looked happier. His dream had come true. They received the highest rehabilitation: Sofia and he were fully exonerated in the eyes of their confused children.

"Maria, how could we live, breathe and do anything, if we were viewed as political criminals in the eyes of our own daughters?"

He believed that with time the whole world would learn the truth about the most inhuman crime of mankind when not the invaders but the demonic government with its political and security systems annihilated more than forty million of their population and destroyed the lives of their beloved.

Maria's hope to be released earlier failed to manifest. Stalin's death did not bring any changes to the lives of the political prisoners. Amnesty was granted to the criminals, but the communist government did not grant exoneration to the political inmates. Maria thought, "Maybe, the head of the government was not a chief demon, or maybe, the demonic system moves under its own momentum?" However, people continued serving and dying in GULAG for never committed crimes.

Maria was allowed again to see Sasha on Sundays. She taught him to pray, though he had not been baptized yet. They started to send kids from the camp to a village school. The kids were good in their studies. Thanks to nurse Masha, they learned how to count and read before school.

One day Sasha asked Maria a question:

"Why do we live in the camp, Mommy?"

It seemed to Maria that she had been prepared long time ago to hear that question. She answered the question many times in her mind, but it was still not easy to explain everything to an eight-year-old boy. Maria repeated the question,

"Why?"

"Yes, why is it so that my Dad lives in another camp? Why cannot we live together?"

She knew that she was the only one who had to explain it to her son in a way that he could understand and believe.

"Sasha, your father and I arrived in 1946 from Germany to visit my family in the Ukraine. During the Second World War, I had lost contact with my father, grandfather, two brothers and a sister. When we arrived with your Dad, we found that everything had been changed in the Ukraine."

"What was different or changed there?" the boy asked.

"The lands and forests of our estate were nationalized, and everything that belonged to our family was not ours any longer."

"What about the house where you lived?" Sasha asked.

"It belonged to NKVD, and my relatives were relocated from our house time ago," Maria answered calmly.

"Did you find your father and the rest of the family?"

"No, Sasha. The NKVD did not give us a chance to look for them. We wanted to find them and take them with us to France. Your grandmother in France prepared everything for them to stay with her."

"What happened later, Mama?"

"The people from the internal service or NKVD decided that we were enemies -

spies and terrorists - and imprisoned us in Magadan camps, where you were born."

Maria took her son's head in her hands and, looking him straight in the eyes, added,

"Sasha, I want you to remember my words: Your father and I did not commit any harm to this country.

I wanted to help my family. My desire was to find my father, grandfather, two brothers and my sister Jennie. I wanted them to go with us and live their decent lives in a civilized country. That was the true reason of our arrival to the Ukraine."

Maria felt as a huge wave of emotional pain hit her with all its heaviness, but she forced herself to continue,

"The only crime I committed was in bringing you and your father to this land."

Maria's eyes were full of tears that started streaming down her cheeks. Sasha tried to catch them with his small hands, preserving her prisoner's dress from getting wet. Then he clung to her and said,

"I knew, Mommy, that you did not do anything bad. I love you so much.

Believe me, Mommy that one day, I'll take you out of here."

Maria looked at her new prince savior, who sounded like his father Alexander, and smiled. She was grateful to the Divinity for giving her the joy of motherhood.

Glory to Thee, o Lord! Glory to Thee!

Chapter 24

After the important conversation with Sasha, Maria started to write her diary, though she knew that it was forbidden in the camp. Maria hoped that one day, he could read her journal, learning and feeling what she felt, thought, understood and sensed about him, her and Sasha's life in captivity. During their imprisonment, when they were unable to see each other, her diary was an invisible bridge between two loving hearts.

Somebody from Maria's cell inmates reported the camp authority about Maria's journal. They found it, and threw Maria in a basement cell, as a punishment. This happened in December of 1955, one week before the New Year. The temperature in the punishment cells was 43 degrees below zero.

Everyone knew that the human body could not withstand such a low temperature overnight. Normally, people fell asleep and died. In the morning, two jailers usually came, remove the frozen bodies and deliver them to the crematory. They joked,

"We are taking the frozen prisoners to '*warm*' them up."

Maria's first thoughts were hectic, and she talked to herself out load,

"How could I take the risk of writing my journal? Alexander will never learn the truthful reason of my death. It was silly to write letters to a beloved person who will never have a chance to read them. What should I do now?"

She imagined Sasha's life after her possible death and felt hot from the thought of how miserable his destiny could be. She exclaimed,

"How can I leave my son? Nothing could be more valuable than Sasha's joy and happiness, when he sees me on Sundays. He lives from Sunday to Sunday with one dream: to see me again and to talk to me about his school life."

Then it was about half an hour or so that Maria's mind was completely paralyzed; she had no thoughts, regrets or feelings. Maria realized her inability to change anything to escape her fatal destiny. She whispered,

"O, Lord! What a situation! I have lost the possibility to survive. I am trapped and cannot see the way out. What am I waiting for? Am I ready for an 'easy' death? When I fall asleep tonight, I will never wake up again, at least not in present life. Lord, have mercy!"

Maria sighed, experiencing deep self-pity,

"I am trapped. Maybe, I underwent too many hardships, and the Universe has sent me a release? What I have been through was too much for any person. Wait a minute! Is this the first time in my life that I have been trapped? Not at all! I have been in dangerous situations like this many times before."

All of a sudden, she recollected her grandfather's prediction: "You'll be on fire, yet not burned down; you'll be drowning in water, yet not be drowned; you'll be kept in bitter cold, but never be frozen; the crowd will trample and torment your body, but you shall survive. You'll be a mother to three children without a husband and a taste of woman's complete happiness. The only good thing I see for you, darling: God Savior and his Holy Mother will support you, and later, your enemies will admit and admire your dignity, knowledge and talents."

The recollection was so vivid than it seemed to Maria that everyone could hear a strong voice of her grandfather:

"Pray, my child. Pray, and our Father will save you."

Maria tried to start her prayers but could not find the right one. The freezing temperature began its merciless combating – paralyzing of her weak body. A blood curling feeling of death interrupted her pitiful thoughts about two Alexanders. She tried to move and realized that her feet in woolen valenki were frozen to the cement floor. Only at that moment, Maria noticed that the jailors poured water on the floor and took away a stool to sit. Maria continue talking to herself,

"They are waiting for my death. The monsters want me to disappear forever. My Lord, what about Sasha? What will they do to my child?"

The thought of Sasha gave Maria additional strength, and she broke the ice and sledded to the plank-bed. She wanted to sit on the plank-bed, but her bed was permanently attached to the wall, in order she could not sit on it. She was not left with a chance to survive. Now,

Maria understood, why the demons were so happy to announce in front of her cell inmates,

"Trust us, a single night that she is ordered to spend in a punishment cell will make this stupid God worshiper, as obedient, as any other prisoner of our camp. We'll teach her to comply with our rules and regulations."

The voice of her grandpa insisted,

"Pray, Marie! Pray with prostrations, low bows and kneeling! You are young. You must live. You cannot leave your son alone among the demons. They will strangle your boy at the first moment that you are not in this world."

The last argument was the strongest one. Maria separated again her feet from the icy floor and started to dance, sliding around the small cell. Then she prayed the entire night. She prayed passionately - a hundred times: *"Our Father, Who art in Heaven, hallowed be Thy name. Thy kingdom come, Thy will be done, on earth as it is in Heaven. Give us this day our daily bread and forgive us our trespasses, as we forgive those who trespass against us. Lead us not into temptation but deliver us from the evil. For Thine is the Kingdom, the Power and the Glory, now and forever and onto ages of ages. Amen."*

Each time at the end of the prayer, Maria kneeled and prostrated, touching the icy floor with her forehead.

Then she prayed about a hundred times to the Most Holy Theotokos: *"O Theotokos and Virgin, rejoice, Mary, full of grace, the Lord is with thee; blessed art thou among women, and blessed is the Fruit of thy womb, for thou hast borne the Savior of our souls. O most Holy Theotokos, save us. Amen."*

Maria moved easily, as she was moving automatically: a bow, a prayer, kneeling, prostration to the icy floor and getting up. It seemed, as if a strong spring was installed inside of her gentle body. She did not experience any tiredness. The longer she prayed, the more energized she felt. In the middle of the night, she did not need the quilted coat that the jailors took away from her; she was hot without it.

Maria kneeled and was about to prostrate again when she sensed: somebody gently touched her right shoulder. She turned around and burst into tears. She saw her Angel. She saw him as clearly, as she could see a real person. The white mist around him did not interfere. He was very tall, with a friendly expression on his face. There was also shiny white mist around his huge wings. Maria kneeled in front of him and continued:

"Thank You, Lord for sending me my Guardian Angel. I believe in his miraculous protection."

Maria saw her Angel smiling. She prayed,

"At this moment *my thoughts and soul I have committed unto thee, o my guardian; please, deliver me from all attacks of the enemy. Holy Angel of the Lord, pray to God. Heal, o immaculate one, the most painful wounds of my soul, and drive away the enemies that ever fight against me. Amen."*

Maria looked up through the tears pouring out of her beautiful hazel eyes: *"Out of the love of my soul, I cry to thee, o my all-holy Angel! Protect and guard my beloved and me always from the hunting of the evil forces, and guide us to the heavenly life, teaching, enlightening and strengthening us. Amen."*

Maria noticed that the Angel was about to depart. He touched her head and disappeared. At that very moment she sensed light and warmth inside of her body.

It was morning. Maria heard the jailers were dragging the frozen bodies of other prisoners from the punishment cells. She looked at the sky and began praying the Creed -Symbol of the Faith.

Just a few minutes later, Maria heard the noise behind the door of her cell. The jailers unlocked the door, opening it widely. They stood still in the doorway stupefied with fright watching Maria with their mouths opened. They were shocked to see steam or mist around her delicate body. Maria walked out of the cell and went back to the barrack. Nobody stopped her. Her one-night punishment was over.

Glory to Thee, o Lord! Glory to Thee!

Chapter 25

Since March of 1956, the prisoners were ordered to mine double norms of gold ore. If they didn't meet the new quota, they were not fed in the evening. Only some were lucky to mine the required amount. At the beginning, nobody could understand the meaning of a new order. Then Maria realized that their camp was supposed to mine the definite amount of golden ore per year. The number of inmates decreased greatly for the last two years, but the plans for output were not changed in Moscow.

The inmates did not see new prisoners coming to the camp. The last mine collapse took the lives of twenty-four inmates and two overseers. Nobody was replaced for five months.

The prisoners joked, "All the '*people's enemies*' were distributed or sent to other planets to mine the natural resources there."

When the camp authority ordered double quotas, it was obvious from very beginning: people were not able to fulfill the task. Then the commandant ordered prisoners to work on Sundays to catch up with the new quotas. The inmates were exhausted due to hunger and overwork. They were unable to move in the mine due to unmerciful cold. They extracted even less ore than during their usual daily mining. The overseers were given whips to "speed up" the prisoners. Some of them frightened women with them, shaking the whips in front of the prisoners' faces. Others, however, used the whips constantly.

One day at the end of April, the most aggressive overseer watched Maria's work and decided that the "obnoxious God worshiper" required some additional "push". He jumped up to her and whipped. Maria turned around, snatched a whip out of his hand and whipped him twice. Two guards appeared there in a moment, pulled her out of the mine, and threw into the punishment cell.

Maria's first thought was,

"Thank God, it's April, and the temperature does not drop too low."

Maria was told that she would stay there to the end of her sentence that meant for more than two years. Since that moment, her daily ration of food was a cup of water (500 ml) and a slice of dark bread (200 grams). The prisoners in the punishment cells were not given hot food. Who could survive such a punishment for two years?

Maria suffered, not because of hunger but because she could not see Sasha. She had a lot of time for praying. She believed that Holy Mother would protect her son, and soon, she would see her boy again. Maria had never lost her hope in the family reunion,

"Two years will pass, and my gentlemen will take me out of this cell. They will love me no matter how I look and feel after staying here for a long time. They will give me strength. I believe that Lord is merciful and will protect all of us. We'll survive."

When Maria had worked her long daily shifts in the mine, she did not have the opportunity to concentrate her thoughts on their personal life after prison. In the punishment cell, she contemplated a lot about her family - two Alexanders, senior and junior, her dearest father, Alexander's mother, grandfather, and her siblings. Every day she prayed sincerely for all of them.

Maria sensed that great changes were coming. She could "smell" them in the air. When she prayed, her Angel delivered repetitive message that she would be released soon and see her family again. The expectation of happy event maintained her inner joy and courage.

Maria focused not on the tragedy of her deteriorating living condition and fear of dying from hunger and malnutrition. All her thoughts were far from the dreadful reality. Her strong connection with the Divinity helped her to survive. Maria thought,

"It is the tenth year of our imprisonment. Sasha is finishing the second grade, and he is one of the best students in his class. He needs a good school. I wish we could leave for France. We are people without citizenship in this country. I hope that they'll let us go back. We suffered enough in the USSR. We were in their slavery for ten years, the best ten years of our lives."

One question disturbed Maria most of all. Doctor Leskov sent several requests to permit Sofia and him to return to their hometown Kaluga. But they were still not allowed to return there.

"What should we do, if they want us, as well, to settle in Magadan? Dear Lord, please do not allow this to happen."

Leaving for France was Maria's strongest desire. In her thoughts she also flew back to Schulenburgs.

"I wonder, how they are doing there. How was their hospitality business developed for ten years? Probably, there is no more business there. The Russians could nationalize the hotel and the lot of land that we purchased for expansion? We had that terrible experience of soviet nationalization in the Ukraine."

Maria remembered her happiest days with Alexander at the Schulenburgs. Their German friends and partners were very nice to her husband and her. An invisible and destructive force tempted her to return to the Ukraine, and for the second time in her life, Maria arrived in dangerous time. It was the second time, when she allowed the evil seeds to grow. Both times, it was connected with her egoistic desire to visit her native land and family, without taking into consideration the warnings of other people.

Maria knew her weaknesses, and every day, she included in the prayers her special requests of the day: *"Dear Lord, deprive me not of Thy heavenly good things... Remit, pardon, and forgive, o God, my offences... Dear Lord, deliver me from the eternal torments... O Lord, deliver me from any temptation... My Lord, enlighten my heart and mind... Dear Lord, as a compassionate God, have mercy on me, seeing the infirmity of my soul and body... My dear Lord, please help me at all times, in everything, and deliver me from every evil thing and every impulse of the devil ..."*

Maria learned and admitted her sin long time ago. However, it was still painful to realize that she allowed the evil seeds that every human keeps inside to grow within her,

"O my Lord, I know the worst thing that happened: it was not just me who was damaged in the demonic fire. I destroyed my husband's and son's lives. Can it be forgiven?"

She often sobbed in repentance, until she sensed the warmth and light inside.

It was the seventh month of Maria's stay in the punishment cell. It was cold outside, and it became cold in the cell. This punishment cell differed from the previous one, where she was thrown into for writing her journal. Last time, she was supposed to freeze and die during one night. In this cell, there was some kind of heating system, although the radiators gave off very little warmth. Maria had lost weight, became very weak, and the doctor insisted in her immediate return to the barrack. The camp commandant did not want even to hear about her release from punishment cell.

"Do not forget, doctor, she whipped the overseer!"

When the doctor tried to explain something about her anemia and critically low blood pressure, the commandant roared,

"I had promised to keep this stubborn God worshiper in a punishment cell to the end of her term. I always keep my word."

Maria thought,

"It really looks, like I'll be here to the end of my sentence. Nevertheless, everything is in God's hands. This time, I feel optimistic. I believe that something is going to be changed for good in a short while."

Maria "confessed" to the doctor, when he was allowed to examine the prisoners of the punishment cells,

"It's my fault, doctor. Why couldn't I bear the blow of the overseer? What had happened to me then?"

Maria worried about Sasha. He needed to see her, and the months of mother's captivity disturbed the boy a lot. The doctor agreed.

"It's true that Sasha is missing you, Maria, but he does not cry and continues learning well in order to please you, when you get out of this hell."

Maria smiled with tears in her eyes. "He is Alexander Jr., and my men do not cry."

Lord, Have Mercy!

Chapter 26

On May 5, 1957 there was a package delivered to the camp office with a stamp *"Confidential: this Document is of National Importance."* All the officers were called to a meeting. However, the camp doctor was not invited there. He was still considered an outsider. They called the nurse Masha instead. When she came back to the hospital after that meeting, she delivered the miraculous news about the amnesty for the political prisoners who had been prosecuted in accordance with Article 58 – High Treason. Those cases were considered as "misconduct of justice."

Doctor Leskov insistent in Maria's release, as soon as possible for two reasons: Maria's health was in life-threatening condition, and her child could not stand longer the separation with his mother. She was anemic, and it was dangerous to keep her on bread and water for over a year. It was a miracle that she survived that long term of starvation. Doctor Leskov was deeply concerned with his last examination of Maria. The young woman was extremely weak, pale, and dangerously underweight. In other words, the doctor was afraid of anorexia, as skinny as she was. She had lost her beautiful voice due to general weakness.

The commandant decided to start the preparation of discharge documents and passports in a week from the delivery of the unexpected order from Moscow. He wanted to be sure that the order was not someone's mistake, though the official letter included the explanation that the imprisonment of countless number of citizens in most of the cases was based on either false information or a politically incorrect approach to the facts. It said that the "difficult political situation" in the country on that time prevented the authorities from properly investigating the majority of the cases.

According to the camp commandant's plans, the prisoners from the punishment cells were the last to be discharged, but the doctor insisted in Maria's release due to her physical condition. The commandant in general was not certain what to do with Maria's liberation:

"Madam Kurbatova is not a citizen of the Soviet Union. She was born on the territory of Poland and was married in France. She is still the citizen of France."

He needed to call to his Moscow superiors to receive the special instructions from Moscow authorities regarding Maria and her son.

"The boy was born in Russia. Maybe, we can issue the Soviet Union birth certificate for him? If not, then the family has to disappear forever, so that no one could find out the facts of torturing and ten-year-imprisonment of the foreigners without *corpus delicti*, which means without *concrete evidence of crime*.

At the moment, the camp commandant was completely confused, and he was not sure of anyone's guilt, especially in the case of that Madam. He was far from being compassionate to Maria and her child. He grumbled,

"It looks like the doctor has been released too early, if he did not understand the danger of his advocacy."

The commandant called the Moscow office and explained the situation of Madam Kurbatov. The answer from Moscow was,

"You have to free the woman and her son now and settle them in the area. Let them wait for the documents from Moscow that probably, will permit them to leave the country. The rest is none of your concern. You have to dismiss prisoner without delay. No procrastination in her case. Our office received a couple of inquiries from France and Germany. Some people there are trying to find them. We'll take care of the rest."

The guards and jailors were also surprised with the new order from Moscow.

"How come that all those '*people's enemies*' were not enemies? How could they stand the long terms of their imprisonment and inhuman life conditions?"

Most of the camp guards and overseers felt guilty and tried to explain their awful conduct to the prisoners, as a general order that was authorized by the camp authorities. The unexpected news about the amnesty of '*people's enemies*' and the order from Moscow that required the release of all the prisoners within a week were the main topics for discussions in every soviet family.

All the guards, overseers and jailors did not know what to do in a week. No one mentioned their retirement or dismissal. The jobs gave them very small but steady monthly income in the area where to earn a living was very difficult. Everybody thought about an amnesty and could hardly believe that one day can change the lives of thousands of political prisoners. Years ago, those prisoners were taken from their families, went through the interrogations, cross-examinations, anguish and assault. The NKVD was always "successful" in discovering the "heart of the matter, root of the crime, and eliciting the truth." The innocent people were stamped with two terrible words, '*people's enemies*', that left them only two probabilities: immediate execution or long-term inhumane imprisonment.

The '*peoples' enemies'* were sentenced to terrible prison life. An enormous number of them were not destined to survive and see the victory of God over the darkness of the Satan. There were painful losses of loved ones in nearly every soviet family, and it was not easy for families and relatives to forgive the inhumane regime for humiliation and annihilation of their innocent mothers, fathers, sons, daughters, husbands, wives, sisters and brothers.

Maria made her fundamental conclusions regarding the national tragedy, and it seemed to her that she found out why it was possible for the tragedy to take place. It became possible because the demonic regime suppressed the faith of people in God and interrupted the vital connection of every human soul with the Divinity. People betrayed the Divinity and accepted the satanic human leaders, as their idols for worship.

Nothing sacred was left to the new generations of Soviet people. They allowed their demonic state rulers to lead them into darkness. Many of them became the monsters, executioners, and hangmen of their own parents, siblings, friends, and children. They sacrificed them in order to prove devotion to the satanic state system. Why? They were afraid to be purged together with their closest people and undergo the same agony. The fear of the satanic system became stronger than the fear of a sin in front of God. God was pushed away and seemed invisible for people. The monstrous authorities were near, and they could easily catch anyone and through into the grinder.

Maria remembered one conversation with co-inmate Kaisa from Estonia, who underwent horrible insult during her nightmarish journey to GULAG. She watched daily Maria's and nuns' worships, and once, on Sunday evening, she approached them with a question,

"Why do you do this? Where is your God, if you and the nuns are in the hell together with us? Do you really believe in His existence? Why doesn't He stop the assaults of the nuns and allow the disgusting camp monsters to rape them?"

Nobody had a chance to answer her, and she instantly continued,

"You were transported here in cold season, in passenger carriages of the trains. I was deported in summer on cargo train. We slept on dirty floors of the carriage. We did not have luxury restrooms, just a big hole in the floor. Every evening ten or twelve guards broke into the carriage and raped us brutally. Those girls and women, who tried to resist them, were pushed out through the toilet holes on the rails. That's why so many sentenced female captives disappeared on the way to this hell, and their mutilated corpses were found on railway roads. So, where was your God? We did not find Him or probably, He is so high up that it's difficult for him to see us and our suffering on the Earth."

Sister Olga embraced distressed woman and answer,

"Wait, Kaisa, and tormentors will be punished. Pray, if not for yourself, then for the souls of those who were slaughtered on your train. Their souls are eternal and belong to the Lord. Those souls will ask for God's mercy on you."

Maria prayed for the victims of inhumane regime: *"O Lord Jesus Christ our God, safe the suffering Russian people from the yoke of the godless authorities... Preserve, O Master, all who live in this house from all harm and every temptation from below; delivere us from fear of the feeble one and the arrows that fly by day, from things proceeding from the darkness and attacks by demons at midday. Let Your servants and Your children delight in Your help, and, preserved by armies of angels, faithfully sing with one accord: "The Lord is Helper to me, and I will not be afraid; what can man do to me? And again, "I will fear no evil, for You are with me. Amen."*

Maria believed that the time of tormentors was over, and the Divine forces would win in the nearest time, as it always happened in human history.

Glory to Thee, o Lord! Glory to Thee!

Chapter 27

On May 15, 1957, the door of Maria's punishment cell was opened. The jailer ordered in unusually quiet voice,

"Take your belongings and follow me."

Maria thought that they were taking her again to the shower and laundry room. "Probably, they did not check the schedule or forgot that I did my laundry two days ago." The jailors led her to the exit and opened the door of the building. The guard at the door of the building did not stop Maria, and she walked out. The day was sunny, causing Maria to squint against the blinding light. Maria could hardly see anything after a year of darkness in the basement punishment cell. All of a sudden, she heard Sasha's voice,

"Mama! Come here, Mama. Our doctor and I are waiting for you."

Maria shuddered, when she heard the voice of her son. She opened her eyes and saw Sasha in the distance, running to her.

She shouted with all her strength,

"Stop there! Sasha, stay there!"

Maria knew that nobody was permitted to run on the territory of the camp without a command. The guards on the watchtowers were ordered to shoot anyone running. Maria remembered, when one of the inmates injured her arm and was severely bleeding. The overseer sent her to the camp hospital. She ran to the hospital. They shot the poor woman to death.

A scared mother rushed to her child. Then she saw the Dr. Leskov with him.

"Mommy, we are free! We are not the prisoners any longer. We are free, Mommy! We came here to tell you this news."

Maria stopped within thirty feet of her son, looked back at her jailer that followed her, and fainted. Maybe, the information was too astounding, or Maria was too weak waiting for this mind-blowing news during long 126 months. When she was conscious again, she found herself in the hospital. Sasha was next to her bed, sobbing loudly. Maria called him with a weak voice,

"Sasha, sonny!"

The boy hugged his mother. It looked like there was no force in the whole world that could separate again those two souls.

"Mommy, do not die! Please, do not die!"

He ran out, and in a minute, the doctor was in the room.

"Maria, why did you decide to frighten us now, when everything is over?"

The doctor tried to look serious but could not keep smiling.

Maria looked at them and asked,

"What is over? Tell me, please."

Doctor Leskov explained,

"An order from Moscow was delivered to the Siberian camps. The order was about the liberation of the political prisoners due to their rehabilitation and amnesty."

Maria almost fainted again. Her blood pressure was critically low, and her anemia was worse than the last time. She looked at the doctor and asked one word,

"When?"

She could not catch her breath and did not have strength to continue the sentence. The doctor asked the nurse to do another injection. They needed to elevate Maria's blood pressure.

When Maria's condition was more or less stabilized, Maria looked at the nurse and asked,

"Masha, when can we leave the camps?"

The doctor was the first who answered,

"In a couple of days, Maria, when you get stronger."

"How is it with Alexander?" Maria whispered.

The doctor answered with a smile,

"He was released yesterday. He'll be here today at four to pick up your son and to move somewhere they want you to live for a while."

Maria asked,

"When will they allow me to leave the camp? Why should we reside in Magadan area? Are they playing again their dirty games with us?"

"Your discharge papers were signed yesterday. You could get them today, but you are not able to breath, Maria. In your condition, it is dangerous to leave."

Maria tried to read the time on the wall clock but could not focus on it. Her blurry vision did not allow her to read the numbers.

She asked anxiously,

"Excuse me, doctor, what time is it now?"

"A quarter to two. Why did you ask?"

The doctor looked at the young woman with concern.

"I want to go to the commandant's office and receive my discharge papers. I must get them today. I cannot wait until tomorrow."

Maria burst into sobbing.

"I can die today or tonight. But, doctor, if I die, I want to be a free person with the document which confirms that my imprisonment was a criminal act of their demonic system."

Sasha came into the room and put his hands around the skinny shoulders of his tiny mother.

"Mommy, do not die! It took such a long time to wait for you and, now, you want to die."

The boy started to cry. The doctor patted the boy on the back, saying,

"No, Sasha. Your Mama wouldn't die. She wants to live. She insists on receiving her discharge papers today."

Maria knew that the camp administration was in the next-door building, but she was not strong enough to walk their alone. She waited for five minutes, then sat down in her bed, catching her breath.

"Sasha, will you call Masha for me?"

The boy ran out of the room. Masha and he appeared shortly together.

"Masha, will you please help me to walk to the commandant's office?"

Maria asked with a pleading look.

"The doctor said that you are not allowed to walk today even in the room, but you decided to be outside. Please, postpone your visit to the office until tomorrow," Masha recommended. She was a very diligent nurse, and she followed all the doctor's orders.

The doctor entered the room, saw Maria sitting on her bed and asked,

"What did you decide to do, Maria?"

He did not wait for Maria's answer. He looked at his nurse and said,

"For ten and a half years, I learned a lot about this woman. If she has decided something, she must go there anyway. Masha, will you please, accompany this impatient patient to the office. Just remember, you go straight to the office and return to the hospital. Maria, you do not have physical strength to walk and talk a lot, especially for arguing with administration of the camp."

Sasha also went together with his mother. At the office, the secretary handed Maria her discharge papers, took her signatures, and explained that they had to live in Magadan area until their passports were ready. Then she sent Maria and Sasha to the next-door room, and a photographer took photos of Sasha and Maria for their new passports.

Maria sensed that there was something fake in the conversation about the passports. She asked,

"Where are our French passports that we arrived with?"

"I was told that they were destroyed in the NKVD office in 1946. You'll be issued new passports soon. They promised to send it directly from Moscow."

Maria looked at the secretary and asked firmly,

"When can I leave?"

The secretary answered,

"Even yesterday, you were free to go."

Maria was about to walk out of the office, when the commandant opened the door of his room and said with uncovered hypocrisy in his voice,

"Ah, Madam Kurbatova is here. I see that you are ready to leave without saying *goodbye* to us. That's not nice. We were taking care of you for so many years, and even now, we have to find a place for you to stay, until your passports will be delivered from Moscow."

He looked with hatred at the skinny, pale but strong noble woman that survived all the hardships of the camp life for ten and a half years. The commandant continued,

"Madam Kurbatov, we'll take you to your flat today, when your husband gets here. You'll stay there, until the French embassy in Moscow issues your foreign passports."

Maria did not trust a single word of this perverted and sadistic person. She did not believe that this monster had become an angel just because of a change in Moscow policy regarding the political prisoners. About three months ago, he yelled in her face that she was lucky that skinny women are not in his taste and promised to rot her, "a stupid God worshiper," in a punishment cell and to send her son to the worst orphanage for young criminals, where every jailor would molest her boy days and nights.

It was he, a demonic beast, who "blessed" the guard personnel for weekly distraught orgies with insulting the women prisoners. It was he, who "assigned" himself to be the first man in lives of virgin nuns and inmates.

Presently, the obnoxious monster enjoyed watching, how Maria hated her further dependence on him. It was the next part of his dirty game. The commandant came up to Maria and hissed,

"What a pity that you are leaving, Madam Kurbatov! Who else will sit in the punishment cell and pray days and nights for us, sinners?"

Maria did not listen to his spitefulness. She thought about more important things,

"Now, it is obvious that there is no repatriation for us. The worst that can be – a settling in this uncivilized and dangerous area. Even after our liberation, they continue dictating us their rules."

Maria felt dizzy and put her arm around Sasha's shoulders. She whispered in a low voice: *"Lord, have mercy! Lord, have mercy! Lord, have mercy!"*

When Maria returned to the camp hospital, she told the doctor that the commandant of the camp had planned to settle the Kurbatov family somewhere in the area until the French passports would be issued and delivered from Moscow. Maria was disturbed.

"Doctor, I do not want the monsters to be involved in the life of our family again."

"But, Marie, you do not have any connection with the French embassy in Moscow. You don't have money and documents to travel. If you decide to travel without passports, they will arrest you and put you in prison again just for traveling without identification documents. This situation is not simple."

Maria saw, how hard the doctor tried to find the escape for Maria's family from under the commandant's control but failed to do it.

Maria said,

"They are liars. I do not believe that anybody from Moscow NKVD will provide reinvestigation of our case and connect us with the French embassy. I am more than sure that they will try to hide such a fact. In order to hide it forever, they can murder us. Then their well-known formula will work: 'No people and no case'."

Maria was exhausted and dizzy again. She laid down in order not to faint. The doctor checked Maria's blood pressure. It was low again. The nurse Masha gave her a shot, and in fifteen minutes they brought dinner for Maria and Sasha. Food always balanced Maria. The doctor came in at the end of the dinner and gave Sasha an apple. It was an apple from the last year, yellow and wrinkled. But the boy, who had not seen apples for a long time, was happy to have it.

"Mama, I'll go and share the apple with my friends."

Doctor Leskov cut the apple in three portions and gave them to Sasha, who ran to the children's room. The doctor smiled.

"Marie, you have a wonderful son. Masha and I will always miss him. He was a big help for us. I mean it, he was a help with the other kids."

Maria's thoughts were circling around the commandant's decision. It was an obstacle that she could not overcome easily.

The doctor noticed Maria's apprehension regarding the settling.

"Maria, you have to calm down, and your God will find something better for you. I am more than sure about it."

"Doctor, the situation like this had happened once before. I remember Alexander's initial request to the NKVD, on the very first day of our arrival to the Ukraine. The NKVD officer promised to find all the members of my family, knowing better that anybody else that my father was shot by his deputy, and my siblings were sent by him to different orphanages under fictitious last names."

Maria could hardly talk, but she wanted the doctor to understand the situation. She continued whispering,

"Alexander asked the officer to connect us with the French embassy in Moscow. He wanted the French embassy to issue the travel documents to take my relatives to France, as soon as possible. I can imagine now, how the demons laughed at my naïve husband, promising sarcastically that their colleges in Lvov would definitely connect us with the French embassy and, just for security reasons, they will keep us in Creeks for another night, a night in hell."

The sad memory and similarity of the situation caused the anxiety attack. Maria could not stop crying. The doctor asked Masha to bring the valerian drops. The doctor understood that Maria had to release the accumulation of old emotional pain. She continued,

"The local NKVD suggested their satanic game. The scenario of the present moment vividly reminded me of everything we went through during the first day and night of our arrival."

Doctor Leskov thought,

"She does not trust the commandant. Who can trust that monster? And she is frightened again for her family and for herself. Poor Maria, nobody can help her. I wish I could."

"Doctor, I know for sure, they involved us again in a dangerous game with their evil rules. I sense falsity in the commandant's tone and ultra politeness. He hates me, and he has prepared a trap for us. We cannot escape the trap. The moment they take us from here, the trap is locked. They can murder us. It's so easy: no witnesses."

"Maria, stay with us for a while, I know that Sofia would not mind your staying,"

the doctor suggested, reading Maria's mind. Then he added,

"If I were you, I wouldn't deal with those monsters. Did he mention, where they plan to settle you?"

"No. If he even mentioned, where they planned to settle us, I would not remember it, because everything here is unfamiliar to me."

The real concern in the doctor's voice made Maria more nervous. She was shaking and unable to stand without leaning on the windowsill or the bed-board. The visit to the camp office and her conversation with the commandant regarding their settlement somewhere in suburbs made her weaker. Maria was so disturbed that for a while, she forgot about her husband's arrival.

Somebody called for a doctor, and he left. Maria stood in front of the window with thick grating on it and thought: "Why did they put the grating? Who can disappear from here? The one-storied hospital is in the middle of the camp."

She was crying and repeating in front of the window. *"O most holy Theotokos, save us. Turn not away from the torrent of my tears. O Virgin, you who gave birth to Christ, who wipes away all tears from every face... O Holy Mother, be the haven and protection, and a wall unshaken, a refuge and shelter, and the gladness of those who flee unto thee."*

Maria experienced a strong sense of dizziness and sat down, continuing the prayer, *"O Virgin, please heal me, transforming my illness into healthfulness. Amen."*

Lord, have mercy!

Chapter 28

Sasha ran into the room with an announcement,

"Mommy, Papa is here. What should I do? Do you think that he will love me, as you do?"

Maria looked at her son and smiled. She stretched her arm and pulled Sasha closer, saying,

"He loves you, Sasha. Your father has loved you even before you were born. Do you remember, I told you a story about a letter that he wrote to you in Blue Creeks? It was our last day together. They took the letter away in Lvov prison. Do you remember, what he wrote there to you?"

Sasha answered, "Papa wrote that he would always love me and miss me very much every day until we meet."

Maria looked at the door and asked, "Where is he now?"

She tried to look strong and sound firm in front of her son. In reality, Maria felt that she was not grounded. She was like a balloon ready to fly with the slightest wind. She heard the steps of people approaching their room. Maria and Sasha stood up and listened with strained attention to all the sounds behind the door, waiting for it to be opened. In a moment, the door was opened. Maria and Sasha rushed forward and stopped. The doctor and Masha entered the room.

Maria felt weak and sat down on a stool. Then she asked in a low voice,

"Where is he?"

It seemed like the doctor did not hear the question and took Maria's wrist to listen to her pulse. He named the medication Masha had to bring to Maria and left.

"Sasha, where is your Papa?"

The boy was confused.

"I saw a tall, limping man in the corridor with a patch on his eye. I thought it was my father."

Maria asked:

"What color was his hair?"

Sasha looked at his mother and answered,

"It was grey and very short."

Maria smiled.

"No, Sasha. It was not your father, because his hair..."

She did not finish the sentence. The disturbed woman realized that she hadn't seen her husband for ten years, five months, and twelve days. The hardships of life had changed everything, and his hair could turn grey.

Somebody was approaching the door again. This time, it was nurse Masha with Maria's medication. Masha looked sympathetically at the nervous woman. She was not the type of a person, who could keep any good news hidden. She said with her soft smile,

"Maria, your husband is in the commandant's office together with our doctor. Doctor Leskov wants you to stay at their place until you can get permission to go back to France."

Masha had been already at the doorway, when she looked around and said,

"In France, you'll be again Count and Countess Kurbatov. Sasha, you'll be Count Kurbatov, Jr. There, you'll recollect with horror about everything what has happened to your family in this country. Let it be your last nightmare in your life."

The nurse Masha came up to Sasha and hugged the boy. In a way, he was her boy whom she gave love, time, and strength for long ten years.

"Take care of your Mama, Sasha. Your mother is the best mother, I've ever met in my life."

Maria wanted to find comfort in the words of the considerate Russian woman regarding the last nightmare. It was true. She could not wait until they return to France. She could hardly wait, until the persistent painful tension in her chest disappear. Maria knew that that terrible chest pain was caused by endless terror, overtiredness and starvation. She cannot be well, until she starts breathing, as a free person again.

Maria thought,

"Maybe, I am a very weak person. But, dear Lord, help us to be out of danger, because we have no strength to deal with it anymore."

At that moment, they heard the male conversation in the corridor of the hospital. Sasha opened the door and stepped back.

"Mommy, he is here."

The boy stood near Maria, waiting eagerly for the first meeting with his father.

For many years, Sasha had constantly asked Maria to tell him something about his father. The boy wanted to know what kind of a person his father was. Nobody was able to replace a father for a boy. Sasha looked for male guidance to discuss his problems and to make the right decisions in different situations in the prison and school.

From age six, the boy used to ask Maria,

"Mommy, what do you think my father would suggest to me in this situation? What do you think my father would do in my place?"

It was not easy to guess or suppose his father's opinion or suggestion in many problems that were vitally important for a child in prison. The most complicated time was Sasha's school years. The boy from the labor camp was an "outsider" to the local children. He was not allowed to have his opinion, and he was not asked to express out load his thoughts. They ignored him for a while, but every teacher admitted that he was the best in math and other subjects.

Being the best in studies, Sasha's teacher still did not want the other children to keep company and friendship with him. A small child learned the bitterness of being an outsider, a foreigner, a stranger to his classmates. His teacher gave him the nickname "professor." It disturbed the child and one day he said to Maria,

"Mama, I wish my father can go to school and talk to my teacher. I don't like her calling me 'professor'. Maria felt sorry for her boy. The child needed his father's protection or defense. It is so natural for children.

The doctor opened the door and let Alexander in. There was a long pause. They were looking at each other and did not move. Alexander turned pale. When he pronounced the first words, no one could hear them. Then he called in French,

"Marie! Mon Chère Marie!"

Maria understood that he was not able to come up closer due to shock. She moved slowly towards her husband with her arms opened wide. They embraced each other and closed their eyes. They had dreamed about that moment for so many years and did not want the moment to slip away. From time to time, it seemed to both of them that they were not destined to feel once again the unity that the Divinity introduced them to in their short but happy mutual life.

Alexander kissed Maria's head, face, and both hands. His eye was filled with tears. Then he smiled with his one-sided smile and stroked the brush of her thick, dark, and shortly cut hair. Maria did not look like a thirty-seven-year-old woman. Her short hair and thin body complexion made her to appear much younger. Alexander mentioned with a smile.

"My love, you do not have your braids again, like in 1945 in Hamburg? But you look great. God preserved your beauty, Marie. I was asking Him for it."

Maria answered,

"Now I don't have my braids, and I am skinny again. Everything is returned to the very beginning."

"Marie, it is true: you look the same, as I found you at the end of the war. Thank God, but the bitterness of imprisonment did not change you, mon amour."

She remembered well that miraculous day in Germany. On that time, she was also an inmate. The prisoners were not allowed to keep long hair.

Maria smiled.

"I hope, it's the last time in my life that somebody decides what hair style I need to have."

She leaned into Alexander, not only because she wanted to feel him, but also because she had no more strength to stand. A wave of light, warmth and joy captured her weak body, reminding her, "The Divine Savior was and is with both of you".

Maria whispered,

"Alex, one more miracle happened in our life: we survived! We are together again! All three of us are together."

Maria and Alexander "woke up" and looked at Sasha, who was waiting patiently, watching a happy moment in the life of his parents. Alexander came up to his son, put his hands on the boy's shoulders, and said

"Good day, my son. I am your father, Count Alexander Kurbatov."

Alexander grew pale and burst into cough with severe wheezing. He did not have the strength to stand and so he kneeled in front of his boy, hugging him. Alexander's and Sasha's eyes met, and then there was silence in the room. The child broke the silence with the words that he had never pronounced out loud before,

"Daddy, I was waiting for you all my life. Mommy, nurse Masha and Dr. Leskov were also waiting for you, and I knew that you'd come. I missed you so much. I love you, Daddy."

Alexander whispered,

"I love you too, sonny. I prayed every day, asking the Lord to give me the strength to survive in order to meet you, to touch you, to take care of you and your Mama."

Alexander needed somebody's assistance to get up. Sasha and Maria helped him. He sat down on the stool and continued,

"As you can see, Sasha, presently, your Mama and I are physically weak, but with time, we'll get stronger again. The God's miracle had happened to three of us, and from now on, we are all together. God blessed us with a re-union. We are free, and today, we start our family life."

Alexander did not feel well and asked for some cold water. Maria noticed that even positive emotions caused her husband shortness of breath and weakness. Masha had brought Alexander a glass of water and suggested everyone to have some tea. It was funny to see people drinking hot water with some herbal taste without sugar or anything else to it. The doctor apologized with a joke,

"We have terrible "service" here. We do not have even dry bread to our tea."

They all laughed, because the invigorating feeling of freedom and human life had penetrated already their minds, souls, hearts, and bodies. They had suffered in captivity for more than ten years. When thorny, fearful, and misfortunate existence affects people for a long time, it usually, makes their senses and feelings frozen to some degree. The Savior keeps them on *self-preservation* regime, otherwise the hyper-sensitivity would never allow them to survive. The feeling of freedom heats them up, causing a blissful but rather painful experience of revitalizing.

The positive changes caused unpredictable effect. The suppressive external pressure in the lifestyle of long-term prisoners was removed. Nevertheless, it made the former inmates completely confused of how to proceed further with their lives. They experienced the dangerous lack of attachment to their families, earthly values, interests and goals.

The mankind learned the regrettable fact of the history: thousands of the released GULAG prisoners, who endured the long-term internment, were unable to survive the elation of freedom and passed away shortly after the liberation. Long-term imprisonment atrophied their ability to think, choose, organize, and succeed in life on their own. The long-term forceful and suppressive mechanism destroyed people's individuality.

Unlike Maria and Alexander, this soviet generation was deprived of rejuvenating and enlightening power of the Holy Spirit due to their communist upbringing and conscious rejection of the Divinity.

Maria saw that Alexander was extremely weak. Being smart, she hustled to "chain" him firmly to their new Earthly mutual life with its danger and unresolved problems. Maria was blessed not to allow Alexander and her to learn another type of freedom - death. It was not because they were too young to die, but because they could not betray their God who entrusted them with life, and Who successfully preserved it throughout all the dangers. They also could not abandon their son who patiently waited for them for his entire life. The Lord gave them their son and helped the boy to survive in order he could fulfill the most important task – to help his parents not to lose the vitally important attraction to Earthly life.

Glory to Three, o Lord! Glory to Thee!

Chapter 29

The camp transport was sent to deliver the Kurbatov family to their new dwelling. Alexander and Maria were concerned about that event. The doctor's request about staying together for a while was rejected by the commandant of the camp. The rejection made the case more suspicious. When the transport was at the door of the hospital, Maria noticed that the driver was alone; no guards or jailers accompanied him.

The doctor whispered,

"God's blessing to you, people."

Maria smiled, seeing how he turned himself to God after the arrival of his daughters. Sofia mentioned that they started to worship regularly, praising the Divinity every evening together. She was sure that it was Maria who brought him to God. Maria tried to argue regarding that, but Sofia knew that the doctor was not the first one who was helped by the Lord and became a spiritual person. The Kurbatovs got into a small truck and waved farewell to their friends. This time, it was again the forceful transporting away that disturbed Maria a lot. The trip took more than an hour and the driver brought the Kurbatovs to an old barrack-like structure in the suburb of a village. One side of the barrack had shifted, causing it to lean. There was a small pile of wood near the door.

The driver pointed to the hill in a distance and asked,

"Can you see the short one-sided trees on the hills? Your firewood is there."

Maria asked him with trembling voice,

"Who stays in those houses?"

The driver answered with unhidden pleasure,

"The discharged criminals from different camps. Remember, that most of them do not have respect for political prisoners. Be careful. It's not your France. It's our wild Russia."

The driver was demonically proud of making that comparison. His mind was twisted with a single thought that was passed to him by the commandant of the camp.

"We'll settle them in a horrible place, so these … frog eaters will remember the camp life, as the most secure time in our country."

The driver recollected how commandant used profanity and neighed like a horse. It was fun for them.

The transport stopped. The driver handed Alexander a key for the barrack and left.

Maria realized clearly that they were caught in a new trap. The situation was more dangerous than she could imagine. Maria was frightened to death and whispered to Alexander,

"Sasha should not know anything about the neighbors. He would not attend the local school. He doesn't need it. He'll go to France and will attend a good school there. Am I right?"

She looked at Alexander and continued out load,

"The first moment we receive the passports, we'll disappear from here forever."

Alexander smiled bitterly.

"Marie, what passports will they issue? Who will issue us French passports? When was it possible for Russian political prisoners to leave the country?"

Maria stared at her husband.

"O, my Lord!" She exclaimed in a weak voice.

They went into the wooden barrack. There was a single room with a huge Russian stove in the middle. None of them had experience how to start a fire in the stove and cook in it. Alexander put the wood in the stove, but there was not a single match in the house.

Alexander said,

"Marie, I'll go to the neighbors and borrow a box of matches,"

Maria was against it. She absorbed the danger from the words of the driver.

Maria thought, "How was it possible that her husband did not understand that they were in a dangerous trap."

She did not want to discuss the topic in Sasha's presence and suggested,

"Alex, please do not go anywhere. We'll pray the whole night with bows and prostrations. One day, I survived forty degrees below zero in my punishment cell, praying hard."

Alexander looked at his frightened wife and answered with an old Russian proverb,

"There are no two deaths for one person, but there is no way to escape a single one." What will be, will be, Mon Chere."

He embraced her for a second and left. Maria heard him knocking on the neighbors' door. Somebody opened the door. She could not hear the conversation. Then the door was closed. Maria started to pray: *"Holy God, Holy Mighty, Holy Immortal, have mercy on us. Lord, have mercy. Lord, have mercy. Lord, have mercy."*

Sasha hugged Maria.

"Mama, I'll go there and help my Dad. I had just found him, and nobody can hurt him or take him from us."

Maria looked at her son with surprise and appreciation. A small boy wanted to defend his father. He was absolutely serious in his intent. Sasha put on his hat and rushed to the door. Maria did not have strength to stop him. She was stoned with fear, or maybe, she was stopped by her Angel. She unfroze when she heard the door open. Alexander and Sasha were smiling. They brought matches, two potatoes, a tablespoon of tea, and some dark bread.

The neighbor's wife was sick, so Alexander had his first professional consultation. They were political prisoners, as well, discharged two years ago. Maria was happy. They set a fire in the stove and had tea and bread for supper. She baked one potato for Sasha. It was a real family feast. Then they pulled the old mattress closer to the stove, covered themselves with their quilted jackets, and fell asleep immediately, as if they were sleeping in the most luxurious beds.

The next morning was the first one in their free life. Maria woke up early and noticed that Alexander was already out of bed. He covered their son with his quilted jacket. Sasha was a tall boy and Sasha's jacket could not cover his body and long legs at the same time, so the boy huddled himself up in order to be covered. The moment his father shared his warm jacket with him; Sasha, still asleep, stretched his legs. Maria was short and so thin that her jacket worked well for her.

She watched how Alex tryed to light a fire in the stove, quietly putting the wood inside in order not to awake his family. It was still dark in the room. Alexander did not see that Maria was watching him. The fire in the stove lit up her husband's face. The torture and ten years in prison left deep imprints on Alexander's appearance. He looked like a man, who was at least twenty years older than he was. Gray thin hair, deep wrinkles on his face, especially his forehead, hunched over posture, harsh breathing with frequent wheezing and only one eye. Alexander's appearance had changed so dramatically that he barely resembled the man Maria knew over ten years ago.

Maria's heart tightened in her chest, causing her pain. She felt sorry for her husband and couldn't keep observing him without tears.

"What have I done to you, mon amour? You probably will never forgive me. How can I help you restore your life, health, appearance and posture? It is impossible to do this restoration. I have ruined everything, and I must be the one, who will work hard in order to bring back some of your strength and rejuvenate your feelings."

Maria moved slowly out of bed, came up to her husband, kissed his head, and kneeled in front of him. She looked in his only eye and asked the question that was the biggest disturbance for her during all the years in prison,

"Can you forgive me?"

Alexander covered Maria's face with kisses and pulled her with strength that she did not expect from him.

"Marie, my dearest Marie, I want you to understand once and forever. I had never blamed you. It happened because it was destined to be. I was so lucky to find you easily in Germany, to have you, to love you, and to be loved by you. One thing I did wrong: I hadn't expressed enough appreciation to God for every single day that we spent together and for our son."

Alexander stopped talking for a moment, trying to control his breathing. Then he continued,

"I survived the incarceration because of you and Sasha, your miraculous existence in this cruel life. I was living for ten endless years in a labor camp with one thought and desire - to see you again, to touch you, to kiss you, to listen to your voice, and to hug my son."

Alexander could not continue talking due to shortness of breath. He whispered,

"Marie, darling, have I answered your question?"

Maria burst into sobbing. She tried not to wake up their son but could not stop crying. The woman sensed her sin, as a large weight in her chest, for more than ten years. It was heavy, icy cold and painful from the very beginning. But with years, the weight of sin from non-stop self-blaming grew significantly. Even the light and warmth from above could not melt it.

The moment, when her husband declared sincerely her "not guilty" verdict, Maria experienced the severest pain in her chest and then warmth and light. The *icy* formation started melting, giving Maria the ability to inhale more deeply. She already forgot the natural feeling of breathing deeply and freely, so compressed she was under the weight of guilt.

What blissfulness and joy Maria and Alexander experienced at their Morning worship! Looking at the first signs of sunrise, they praised the Divinity that made that morning possible. The emptiness of the room meant nothing for them - the family was together, and they had much to be grateful for. A new chapter of their life had begun. They were blessed to joyfully continue their living, no matter how poverty-stricken the quality of their life was.

Glory to Thee, o Lord! Glory to Thee!

Chapter 30

Sasha woke up about nine o'clock in the morning. On that day, he did not go to school. He saw his parents sitting near the stove, discussing something very important. Sasha got up and went to them. Maria noticed him coming and lowered her voice. The boy wished them good morning and put his arms around the shoulders of both parents. They smiled happily and answered simultaneously,

"Good morning, Sasha".

The boy stood for a minute, enjoying with his kid's heart the most pleasant moment of his life, and then he went back to sleep with a smile on his lips. Sasha's nervous strain during the last year was enormous. It was difficult for a boy to wait for his mother to be released from the punishment cell. Maria, being a physician, noticed that her son was more disturbed than ever.

Yesterday, the boy was stressed out again, when he met his father for the first time in his life. He spoke a lot about his father with Maria, Dr. Leskov, and nurse Masha. Sometimes it seemed to him that he knew his father very well, but it was from the words and stories of other people. It was still a huge trauma to see his father's mutilated body, hand, and especially face. Maria prepared Sasha, describing in a gentle version what his father and she went through, but without dramatic details that could harden his heart and seed the anger and hatred in his mind. The child was not ready to learn all the details of the terrible September night of 1946. The real appearance of his Dad told him much more. The boy felt sorry for his tormented father.

It was good that Sasha went back to sleep. His parents had to find a way to feed him and to get something for themselves, as well. Maria went to meet the neighbors. She knocked on the door, and it was opened immediately. The woman was washing the floor by the door.

Maria introduced herself.

"I am Maria Kurbatov, your neighbor. I am really sorry that I came to you at the wrong time. I did not mean interrupting your cleaning. I can come later."

The woman looked at Maria with surprise.

"Why later? I have finished. Come in."

The hostess went straight to the stove. With her back toward Maria, she put some wood in the stove, turned around, and then introduced herself,

"I am Lena. And you are?"

"Maria Kurbatov," Maria repeated and continued,

"I do not want to bother you. I was wondering, if you could tell me, where the nearest grocery store is. We need to buy some food."

"In the center of the village," Lena answered.

"Is it far from here?" Maria asked.

"Twenty minutes of walk," Lena replied.

The next question was about the work.

"Alexander and I have to find some job."

"What are you?" Lena inquired.

"I am a physician."

"You are a surgeon, like your husband, aren't you?" Lena presumed.

"No, I am a general physician," Maria corrected.

"Understood," Lena replied coldly.

It looked like the woman did not have any wish to keep a conversation with a stranger. Who could blame her? Maria guessed that probably once in her life she learned a lesson and paid with long term of imprisonment for a brief conversation with a wrong person.

Lena thought for a while and suggested to Maria,

"Go to the hospital. Ask them. They could find something for you."

Then she added,

"Nobody likes us, but if they have shortage in personnel, they can allow you to wash the floors in the clinic."

The woman smiled bitterly. Maria realized that Lena had uneasy experience in her "free" life. Maria was about to leave, when Lena stopped her.

"I know that you do not have anything to eat in the house, do you?"

Maria was surprised that the "icy" woman asked about something human. Maria's eyes got filled with tears, ready to roll on her pale and bony cheeks. She tried to answer without emotions,

"You are right."

Lena continued,

"I remember our own moment of discharge two years ago with no money, food, or job. Employment for us was extremely difficult."

Maria asked,

"What was the difference?"

Lena explained,

"Your advantage in comparison with us is that they admitted that your long-term imprisonment was a 'mistake' of their internal security service." We were discharged as '*people's enemies*' due to the end of serving the sentence."

Maria could not see the difference. Lena, seemingly read her mind, clarifying further,

"I hope that now it's easier for you to be hired for work positions. It was very different with us. After we served our sentence and were discharged, we were still "people's enemies", and nobody wanted us. They were afraid to hire us. Most of the scared population preferred us to disappear, probably to parish in the labor camps and forget about our existence."

Maria tried to determine Lena's age – perhaps, she was between forty to fifty. Lena continued with the anger in her voice.

"I had my liver attack yesterday. It was damaged with beating up at the very first interrogation. Your husband diagnosed it right away. He is a good specialist, but I doubt they can hire him, as a surgeon. They will always be afraid that with the first opportunity, you'll take revenge, especially, if their lives are in the hands of a surgeon, who is a former 'people's enemy' and served for ten years without committing any crime. They prefer to protect themselves."

Then Lena shook her head and suggested that Maria bring her men for dinner,

"We do not have anything special, but you do not have anything at all."

Maria was surprised with an unexpected invitation and answered,

"You are right about nothing at all."

Lena continued,

"My husband is coming at two. He works in a tractor repair shop not far from here and comes for dinner every day. He wanted me to cook more soup and vegetable stew in order to feed your family."

Maria did not want to refuse. There was one more thing she came for: a pot. Yesterday the neighbors gave Alexander two potatoes. Maria baked one for Sasha. They would boil another one for his breakfast. Lena gave her a small pot, an onion and some more bread, and Maria promised to bring her "men" at two for dinner.

She flitted into the room and saw a picture of her dream: Sasha and Alexander were sleeping together. Their foreheads were pressed to each other, and Alexander was sleeping with his arm around his son. Maria watched them with adoration:

"Thank You, Lord!" she whispered and sighed.

"Poverty is the only difference between my dream and the reality. But poverty could not affect our happiness. I know for sure that poverty is not eternal. We'll work hard or leave for France, and we'll be rid of it."

Maria noticed with the smile that they put her valenki under their heads, and this way, they fixed the problem of the absence of pillows. That morning brought her the feeling of forgotten happiness. She praised the Lord for so many things, He allowed to happen: Alexander's forgiveness, her son's joy due to having both parents, and reunion of three hearts and souls.

Maria whispered, *"Glory to God in the highest! We praise Thee, we bless Thee, we worship Thee, and we give thanks to Thee for Thy peace on Earth and good will among men. Amen."*

Maria poured some water into the pot, washed the potato, and put the pot with a single potato on the stove. When she went out to bring another armful of firewood, it started boiling and the lid rattled. The loud noise woke up both men. They looked at Maria's shining face and could not define what had made her so happy. It was a quarter after ten in the morning. Maria pulled the quilted jackets from her gentlemen and pretended that she was angry with both of them.

She said in a strict voice,

"Get up, lazy bones! We have a lot of work to do. We are invited for dinner at our neighbors' place. The dinner is at two. Before dinner, we have to bring water from the well, wash the floors in the room, and go to the forest to bring some firewood. We have firewood left for just one more day. Tomorrow, we do not have time to go to the forest. We have to go to a local hospital and apply for a job."

Maria talked and moved near the stove quickly. Alexander enjoyed watching his wife in such a mood, and ready to do plenty of work. She looked pale and fragile, but she was his wife again from their previous happy life. He noticed a strong desire to be with her. The years of suffering had turned off that desire, and she switched it on again.

Maria continued,

"Alexander, any job is good. We need money to buy our food and clothing. Nobody knows, how long we have to wait in Russia, until something will be resolved with our documents."

Sasha went outside to the lavatory. It was nothing new for a boy. He was born and grew up in the camp, where normally, there was no plumbing inside of the barracks.

Alexander was not able to get up quickly. He moved slowly. He came up to Maria and embraced her from the back. In spite of everything, the rejuvenation of his body was going briskly, and he desired only one thing: to clasp this tiny bird in his arms and never ever let her fly away.

His arms were strong, and Maria did not have strength to move. She forgot what she was talking about. The two of them stepped again on the path of happiness and flew away together into another world. Sasha's voice delivered them back to earth. The parents felt confused.

"That's why the children are born, just to stop us from silly things," Alexander whispered in Maria's ear. They burst into laughter.

Sasha had finished washing in washbasin and dripped some water on his parents. All three of them laughed. The spirit of domestic life and happiness settled in the empty room. It seemed that nothing could affect the atmosphere of joy in their uncivilized life.

Before breakfast they cleaned the room. The table and the floors were scraped and washed with warm water. The color of the fresh wood was light, and the smell was pleasant. It took less than an hour and the three of them had finished with cleaning. Alexander joked,

"It's really easy to clean when the room is small, empty, and there is no furniture in it."

Maria sliced the potato, onion and bread, and put it on the table. They did not have a single dish in the room. They haven't been sitting around a table, as people normally do. They had only one stool in their room. Maria suggested that Alexander sit on the stool because of his persistent back and leg pain. It was easier for him to walk than to stand straight. He performed all the surgeries leaning on the operating table and standing most of the time on his less damaged leg.

Alexander looked at the table and said,

"Marie, I was given some money at the camp, when they discharged me, and your doctor added some for food. Let us go and buy two more stools."

Maria asked Sasha to give her a sheet of paper. She wrote a long list of necessary things they needed to buy, as soon as possible. The list was long because they did not have anything. Maria looked at the list and named everything out loud. They needed a pot, a frying pan, three of each - cups, plates, forks, spoons, and one big knife for cooking. She had been using Alexander's small pocketknife. It was too small for slicing and cutting the food, especially the raw produce.

Alexander suggested,

"We have money to purchase only some things from this list. First, we'll get firewood, and then we'll go shopping for food and kitchen supplies."

"What is more important, to go food shopping or to gather brush-wood and firewood?" Sasha asked.

Maria had the answer ready,

"First of all, we have to bring water into the house, put it on the stove, and arrange a bath at night. Then we go and gather wood."

Alexander added,

"We have to buy a couple of more things: two pillows and two sheets. If we have enough money, we'll buy a quilt. If not, we can wait until we earn something."

Sasha concluded,

"Water and wood first, and then - shopping and dinner. Dad, we got up too late. Mama was absolutely right, when she called us "lazy bones."

They laughed again. That time, Maria was near the stove and hadn't seen her husband's face, but

Alexander's laugh sounded like his old, forgotten one: that Maria had always enjoyed listening to.

It was such a pleasure for Maria to hear the laugh of her husband again. She recollected the scene from her fairy tale life before the war. Maria was a freshman year student. Her friend Anastasia and she were leaving after class, when she heard Alexander's laugh for the first time: so pure, natural and pleasant. The girls burst into laughter too. Anastasia noticed that Alexander had a contagious laugh. Maria could not get rid of the desire to be introduced to the laughter.

She believed that their relationship was destined from Above. They fell in love on the second day of their acquaintance. They knew that the intimate relationship was forbidden until the church wedding. Both of them could not keep waiting for the beauty of the wedding ceremony that they dreamed of. The cruel war postponed their happiness, but even the war and Nazi concentration camp did not kill their love and desire to be one body and one spirit in front of the Universe. Only in 1945, God blessed them with marriage.

Glory to Thee, o Lord! Glory to Thee!

Chapter 31

Maria looked at her husband and saw that Alexander's face was different. It was not a face of that Alexander from the fairy tale, but it was not so ugly anymore, as she found it after the tortures. Since then, she was unable to look without sympathy at her dearly loved husband. She loved him undoubtedly. It was unconditional love, but for Maria, his disfigured facial features and lop-sided posture were like the pricks of conscience and painful reminders of her imprudence, to the point of foolhardiness, with the desire to go to the "soviet or red" Ukraine.

Her eyes grew dim with tears. Maria prayed silently,

"O Lord, forgive me a sinner, have mercy on us and save us."

She shook her head, fighting back the unpleasant thoughts.

"I need to move forward. I cannot live and blame myself constantly for everything that has happened to my family, and the hardships that we continue to go through. We cannot change our past. With God's help, all of us will move forward. Move forward… How?"

Maria wondered,

"What do we need to do this?"

Instantly, she received the guidance,

"When people want to interrupt the vicious cycle, they need to become stronger in faith, obtain lessons from the past experiences, and become wiser in their choices. Otherwise, they keep attracting negative chain of events, as a form of self-inflicted punishment, that wastes their physical and mental energy and ability to build a better new life."

The family finished the meal quickly, with only a single potato, onion, slice of bread, and some tea that was made in the same pot after cooking the potato. They went to the well with three buckets that the previous inhabitants left on a small bench in their room together with two sheets and a towel. One bucket of water they left for drinking and cooking. Two others they put on the stove to warm up for baths. The roundtrip to the well took about ten minutes. The well was in the middle of their block. The Kurbatovs considered it very close to their barrack. The barrack had four entrances that meant four families lived there.

After bringing the water, the family went to the forest to gather firewood for the stove. The forest was also not far from the barrack, but it took about half an hour to reach it. Alexander and Maria were not able to walk fast, and they needed to stop several times to rest. The severe pain frequently shot into Alexander's spine and legs. Sometimes, it was shooting nearly every minute. At that moment, the excruciating pain did not allow him to be in motion, and he had to stand for a while before it allowed him to move on. This pain prevented Alexander from forgetting the inhuman brutality of 1946.

Maria and Sasha wanted Alexander to go back home, but Alexander insisted going everywhere together. Maria asked,

"My darling, you are not going to carry the wood, are you? Maybe a little bit of brushwood, Mon Cher."

Alexander smiled,

"May I ask, my love, who is going to carry the wood?"

Maria was not given a chance to answer.

Sasha stopped him and begged Alexander looking straight into his father's face,

"Daddy, please do not carry a single piece of wood. I'll do it by myself. I know how to do it, trust me. They sent us to gather the brushwood all the time. It's nice that somebody left these good ropes for us. I was five. They gave me a bad rope, and I was losing the wood. The overseer walked behind me and kicked in the back with his heavy boot all the way to barracks for every lost piecc of wood. I was small and cried every time when I fell after his push. Later, I learned how to bind the wood and carried a lot and did not lose a single brush."

Maria saw, how Alexander's face turned pale. He hugged his son and Alexander's tears were rolling on Sasha's hat.

"Sonny, forgive me. I beg your pardon, Sasha for my weakness, and I am sorry for my absence in your life for more than ten years."

Sasha pressed himself with all his strength to his father's body and said,

"Daddy, there is nothing to forgive you for. You are my Dad, and I love you so much. We will never separate again. I'll do all the male work in the house instead of you. You'll teach me, and I'll do it. I promise to help you every day."

The child burst into tears and cried out loud. All the feelings that were suppressed for ten years in his small heart, exploded. Maria knew that she felt better after her morning "outburst" and did not want to interrupt the release of the negative emotions of their child.

Maria left her two dearest men together and went to the forest, crying bitterly. She thought,

"All three of us stored a lot of emotional pain for ten years, and it is wonderful that the Creator gave us the opportunity to release the enormous emotional overload, the suppressed feelings, disturbing thoughts, and painful memories during the first day of our reunion. From now on, we start feeling differently about our life experiences. They will not be so damaging. Today, we were blessed to cleanse ourselves from phyco-emotional build-up. Nothing will interfere to see clearly the future of our mutual lives."

Maria was right in her understanding that the improvement of the physical and psychological conditions was possible only when people acknowledge and release the painful memories, offensive feelings, negative thoughts and traumatic experiences. That heavy waste that mounted up for years of hardships always developed physical fatigue, slow healing, emotional exhaustion and frequently led to death.

She praised the Lord out loud for His explanation to her the vitally important phenomena in human lives,

"Glory to Thee, my God! Glory to Thee!"

Chapter 32

Sasha noticed that his mother was not with them. He looked around and saw her near the forest. Two Kurbatovs continued walking. They came up to the first chain of short, one-sided trees. Alexander paid Sasha's attention to the color of the forest. It was no longer gray. The first warm sunrays turned the dull gray color into a hazel and light green. Tiny leaves were peaking out, and they had changed everything around. Alexander smiled and told Sasha,

"Look, sonny: the forest is awaking from winter freezing. It's like us. The warmth of our love and freedom brings us back to life."

Alexander put his right arm around his son's shoulders and continued,

"I am the happiest person, Sasha. God gave me your mother and you. The two of you kept me alive in captivity. Even there, the memory of your mother and you warmed my heart and soul, and I believed that with time, my body would be healed and become stronger because there was a reason to survive."

Alexander smiled and added,

"I must live forever because I have both of you with me."

The boy looked up at his father and said,

"Daddy, you are the best father in the whole world. I missed you in my life. I did not know how nice it is to have a father, to stay with you, and to talk to you. I liked to speak to my Mama, the doctor, and our nurse Masha. They had always been good to me, but you are different..."

Sasha could not define, what made his father different. Alexander was weak, limping, and emaciated. His facial features were repulsive. But it seemed like the boy did not notice any of those defects. A strong invisible cord sent from Above bonded two souls together at the moment of conception. The demonic force pulled their souls apart, making the separation tormenting for both. Their father-son love on the level of the souls was unchangeable for ten years, because the Lord protected the cord from being torn. Any transformations in physical appearance did not mean anything for the father-son connection.

Sasha asked,

"Dad, do you know who made us prisoners? Who separated us for so long? Why did they put us and others into the camps? Was it Stalin?"

Alexander was surprised to hear such philosophical questions from his ten-year-old son. The boy wanted to define a person, who was guilty in imprisoning of innocent people. Alexander answered,

"I do not think that Stalin was the only one guilty in this situation. The whole satanic system was against decent people and definitely against those who belonged to nobility, like us."

Sasha listened attentively, and then asked another question,

"Dad, but Mama is not Russian. She is Ukrainian who was born in Poland. She told me that her ancestors were respectable Ukrainian people. Why they hated her, as well?"

"The answer is the same, son. The people, completely illiterate or with two-three classes of school education, built '*the dictatorship of workers and peasants.*' They based it on humiliation of well-educated people, nobility, and clergy. During the years of their communist power, they killed the spirituality of people, destroyed the ethical judicial system and created the discriminating laws in their country. Normal people cannot exist and function successfully in the society without faith, public morals and human rights laws."

They worked silently for some time, and then Sasha asked,

"Dad, how come that you have survived the camp life in your physical condition, and other people could not do it? So many inmates in our camp killed themselves."

"The Polish, Ukrainian, and Russian people were historically spiritual. They believed in God and were supported by Him for centuries. Suicide was always considered, as one of the unforgivable sins. Those who committed suicide were not buried at the cemetery. I believe in God. I did not allow myself to betray His trust in me, your mother's love, and my devotion to your mother and you."

Sasha was satisfied with father's explanation and smiled.

Alexander continued,

"Sasha, look at your mother. She has a strong faith in God, and she always relies on His support, guidance and protection. She is His child. She has never betrayed Him. She has never blamed Him for her hardships, as many other people do. Even under the most intolerable life circumstances, she did not allow her mind to arise a thought about committing suicide. Why? She believes that suicide permit the satanic force to capture and torture the person's soul – the most valuable gift from God. Presence of the eternal soul differs us from all the rest God's creatures. The heartbreaking life events did not diminish your mother's hope for positive changes with God's will."

Sasha asked,

"Why were those people who killed themselves not afraid to do it?".

Alexander looked at his son and answered with sadness in his voice,

"Poor people, they have lost or never found the spiritual connection with the Divinity and did not know anything about the eternal suffering of the soul after their death. If they knew, they would never commit such a sin."

Sasha listened attentively to his father, and every word was planted in the boy's mind. He was proud of his parents. The difficult life did not break them, as it happened to many others.

"Dad, how is it possible that good people become bad, or even demonic?"

Alexander picked up Sasha's concern. The boy wanted to understand the process of transmutation or descension, keeping deep fear in being unwillingly turned into monstrosity.

"Looking for power or popularity, many people deny the worship of God. These socialist and communist '*leaders*' pursue one goal: to withdraw other people from worshiping the Divinity and force them to worship the political idols, instead."

"What happens later with those who betrayed God?" Sasha inquired with impatience.

"At the beginning, nobody sees the danger. People just refuse to honor the Divinity. With time, they lose their connection with the Lord, His support and protection. Without the Lord's protection and guidance, people are lost in this life. They become an easy target for the satanic force and are pulled to the evil side. The satanic structure turns them into Satan servants - demons or monsters."

Sasha did not receive a complete answer to his question and continue inquiring,

"Dad, you are talking about the authorities. But what happened to the regular people?"

Alexander explained,

"The leaders involved different people in satanic darkness through pillage, corruption, moral degradation, crime, alcoholism, brutal violence, and cowardice. The soviet political structure successfully planted the seeds of fear."

"Who were they afraid of?" Sasha asked with surprise.

"At the beginning people were afraid of the authorities, any representative of a punitive power. With time, they saw danger in co-workers, neighbors, and relatives. The satanic fear paralyzed human will, consciousness, thoughts, and feelings. The frightened people wanted to 'protect' themselves and get rid of danger. They sent the anonymous denunciations on the people to NKVD with accusations of the innocent people in '*suspicious activities*.'"

"Dad, are you afraid of anything?" Sasha asked.

"Yes, Sasha."

The boy was surprised to hear such an answer. He had built the image of his father, as one of the most intelligent and brave men.

"Dad, what are you afraid of?" Sasha asked in a low voice.

"I am afraid of two things: the Lord's punishment for a sinful deed, and the loss of my family."

Sasha stared at his father with admiration and decided to ask the most difficult question.

"If our Lord sees all the cruel and dirty tricks of the satanic force, why does He allow them to take place?"

Alexander looked in the eyes of his son and affirmed,

"There is only one reason, why God allows the satanic force to exist in this world, and that is to put us and our faith to the test."

Alexander's voice became stronger,

"My dream is to leave this country, as my parents did in 1917, without further investigating which demonic department made our lives miserable: NKVD, government, or communist leaders of 'the dictatorship of workers and peasants'."

The interesting conversation energized the Kurbatovs. They gathered the wood, tied the bundles quickly, and carried the bundles home on their backs. It took more than an hour to get home with heavy firewood, making several stops to rest. All of them were tired but joyful.

Glory to Thee, O Lord! Glory to Thee!

Chapter 33

What was a surprise! In half an hour after they returned to the barrack, there was a heavy snowfall. It lasted for ten minutes, covering all the paths around the barrack. Maria commented,

"Look, our Lord gave us a wonderful morning. It was pleasantly warm and sunny. You see, gentlemen, how He was merciful to us. Thank God for giving us the opportunity to bring some firewood without fighting the snowfall in the forest or on our way home."

Alexander looked out of the window, watching the changes of the weather. Then he concluded,

"We have to postpone our shopping until tomorrow. Then we'll stop at the hospital to apply for job. You are right, Marie, any job is good for now."

At two o'clock, the Kurbatovs were ready to go for dinner to their neighbors, when somebody knocked on the door. It was Vladimir, the neighbor who came to hurry them for dinner.

"Let's go," Vladimir said. "Dinner is ready and waiting for us."

The Kurbatovs were glad to go. They were hungry after the work in the forest but did not have anything to eat at home. During the dinner, Vladimir and Lena shared their story. They were born in Voronezh and imprisoned in 1939. Vladimir was one of the leading engineers at the military plant. His projects were well-known by the military leaders of the soviet government. The tragedy happened unexpectedly. His last changes in the blueprints were disapproved by the chairman of the committee, and that fact grew into 'incontrovertible evidence of a political disorientation and sabotage.'

Vladimir said,

"I was sentenced to fourteen years in Magadan labor camp for no crime. Lena, as a wife of the "people's enemy," was sentenced to eight years. Our son was taken to an orphanage, and since then we have not heard anything about him. He is twenty-six now. At that time, our boy was nine."

Lena continued their story with deep sadness in her voice,

"We had served the full term of imprisonment. After Vladimir's discharge, we wanted to go back to Voronezh and find our son. We were not allowed. Nobody issued us the passports. We are waiting for passports for three years. The endless waiting made me sick and depressed more than during the years of slavery work at the camp."

Maria was shocked. She couldn't believe that they had to spend additional years in poverty, in the terrible barrack with rats, mice, and cockroaches. Listening to the sad story of the neighbors, she could not eat and say anything due to the spasm in her throat caused by a new stress.

The Pavlovs introduced them to the life story of another couple – the Nikonovs, who lived in the room from the other side of the barrack. The people were discharged (not imprisoned) in 1949, after twelve years in the labor camp "without the permission to return to the central part of the country."

"Elizabeth Nikonov died a year ago," Lena said. "She could not stand the climate and the terrible living conditions after her heart attack. They had three sons, but who knows what happened to them? They were taken to the orphanage for small kids due to their age: one, three and five years old."

Vladimir continued,

"Since the death of his wife, the old man is absolutely alone. Lena takes care of him by bringing some food, cleaning the room, doing his laundry. I help with wood gathering, taking the old man to the village bathhouse on Saturdays and visiting him in the evenings. You can understand that he is not interested in life after his wife's death, but he can't die earlier than destined."

Both of the life stories sounded horrific to Maria: the more she learned on that day, the more upset she became. The neighbors told the Kurbatovs not a tale, it was the reality of post-GULAG life.

Maria understood one thing – they are in a cage. There is no visible exit from it.

"Alex, what we heard was terrible. Realistically speaking, who would issue the French passports to us? They would never contact the French Embassy on our behalf. They did not issue the passports to their soviet citizens. What inestimable price would we need to pay for leaving Magadan?"

Alexander listened to Maria's conclusion without interrupting. Maria continued,

"The tragic mistake was admitted by the new soviet government. However, it was admitted inside of the country, but nobody would do it in front of the whole world."

The stories they had heard on that day did not bring even small consolation to the Kurbatovs. Maria exclaimed,

"Dear Lord, I do not want to be one of them. I do not want my family to live in this village, in this wild zone, and in this unpredictable country."

She burst into tears, when they entered the barrack. She was inconsolable,

"Alex, dear Alex, they want to bury us here. I learned their formula - *No people and no crime*, especially international crime."

Alexander tried to calm his wife down, but it was not easy. The decade in captivity affected Maria's nervous system. It was good that Sasha left earlier and fell asleep. The boy was exhausted. All the news, stories, exiting emotions with his father, and spending half a day working outdoors knocked the boy out.

"Marie, we have to live one day at a time. We should not expect the great changes tomorrow. If we learn, how to live constructively instead of destructively under these circumstances, the Lord will help us to find the way out. I believe that for fifteen years of your life during the war and in prison, your tolerance grew, and you had learned how to be patient. You have been blessed with inner strength. Don't lose it now, when we are all together."

Maria listened attentively, looking at her husband with trust, love and respect. He experienced again shortness of breath, as it always happened to him with any stress or excitement.

Alexander waited for a couple of minutes, catching his breath and continued,

"Marie, we are not given the alternatives. We have no right to spoil our mutual life. I agree that it's not a normal life in our understanding. Nevertheless, when we live with appreciation and enjoy every moment together, the Lord will find for us the way out, as He had unexpectedly found it in 1945 and on the day before yesterday."

Maria noticed that Alexander wanted to add something but did not dare to say.

"What do you want to say, Alex?" she asked him.

"I dream of one more Count Kurbatov to be born."

Alexander gently pulled Maria toward him and sat her on his lap.

"No, Alex. Not now, and not in the wild Russia. We have no strength to breathe and to work. What child can be born from scrawniness? We are two walking undernourished skeletons with shortness of breath, low blood pressure, tachycardia, and so on. I can easily continue this list, if you insist, my darling."

She was ready to bring a hundred of arguments against his unexpected wish. Alexander laughed.

"Marie, you drew a funny picture. Darling, I'll be better, I promise. I'll heal fast, as well as you will.

When we are stronger, we'll have our second son. Do you agree?"

He elevated her mood with his unexpected desire. Now Maria laughed, making her assumption,

"It could be a Countess, darling. What do you think about that?"

He pretended that he did not understand his wife and asked,

"What should I think about what?"

"About having a girl?"

"Oh, I agree, my love, but upon many conditions...," Alexander answered.

"It's interesting. Alex, what are your conditions for a girl to be born?"

"Marie, she must be as pretty, and as smart, and as patient, and as sweet as her wonderful Maman."

They burst into laughter. Maria noticed that it was painful for him to hold her on his lap and jumped off with the words,

"You are right, darling. You are always right. How can it be different? In general, today was a wonderful day. Do you know, what was the most significant in this day?"

"What was it, Marie?" Alexander inquired.

"It was a day of release," Maria answered.

Alexander asked with interest,

"What release do you mean?"

Maria explained,

"We released the vast accumulation of our heavy emotional pain. This pain could interfere with our health, success and happiness. You saw, how psycho-emotional pain overloaded even our little boy. I hope that he got rid of it completely and forever."

"Marie, I wanted to tell you, that we have a miraculous child. You delivered and upbrought a miracle."

Alex came closer to Maria and kissed her. Then he returned to his stool and continued,

"From the very beginning, everything was miraculous in our mutual life."

Maria enjoyed listening to Alexander's calm voice. She seemed to be ready to stand, leaning to the warm stove until the morning, just listening to her husband. She missed him so much. The separation was extremely painful for both of them.

Alexander continued,

"Just imagine, Marie, I found you in fire of war on that very day, when they planned to execute all the inmates from the concentration camp. Then you got pregnant and took a risk to come to the Ukraine. The Lord miraculously protected you and the child during the long deporting to the camp. You remember that so many misfortunate people could not stand cold and hunger, and they died on the way to the camps."

Alexander sipped some warm water from the pot in order to interrupt a new attack of shortness of breath. Maria leaned toward him with the words,

"Come down, Alex. Please, come down."

She was afraid that the excitement could extend the attack.

Alexander continued,

"Mon Chère, God created another miracle, sending you with a group of nuns, who shared every day their food with mother-to-be. Wasn't it a miracle? When Sasha was born, he was surrounded with warm attention of Dr. Leskov, and later, nurse Masha. The Creator blessed the boy with miraculously strong stamina, and our son survived 10 years of camp life."

Maria agreed, "It's true. Everyone was surprised to see a big and strong baby, that was born after everything I went through."

Then she corrected herself, "Sasha and I went through. The last week of pregnancy with 12 hours of mining was unpredictable. Both of us could die in the mine."

Alexander continued,

"Regardless of our boy having been born and raised in the camp, the Creator preserved his heart, mind and humanity. I know, Mon Chere, it was you who kept him in light, warmth and love. I am so much obliged to you, Marie. Dr. Leskov was right. You are a loving and devoted mother. I worried a lot about you, when you kept our baby on breast feeding. You slept just a couple of hours at night and worked long shifts with mining double norm of gold raw, in order to be permitted to feed our baby. It was you who preserved the kindness of Sasha's heart."

Maria leaned to her husband and said,

"Sometimes, Alex it was not easy to pull Sasha out of peevishness and keep him in light. His lot was not stress-free, because he had to wait for extremely long

10-year term for everything that normally is granted to children from the first moment of their coming into this world. He waited for us, his parents and for normal family life. I tried to bring him up, as a nice, obedient, helpful, understanding and compassionate person, keeping his soul in light and warmth. We always prayed together for you and other nice people."

Maria signed and continued,

"Sorry to say, my child was not with me most of the time. They violently forced the small children to work by threatening to leave them without food. On those days, I found Sasha despairing. Those days were the most painful for me. On the top of my struggle for my spirit uplifting, I had to support Sasha's spirit, as well. Thank God, everything is over."

Alexander listened to his wife with admiration. He thought,

"Marie did her best to preserve our son physically and emotionally."

Alexander kissed his wife, thinking, "What a strong person Marie is! God blessed me not only with the best wife but with the wisest mother of my child! I must be the happiest man in this world."

Glory to Thee, O Lord! Glory to Thee!

Chapter 34

That day in May was the second day of the Kurbatovs' free family life. They got up at eight in the morning, borrowed a wheelbarrow from the Pavlovs and went to the village store for the first shopping in their free life. People could hardly use the words a *market* or a *store*, entering a strange structure in the middle of the village. There were two railway freight carriages put on a platform. The Kurbatovs noticed from the very first moment that the customers knew each other well. When the new couple entered the store, all of them paid attention at Maria and Alexander. Sasha was left outside to guard the neighbors' wheelbarrow.

They were hungry, and Maria went straight to the food corner. She bought some bread, oil, salt, flour, rice, dry beans, dry mushrooms, oats, and buckwheat. Alexander found some half rotten onions, beets, carrots, turnips, and potatoes. The vegetables were partially frozen while being delivered to the store, and they had unpleasant smell and looked ugly. Maria thought that only the prisoners in the labor camps ate food of that quality, and suffered later with indigestion and intoxication, but she was mistaken. The population of their village dug in the heap of dirty, half-rotten and half-frozen produce, trying to find at least some pieces for cooking.

Maria looked at the produce and made a conclusion for herself,

"O Lord, it was my huge mistake when I thought about the discrimination of prisoners with low quality food. I am sorry, but now I can say that the government does not discriminate anybody in this country, feeding all the soviet citizens with foods of terrible quality."

Maria looked at the faces of the people around and continued thinking, "Perhaps, only the inhabitants of this area have low quality food? Poor people! They forgot about fresh produce and delicious dishes, or maybe, they did not know them at all?"

For a decade in the camp, Maria's body missed the vegetables and fruits very much, but she could not eat the food of the camp quality. She got a suspicion: "Nobody takes care about the delivery of fresh, or at least not damaged, produce to the far east of the country. I can understand, they do not grow anything locally due to a very short summer and ever frozen soil. Lord, have mercy for these people."

Maria continued shopping and picked up some cookware, necessary for cooking and serving foods: three spoons, three small aluminum bowls, one big knife, and two cast-iron pots. She planned to use one for frying and another for boiling vegetables and grains. They were unbelievably heavy, but they were good for the firewood stove. Maria could hardly carry them to the cashier.

Maria wanted to buy a tea kettle, but Alexander reminded her about soap, towels, pillows, toothbrushes, and tooth powder, as well as Sasha's ink and notebooks. All of those things were of higher necessity, so Maria chose a small cheap pot for boiling some water for tea. It was much cheaper than a kettle. When the Kurbatovs left the store, they had no more money. The parents silently loaded their shopping into the wheelbarrow and pulled it to the hospital across the street.

The so-called hospital was housed in two long barracks that were connected with a veneered corridor. The corridor was built to protect the medical personnel from wind, snowstorms, and rains when they needed to get from one part of the hospital to another. Maria remembered that the camp hospital was connected with the administrative building in the same way. Alexander looked at the hospital and said to Maria,

"The hospital looks like it was built a long time ago and never renovated."

Maria agreed.

Alexander asked the nurse on duty if he could see the chief physician. The nurse looked at them attentively and answered in a very cold manner,

"We do not hire now."

Maria understood. The way they looked manifested who they were and from where they came to the hospital. She shared with Alexander in a low voice,

"Alex, the way we look gave the nurse the understanding of who we are and, as Lena predicted, they do not want to hire former '*people's enemies*.'"

Alexander insisted in seeing the chief-of-staff. The nurse shrugged her shoulders and disappeared behind one of the doors. In five minutes, she returned and "ordered",

"Sit and wait for him in the waiting room because now he is busy with the morning rounds of the hospitalized patients."

Her intonation was so familiar to the Kurbatovs. They knew for sure: the nurse had worked earlier at one of the labor camps.

They did not wait longer than five minutes, when the doctor flew into the waiting room. He was in his early forties, with thick red hair and a few bright freckles on his nose and cheeks. The doctor was full of energy. Passing the Kurbatovs, he introduced himself,

"Doctor Belikov."

He continued,

"Let us talk on my way to the other building. The patients there are waiting for the doctor's check-up."

He was surprised to see two specialists at once, looking for working positions at the hospital. The doctor asked,

"How long are you supposed to stay here?"

Alexander was honest,

"We don't know. Our neighbors were discharged in 1949 and have never received permission to leave."

The doctor stopped abruptly and said,

"We need a surgeon badly. Today, I have to call to the camp, where you served your sentence and worked, as a surgeon to find out the information on you, as a specialist."

Then he turned to Maria,

"As for you, Dr. Kurbatov, I know that there is no physician in the children's and maternity department. For seven months, the doctor's assistant took care of the kids. There were twelve fatal cases during last winter. You know, it's a lot for such a small hospital."

Maria asked,

"Where is the children and maternity department?"

"Department" sounds too impressive," the doctor responded.

He pointed to one more structure in the back and asked with some disappointment in his voice,

"Can you see a smaller structure behind you."

He motioned to a smaller hut behind the long barrack.

"Are you ready to work in that *department*?"

Dr. Belikov sounded a little bit sarcastic.

"How long have you been here, doctor?" Alexander asked.

The doctor continued walking. He looked at Alexander and answered,

"Trust me, long enough in order to learn the hospital matters."

Then he looked at the couple and said,

"I can see that you are from another world."

Maria and Alexander smiled. Then Alexander asked,

"If you mean GULAG another world, then you are right, doctor. What else makes us so different?"

The doctor looked at the couple and explained,

"I cannot pick up from you any anger, jealousy or hatred. During the last five years, so many former inmates were looking for positions in the hospital, and they hated me just because I was not one of them."

Maria preferred not to continue this topic and asked,

"Do you want me to go to the children's department and talk to the person in charge?"

The doctor answered with a smile on his face.

"I am the only one "in charge" here. Where can I get the info about your education?"

"At the medical school of Sorbonne University in France," Maria answered.

"Where?!"

The chief-of-staff could not hide his surprise and satisfaction.

"I was right a hundred percent, when I immediately picked up that you are from another world. It was not a mistake."

Somebody tried to interrupt their unusual interview and asked the chief physician a question. He answered with the question,

"Is it an emergency? If not, wait until later. I have to introduce a new doctor to the staff of the children's and maternity department."

Maria did not believe that she was admitted, as a physician. They went quickly through three rooms. Maria looked at a big room with twenty beds in it and asked,

"I hope that there are no children with contagious diseases in this room?"

The doctor answered honestly.

"We do not know about their diagnoses, when we admit them to the hospital, so we hospitalize all the kids together."

It was terrible reality that the children with different diseases, including the infectious, were kept together in one big room.

Maria was shocked and thought: "O, my Lord! Who could be surprised with the high mortality rate of children in this hospital?"

The children's room was connected to a tiny procedure room, and there was a separate entrance from the corridor to the maternity room with three beds and an old operating table for delivery of the babies. The table was separated from the beds with a white curtain. Maria saw the poverty of the hospital and thought, "It's a hospital from the Middle Ages or even earlier."

The chief physician continued,

"The lab and X-ray are in the Magadan Central hospital only. And the truth is that we do not have an additional room in the hospital for adult patients with infectious diseases. We can separate them from the other patients only with the curtain wall."

The doctor saw the expression of concern on Maria's face and thought,

"This tiny doctor is not scared at all. She is just concerned."

The chief physician looked at Alexander and asked,

"Is she always so serious about things?"

"She is a very responsible person," Alexander answered.

The doctor came up to Maria and said,

"Doctor Kurbatov, I hope to see you here tomorrow at seven thirty in the morning. We have a lot to discuss. I think that one hour will be enough for your meeting with your colleagues and introduction to your daily routine."

At that moment, he entered the door to the second barrack, leaving Maria and Alexander stunned with his decision.

Glory to Thee, o Lord! Glory to Thee!

Chapter 35

The visit to the hospital was so unbelievably successful that Maria could not keep silent.

"Alex, the Lord created a miracle. They hired a person from the street, without a diploma and work history in this country. It's one more miracle in my life. Thank you, Lord! Glory to You!"

Alexander smiled.

"I agree, Marie, it's a miracle. Dr. Belikov is a smart person. He has seen a lot in his medical practice and administrative position, and he understands people well. They did not have a physician for such a long time just because they could not find a specialist. They paid for it with deaths of the children. He wants a real doctor to be in charge of the children and maternity department."

Maria was concerned that there was no laboratory and X-Ray at the hospital. She asked,

"How do they provide the diagnostic studies without lab testing? They must be trained in absolutely different way."

When the parents came up to Sasha, he was talking to a boy. Sasha introduced to them his new friend. The boy was one of the children who was also born in the labor camp. His mother died when he was nine months old, and he was sent to the hospital in critical condition with severe anemia. He turned seven years old last week, and was allowed to be outside every day, walking around the hospital and breathing fresh air. The boy looked anorexic, with bluish skin and dark circles around huge blue eyes. He walked slowly and talked so quietly that it was difficult to hear what he said.

Maria thought,

"There are so many camp children, like him, dying from malnutrition, anorexia, and anemia. It was Sasha's luck that God sent him two angels: doctor Leskov and nurse Masha."

Maria did not hear the conversation of the boys because her thoughts were still there, in a big room of the children's department.

"Alex, there is a possibility to separate children with infections, if we subdivide a spacious room this way."

Maria picked up a stick and drew a big square in the dirt. Then she sketched all the existing windows and doors. After that she separated some small portion at the end of the square with one window.

"The only thing we need to add is a separate entrance from the opposite side of the hut, as a detached corridor. So, four or even five beds could be separated easily for the children with contagious diseases."

Alexander looked at her drawing. Maria continued,

"It is the only decision possible in the situation. The existing stove will warm both rooms."

He pulled Maria toward him, looked in her eyes and said,

"Marie, I am so grateful to God for my smart wife! You always impress me, my love."

He kissed the hand in which Maria was holding the stick. Maria thought,

"Alex preserved his wonderful manners. He was always polite and kissed my hands."

Maria noticed that two women in medical uniforms were looking out of the window, watching the Kurbatovs with curiosity.

"They are probably shocked with Alexander's gesture," she thought.

Maria turned to the boys, apologized for the interruption, and said,

"Sasha, let us go home. I'll start my work tomorrow, and you will go to school. Now, we'll stop at your school and register you there. The "vacation" is over. I have a lot of chores to do at home."

Maria pulled the wheelbarrow with the groceries, feeling new strength in her body. Alexander wanted to help her with pulling but could not catch the pace.

"Marie, you pull, turn and push the wheelbarrow, as it was your permanent job, and you did not do anything else in your life."

Both gentlemen laughed.

Maria answered,

"I had good experience with pushing a cart. This is not as big and heavy, as I used to push daily for some time."

Alexander asked his wife,

"We did not hear anything about that. Will you, please tell us about your great experience with the cart."

Maria hesitated for a moment. She recalled her heavy wheelbarrow in Germany, when she used to do morning shopping at the farmers' market for Frau Martha's bakery and restaurant. Then she decided to "open the secret", telling her men a horrible story about her escape from the nasty Bauer, her work at the restaurant for two nice women, and her arrest with tortures at the concentration camp, where they wanted to burn her together with some other prisoners in the old barrack.

Maria's men were listening without interruption. At the end, Alexander said,

"Marie, I feel sorry that I asked you to bring up such a painful memory." Sasha hugged his mother.

Maria sensed light and warmth inside. She asked with her beautiful smile,

"What do you think has saved me?"

Alexander answered without hesitation, "Your willpower, Mon Chere."

Maria shock her head. Sasha looked at his mother with interest and inquired,

"What do you think it was, Mama?"

Maria kept walking in silence for several minutes.

"It was God's miracle. When everything has been against me, and look – I am with you, it must be only God's miracle. Sasha, you should not even doubt it. Doubts insult our Lord. He does His best for every single individual in His fight with satanic forces.

You'll be always given everything in accordance to the strength of your faith."

The initial days of freedom were transforming, as many things happened for the first time in the Kurbatovs' family. All the events that took place were new in their mutual life.

In the morning of the next day, Maria planned to leave early for work, and Alexander needed to take Sasha to school. Maria did not have any other dress to wear except her camp dress. She did laundry in the evening and dried it around the stove. In the morning, Maria looked absolutely different, wearing the same dress. Maria warried about her poor appearance, but Alexander came her down,

"Marie, you look glowing today in the same dress. Your inner transformation took place. Everyone could notice that you are a professional, educated, and knowledgeable specialist. Besides, you are an attractive woman."

Alexander came closer in order to see better her face, calm expression of the eyes, and pure, baby-like smile. Everything has been changing - the way she walked, the manner she talked to her men. She became again Madam Kurbatov with confidence and strength of character.

The chief physician Belikov briefly introduced Maria to the hospital staff and then ran to examine an emergency case. Maria started her first working day with morning round and examination of all the children in the room. She asked the doctor's assistant and a nurse to help her during that long procedure. They entered the room, where all the children were in beds, waiting for a new doctor to come. The doctor's assistant was giving the reports regarding each child, and the nurse named all the medications the patient was ordered and the procedures he or she was undergoing.

It took about three hours to collect all the information and examine the children. Then Maria went to her office to study the test results, if any. There were four children from the camps. Two of them did not have mothers. Nobody knew about the existence of their fathers, as well. Maria thanked the merciful Lord one more time for her Sasha. He was stressed, as all the camp children, but he was healthy, and had both parents.

Long hours of studying the cases made Maria tired. Alexander and Sasha came to meet her after work, and she was happy to see her gentlemen. They gave her new shot of energy and joy. They brought good news: Alexander was admitted, as a surgeon assistant with one-month trial. Alexander was surprised.

"Can you imagine, Marie, the chief physician mentioned that the administration at my labor camp gave a good rating of my work. It was strange to hear that sometimes those monsters can tell the truth about their inmates."

Maria was grateful to God and proud of her husband. She found the explanation.

"You saved the life of the commandant of your camp. He remembers this fact very well."

Maria asked about Sasha's school. The location of the elementary school was one block from the hospital, and it was convenient for the parents to bring Sasha in the morning and pick him up after school. The next morning, all three Kurbatovs left the house early. They started their new life in Russia.

The Kurbatovs' salaries were miserable, as was the salaries of all soviet doctors, engineers, and teachers. The income of educated people was lower in comparison with the house builders, plant and factory workers, road workers, miners, etc. The whole structure was turned upside down, supporting the low educated majority of the population in order they could always vote for the communist party - the only party that existed in the country and the only one that was "politically correct and represented the dictatorship of the workers."

It was hard to explain, but with all the complications and difficulties of their new life, the real human happiness was returned to the Kurbatov family. Maria confirmed,

"I was told as a child that happiness is not in money or not only in money. Now, I agree. I am happy to see both of you, to help my patients and get back my dream that one day, I will find my family, and we'll leave for France."

She remembered her father's loneliness after her mother's departure. He had assets for life, but he was totally unhappy.

The Kotyks were always financially stable. They inherited money from the previous generations and increased their wealth from income derived from their stables, cattle and poultry farms, bee-keeping, crops, hunting, fishing, gathering berries and mushrooms from their forests, preparing jams and preserved fruits, marinated and salted vegetables and mushrooms, smoked fish and meats, developing delicious dairy products, and exporting to different countries in Europe.

Nevertheless, possessing the significant resources, material goods, and properties did not make her father happy. He was a devoted father to his children. He enjoyed his work, but most of all he loved his wife. He adored her and became internally destroyed after their separation. That state lasted for a rather long time, not less than for three years. A painful emotional wound turned into a deep scar that ached most of the time.

In Maria's life many things were opposed. She lived in an uncivilized country and in complete poverty. They had only one set of clothes. They did not have food, as food is normally understood. But she experienced internal happiness. She was happy in the land of her enemies. How could it be? Only the Lord's grace made it possible.

In the evenings, they enjoyed gathering together around the table at their supper, when they shared news, problems, and disappointing or successful events of the day. It was life, difficult, but real life. They made a list of clothes, furniture, linen and stationery, they needed to purchase in accordance with their salaries. Maria and Alexander borrowed a book of Russian pharmacology from Dr. Belikov, in order to learn everything about the

Russian drugs and medications. They studied at night and enjoyed the very process of studying together.

They were extremely busy and tired a lot, but one thing they did not forget to do at the end of the day. They thanked the Savior and his Virgin Mother for everything they went through on that particular day.

The neighbors Lena and Vladimir moved to another part of the village and wanted the Kurbatovs to follow them. Maria asked the administration of the hospital to help them with a flat near the hospital. She knew that in wintertime, it would be difficult for Alexander to get to the hospital and for Sasha to get to school in darkness early in the morning with frequent snowstorms. The administration promised to assist their two specialists with getting a flat by winter.

The last week of August was wonderful. Miraculously, the Kurbatovs were given keys to a two-room flat in a nice new house. It was within five minutes of walking distance to the hospital and nearly across the street from Sasha's school. They moved on the next day, on Saturday. Alexander joked,

"Sometimes, it's nice to live in an empty room without furniture. We have packed our belongings for half an hour and are ready to go."

The hospital personnel collected some money, as a housewarming gift for them, and the Kurbatovs added it to their two salaries in order to purchase a sofa for Sasha, a bed for themselves and a kitchen table.

They couldn't help admiring the view out of their bedroom window. The nature at the end of summer was picturesque: many colored dwarfy trees near the creek and on the hills. And the creek itself was, as blue as the sky. It was already cold with slightly freezing temperatures at night, but it was sunny during the day when they moved in, and everything looked very joyful.

Maria said,

"It seems like our souls in some way have already been connected to this harsh land."

Glory to Thee, o Lord! Glory to Thee!

Chapter 36

Every working day Maria got up at six. She washed, dressed, did her hair, and had half an hour for her morning prayers, including her favorite one: *"Having risen from sleep, I hasten to Thee, O Master, Lover of mankind, and by Thy loving kindness, I strive to do Thy work, and I pray to Thee: help me at all times, in everything, and deliver me from every worldly, evil thing and every impulse of the devil, and save me, and lead me into Thine eternal kingdom. For Thou art my Creator, and the Giver and Provider of everything good, and in Thee is all my hope, and unto Thee do I send up my glory, now and ever, and unto the ages and ages. Amen."*

Then she woke up her gentlemen. It was such a pleasure to open the door and see her son sleeping. He was a very obedient and happy boy. He did not cause any trouble for the family. He was also loved by everyone at school. Alexander noticed that his son was a very loyal friend. He was the one who was always surrounded by children, helping them with homework, patiently explaining the material that they did not understand at school.

The teachers loved him for his multiple talents. He was good in studies, music, singing, dancing, and sports. Sasha was a good leader and splendid assistant for his teachers when they participated in different school events. Sasha liked his school, friends and teachers very much. In this school, nobody tried to hurt him or put him down, mentioning that he was a "camp kid."

Every morning Maria used to come quietly to her son and touch his shoulder. The boy always smiled and tried to catch her hand with a kiss. Then she kissed him on both cheeks. That was their morning ritual, and it contained something they could not live without. After the ritual, Sasha opened his beautiful eyes and jumped out of bed.

There was a constant competition: who of two gentlemen would be the first to occupy the bathroom. Every morning the joy "woke up" in the house at seven o'clock. They experienced a permanent pleasure to belong to the family. Long years of forcible separation and inability to see each other taught them to treasure every single moment spent together. They were nice and thoughtful, ready to help and to share everything.

It was the end of October, when Maria noticed that she did not feel well. She was not ill. She felt different. Maria was disturbed with the smell in the patients' rooms. She asked that the patient's bathrooms to be cleaned again. All the unpleasant smells made her nauseous. The prior week, she was the doctor on duty and at night, assisted the surgeon with the emergency case. She nearly fainted when she detected the smell in the operating room.

Alexander noticed that she became pale and was extremely tired after work. Normally, she did not come back home at 3:00 p.m. They paid the physicians in Russia for a six-hour workday, but being the head of the department, she had a lot of additional work. She did not have any one during the second half of a day who could substitute her with completing the paperwork, ordering medical supplies, as well as cleaning materials for sanitation of the children's department. Usually she returned home by 6 p.m. It was nice that Sasha did not expect her to give him dinner; he knew how to warm it up and wash the dishes. During the previous week Maria started to come home earlier, around 4:30, and took a half hour nap every day. When Alexander returned from work in the evening, she was already up, cooking supper for evening and lunch for the next day.

On that day, they had just finished supper, when Maria ran to the bathroom and vomited. Alexander was in the doorway, watching her with a big question mark on his face.

"What is this, Marie?"

Maria answered with her smile,

"Somebody promised to get stronger and with God's blessing, to create one more Count Kurbatov. I think we can see the results of getting stronger, Mon Cher,"

Alexander stood in the doorway, as still, as a statue. Maria made a curtsy and asked politely,

"May I pass you, Your Grace?"

Alexander woke up from the shock.

"Your Grace, you want to pass me, do you? You want just to pass the father-to-be of a new Count?"

Alexander burst into laughter, like he used to do. It seemed to Maria that she heard this kind of laughter a century ago. He pulled Maria out of the bathroom and squeezed her in his embrace, covering her face, eyes, neck, and chest with kisses. He kneeled and kissed her belly, repeating between kisses,

"Thank you, Lord!"

Sasha ran to them, trying to find the reason for such irrational behavior of his usually reserved father. Alexander noticed the boy watching them, got up, and made an announcement.

"My dear son, we have wonderful news for you. You are blessed to be an older brother of another Count Kurbatov."

Sasha listened to high-flown language of his father and could not understand the reason that caused his father to be so excited. Maria looked at her confused son and explained.

"Sasha, you'll have a baby brother or baby sister in May. How do you like the news?"

The boy was hesitant with the news. Alexander wanted to get in on the act. Maria stopped him with her head motion. Sasha was looking at his mother and responded,

"Mama, I like it very much, I mean the news. But I don't know, maybe, he will not like me. I was waiting for you and Dad for ten years, but I knew that you loved me, and I was ready to wait. Will you love him in the same way, as you love me?"

Maria smiled, watching for the first time her son's unwillingness to share his parents with anybody else. She embraced her boy.

"No, Sasha, I cannot love him in the same way. You were my first child, who was born in prison, in appalling slavery, who gave me strength for survival. It is so different. Being a mother, I will love him very much, but in another way, sonny. All babies are very tiny, weak, and dependent, when they are born. They need our love and care in order to survive, grow and develop."

Maria saw that Sasha was pleased with her explanation.

"Don't worry, Mama. Three of us will share our love and food with him. He will grow fast, and I promise you to protect and help my younger brother."

Maria kissed her son and said,

"You are right, my boy. You are absolutely right with sharing your love with your brother. But do not forget, it could be a sister."

Alexander asked with a smile,

"Sonny, then we'll love her, wouldn't we?"

All of them were happy.

Maria's pregnancy greatly affected her husband's and son's attitude toward her and everything in the house. The gentlemen had a long talk and divided the chores. From that time on, Maria was not supposed to bring water from the well. She did not take garbage out of the house. The firewood was always ready at the stove. Maria realized that they could be very helpful with chores, washing the floors, doing laundry, or even cooking supper. Maria felt herself, as a queen, and found time to walk outdoors every evening, breathing fresh air and digesting her supper that was frequently cooked by her with Alexander's help. Her husband liked to accompany her walks after supper, while Sasha did the dishes and prepared himself for going to sleep.

Maria loved her gentlemen even more, if it was possible to love more. She saw, how her pregnancy positively changed the life of the whole family. They were more sensitive and helpful, sharing their love and care with Maria, so that Maria could provide a stronger channeling of their mutual love to a baby.

Maria's appetite grew at last, and she started to eat larger portions. Alexander was glad to see the positive changes in her appetite. After the camp, Maria could hardly eat the portion of a two-year-old child. Her weight was always a big concern for Alexander. At the same time, she had to work long and intensive hours in the hospital. He was afraid of health complications due to Maria's pregnancy, malnutrition, and everyday overwork. The gentlemen tried their best with home chores. After Christmas, Maria started to gain some weight, and in March she was on her maternity leave.

Maria did not like to stay at home. She did not consider her condition, as a medical illness. Every morning she went to the hospital and stayed there with the patients and paperwork for four hours and longer. She was a very dedicated doctor, and Alexander did not mind her part-time work. The chief-of-staff found the means to pay her for her hours in March and April. It was so generous. They could buy everything necessary for their baby, without squeezing from their tight family budget with just Alexander's salary.

The two men liked talking about the future baby. Sasha suggested putting the baby's crib only in his room, so that his Mama could have better rest at night. It was so thoughtful of him. Maria knew that her new-born child would definitely stay in her bedroom, but she was pleased with Sasha's suggestion. Two times on Sundays, the family visited Magadan. They took a working train there. The train for the local workers reminded Maria and Alexander of their endless journey to Magadan in 1946.

Magadan was a rather big city in comparison with the village, where they lived. Sasha was in a city for the first time in his life. He concluded that he preferred the city to the village. His parents bought new warm quilts for both children and themselves, as well as some fabric for Maria to sew.

When the family stopped at a big grocery store, Sasha liked the city even more. The boy tried the sausages there, and he was very envious that city residents could go and buy such delicious food at their grocery stores.

When they returned home, Sasha could not stop talking about moving to Magadan.

"We'll see what we can do with this idea in future," Alexander promised and explained to his son some issues.

"Sasha, you have to understand that here God was so merciful to us with our work positions in the hospital. Your mother and I were admitted by the hospital for doctors' positions and no one insisted on seeing our diplomas. It could be different at a new working place. In a very short time, your brother or sister will be born. Here your mother is allowed to work part time. It's important for the family. With mama's part-time salary, we can pay the baby-sitter."

Sasha was surprised to hear about the baby-sitter.

"Who will take care of the baby, when Mama is not at home?"

Alexander answered,

"We talked to aunt Zina, our next-door neighbor. She took good care of her granddaughter for five years, but two months ago her granddaughter started to attend the kindergarten, and aunt Zina agreed to babysit our child."

It looked that the boy understood his father, but the hope of a future move from the village to Magadan was preserved deeply in his heart.

Alexander did not want to mention to his son that he decided to visit the KGB committee in Magadan. He wanted to inquire what alternatives were given to his family: to stay in Russia forever, or there was still a possibility to leave for France. If they insisted that the Kurbatovs stay in Russia, Alexander wanted them to issue his family Russian passports, so that the family could move to another part of the country.

Alexander could not imagine living in Magadan region forever. The climate was killing him. Long and severely cold winters affected his damaged spine and legs, making standing over the operating table a real torture. This climate was also not easy for the kids. The shortage of sunny and warm days, and absence of fresh produce made the children in the area malnourished and anemic.

Alexander believed that they would get the French passports more quickly, if they moved to a more civilized part of Russia, closer to Moscow. He constantly thought about visiting the French embassy in Moscow to straighten out the situation. Alexander was certain that the French diplomats could understand him better than the Russian communist authorities or internal service. He had no doubt that French embassy would return his family and him home to France.

Very often Alexander's thoughts flew away to his old and lonely mother. He pleaded her,

"Wait for me, Maman. Wait for us, please. Do not die, and one day, we'll return to you. I know that I was not a good son for you, because I did not take care of you for these long years. I prayed, asking the Lord to save you and to bless you with good health and angelic patience."

Alexander knew his devoted mother well and believed that Countess Kurbatov was looking for her son everywhere, sending numerous inquiries to French embassies in Germany and Russia. Alexander directed his thoughts to his mother again.

"One day, Maman, I'll be back to our cozy French home and not alone: I'll bring my family with me. You'll be delighted to see all of us. You loved Marie, as my beautiful, fragile bride and a successful, talented graduate from the university, but you cannot imagine her transformation into a strong and devoted wife and mother."

Alexander sensed the warmth of his mother's daily praying and felt God's support in passing the hardship of his life tests. His mother asked, and the Lord gave him, as a reward, his miraculous wife and children. He was grateful to his mother for that.

Glory to Thee, o Lord! Glory to Thee!

Chapter 37

It was a typical day in May. Maria cooked and served breakfast for her family. Then she prepared the sandwiches for lunch and led her gentlemen to the door. They kissed her and left. The last six days, Maria did not go to the hospital because of a hepatitis epidemic. Dr. Belikov and her colleagues warned her not to take such a risk in the last days of her pregnancy.

Maria looked at the clock. It was 7:45 a.m. Alexander had made the bed, but Maria felt sleepy and lay down on the bedspread, covering herself with a big beautiful Russian shawl. In a few moments, she fell asleep and had a very strange dream. She saw, how Alexander was presenting her a beautiful engagement ring, but different from the one, he gave her years ago. Her groom looked, as he looked before the war: strong and handsome. He was in his off-white linen suit and his favorite beige shoes. He took off his hat and did not know, where to put it, because the hat was white, and everything around him was dusty.

Maria heard his contagious laugh, and then he put a ring on her finger and lifted her, as if she was weightless for him. They were dancing and spinning around for some time. Maria saw the light covered them and felt warmth inside. She pressed herself to Alex and closed her eyes. The shadows appeared from both sides of them.

The shadows tried to separate them, but Alexander held Maria tightly, maneuvering between dark shadows, and continued dancing and spinning around.

When Maria opened her eyes after spinning and dancing, she saw a steep cliff behind Alexander. Maria screamed, and Alexander put her on the ground. The moment she touched the ground with her feet, the shadows surrounded him. Maria saw her feance losing his balance on the edge of the cliff and falling over the edge. She screamed loudly. It seemed that she screamed in reality and woke up.

Maria stayed in bed for a minute or two until she felt something warm leaking.

"Here we are," she said, and tried to get up slowly.

Two days ago, the phone was installed in their flat due to frequent emergency cases delivered to the hospital from near-by villages. Alexander, being already the head of the emergency department, had to be ready to go before the ambulance was at the door to pick him up. Maria was proud of her husband. He was named in front of the hospital personnel "the person of the highest professionalism and dedication." The Region Health department found the funds to build, as an addition to the renovated hospital, an emergency department with four beds, supplying the department with an X-ray machine, a lab and a separate operating room.

Last month, the reconstruction of children's department exceeded Maria's expectations of the project. From that time on, the children with infectious diseases were separated from the rest of the kids. And a new entrance was two times bigger than Maria drew in her project. The chief-of-staff joked,

"It's a pleasure to have these two "from the other planet" on our board."

Maria dialed **03** and asked for an ambulance. She was happy to have a phone installed. The dispatcher recognized her voice, and the ambulance was sent. Maria had finished the necessary preparations for both her and her baby two days before. What Maria made for her baby from the fabric that they purchased in Magadan, was so pretty. Alexander enjoyed her everyday preparations with sewing, embroidering and knitting the baby cloths. Every two or three days, Maria demonstrated to her gentlemen something cute and beautiful. She packed the necessary things for the baby and her in a small suitcase and waited outside for the arrival of the ambulance.

Maria did not have painful cramps. The midwife was sure that the doctor appeared at the hospital too early. They put Maria on the table for an examination and preparation. At that moment, Maria had her first strong and tearing contraction, and it was so unexpectedly strong that she screamed loudly.

"I am sorry," Maria apologized.

The midwife smiled, saying,

"Oh, doctor Kurbatov, I did not know that you have such a loud voice."

Maria's second contraction was even stronger, but she did not allow herself to scream. Someone told her husband that she was in labor in the maternity room of the hospital. Alexander rushed in and covered her face and hands with kisses. Her husband did not pay any attention to the presence of a midwife and a nurse in the room. He was nervous and his voice was lower than usual.

"You are doing great, mon amour. Two to three more contractions and a strong push and our baby will be released."

Alexander tried to support his wife in that situation, but at the same time, he looked frightened and helpless.

Maria was working hard but could not deliver the baby. She tried to pray and could not. The frequent and painful contractions did not allow her to get into the tranquil condition of praying. A new ripping pain forced her to scream. Alexander walked out of the room and started to pray,

"O Lord God Almighty, Creator of all things and Giver of knowledge to mankind... I fervently entreat You who loves mankind to bless Your servant Maria, who is with child, granting her help and comfort at this trying time. Ease her labor and bring her to a safe delivery. Yea, O Lord, open the treasury of Your mercies and Your compassion to her, and let her give birth to a fruitful vine. For You are glorified, together with Your Only-begotten Son, and Your Most-holy, Good and Life-creating Spirit, now and ever and unto ages of ages. Amen."

Alexander returned to the room. Maria was pushing hard but with no result. Alexander turned pale. The midwife noticed it and sent the nurse-assistant to bring him some cold water.

"Marie, let us breathe together," Alexander suggested.

Maria tried to breathe, but there was no break between contractions.

The midwife saw a head of the baby coming. It was big and could not get out. Maria was pushing harder. She grabbed Alexander's healthy hand, squeezed it and made a push. The dark-haired head was released. Maria had no more strength to push. The baby stuck with his head out. The midwife screamed at Maria,

"Do not stop! Not now! Continue pushing!"

Alexander looked at Maria's face and begged her with tears in his only eye,

"Marie, Mon Chere, please, the last hard push!"

She breathed in, collected all her strength, and pushed. The midwife screamed,

"Coming, its coming. Do not stop now, please!"

The mid-wife helped the baby at the end and put him up on Maria's chest so that the parents could see: their baby boy was born. The baby had rather long hair. He started to scream and turned purple. His hands were clenched, and he was moving his hands in a circular motion. The midwife noticed.

"It looks like he is not so happy to be out. He enjoyed more his staying in his mom. As for him, it was warmer and more comfortable there."

Alexander crossed himself, saying,

"Thank You, Lord!"

Alexander kissed his wife on both cheeks and whispered with appreciation,

"Thank you, darling! I am so happy!"

The mid-wife handed the scissors to Alexander to cut the umbilical cord. He did it easily. He was truly happy that his healthy boy was already born, and his wife was strong in labor. The nurse swaddled their boy and return him to the parents. Alexander took his son but could not see him well, because his eye was filled with tears. He pressed the child cautiously to his chest and the tears poured down the cheek of a happy father, rolling fast and dripping on his baby's quilt.

"Marie, does he look like Sasha, when Sasha was born?"

Maria looked at the baby.

"I cannot say so, Alex. They are different."

Their younger son was a small version of Alexander's mother. It seemed that Alexander read Maria's mind and whispered,

"His face is a tiny copy of his grandmother's face, Countess Kurbatov. Am I right, Mon Chere?"

Maria nodded and closed her eyes. She was satisfied with herself, but she was too exhausted to talk. Maria thanked the Lord and His Holy Mother for their gift of a new son and fell asleep, smiling.

On the third day, Maria felt rejuvenated and strong enough to go home. She remembered her horrible condition after Sasha's birth, but now, she had nothing to do in the hospital. The young obstetrician was not sure that she was ready to go and insisted in her staying for another day or two. Maria did not want to hear about it and asked Alexander to take her home. He was glad to see his wife in a joyful mood and healthy condition.

Maria looked like nothing had happened to her, and it was not her who went through the labor. Maybe, Maria was stronger now, or this boy was smaller than the first one, but there were no complications during the delivery and after. They found just a trace of anemia.

"Thank You, dear Lord, for everything You've done for my baby and me,"

Maria praised.

Alexander asked the obstetrician to discharge the "disturbing" patient.

"You have my word that I will be in charge of our baby and my wife for this weekend."

Maria was happy with her release. Her family stayed together for a weekend, enjoying a new toy – a baby boy. He was asleep most of the time. Sasha waited for hours to talk to his brother, but there was no progress, because the baby continued sleeping or eating with closed eyes. Alexander explained to Sasha,

"Usually, it takes a week for a newborn infant to get strength and keep his eyes opened."

Sometimes the baby smiled in his dreams, and Sasha was sure that his baby brother could hear him, so he talked to him in a serious voice. He was getting a new feeling: being an older brother. Maria tried to arrange the schedule for herself and the baby, so that she could have rest and walk outside every day. She was always well- organized, no matter where she was - school, labor camps, work, or home.

Her gentlemen were of great help to her. She returned from the hospital to a freshly cleaned appartment.

Alexander cooked their food and did the baby's laundry, while Sasha did food shopping, washed the dishes and brought water from the well twice a day. Both of them took care of the firewood and heating of the house. It was the second half of May, but it was still cold outside.

Alexander looked out of the window and noticed again the same transitional hazel color of the trees, exactly as a year ago when they were released from the camps. He thought about the cycle of life:

"In a week, these one-sided dwarfy trees will turn light green, then emerald green, and in two and a half months, they will become multicolored for a very short time. The frost and rain pull the beauty off the trees and cover them with snow."

Alexander observed his wife who nursed Tisha every three hours, and then held a sleeping baby after breast feeding. She reminded Alexander Madonna from Renascence period. Maria was explaining something to Sasha with her pleasant voice and in a usual calm manner. Her face radiated peace and joy. It was obvious to Alexander that his wife was filled with a woman's happiness. Maria noticed that Alexander was watching her and smiled. She was grateful to God for her loving husband and two wonderful sons.

Glory to Thee, O Lord! Glory to Thee!

Chapter 38

On July 22, 1958, a baby boy was baptized secretly together with his older brother Sasha in a small Russian Orthodox Church in Magadan. He was given the name Tikhon, after St. Tikhon from Kaluga, the healer and founder of the Russian monastery. Alexander's ancestors were from that area, and he was glad to be connected through the name of his younger son with the place of his father's family.

The summer was always short, and Maria tried to spend most of the daytime outdoors with her baby son. She remembered from medical school that the sun is important for people, particularly children, to secrete vitamin D required for utilization of calcium in the body and prevention of rickets disease that was widely spread among the children in the area.

Winter lasted for nine months and was always difficult for people who lived in Magadan zone. The temperature dropped to 35-45 degrees below zero. The absence of warm clothing and boots, malnutrition, anemia, severe colds, frost-bitten faces, legs and hands, as well as pneumonia were frequent causes for children's hospitalizations. They needed Maria at the hospital, so she could not stay long at home enjoying her baby son. She returned to work at the beginning of September.

The next-door neighbor Zina, an experienced mother and grandmother, was staying with Tisha at home. She loved the three-months-old boy, and the money the Kurbatovs paid her for baby-sitting was a good addition to her minimal pension.

Maria tried not to be in the hospital longer hours, but sometimes the cases were complicated, and she returned home later, knowing well that nobody would pay her for overtime. Zina was a very kind woman and never complained. She liked not only the baby, but the whole family.

After one week of work at the Kurbatovs, Zina concluded,

"You are so different. You live with love towards each other. Your love made your home warm and beautiful, opposite of my children's homes. I have four children. All four were married, but from the very beginning, in their families there was no peace and care for each other, as well as for their children."

Maria listened to the babysitter's stories, inquiring,

"Why is it so that there is no peace in their families?"

Aunt Zina explained,

"They are drunkards. They love vodka more than they love each other or their poor children."

"What about the women in the families?"

Zina sighed bitterly and answered,

"They can drink more than their men. My oldest daughter had lost her baby after eight months of pregnancy."

"Why? What's happened?" Maria asked.

"She was so drunk that she did not remember, how she fell down and did not go to hospital until morning. When she got to the hospital, the child was dead."

Maria sensed Zina's enormous emotional pain but did not know what to say, because it was difficult to find the right words of support. Zina was fifty-seven. She became a mother at sixteen, which was normal in Russia at that time.

Zina continued with her story,

"We were young in 1917, when George and I got married. God blessed us with love and children. We lived a very happy life in one of the villages near Kaluga."

When Zina talked about her former life, her face became younger and very beautiful. Maria realized that it was pleasant for Zina to recall the time from her and her husband's youth.

"In summer, we worked hard in the fields from early morning to sunset. The family began the field work after Easter and finished with harvesting at the end of October. We had nice rest for more than three months in winter and March. I remember beautiful, frosty and quiet winter days. Sometimes, there were snowstorms, and we enjoyed staying in the warmth of our spacious house that my husband built with his own hands. As a woman, I always had much to do in winter. There was sewing, knitting, or embroidering. My husband was making new furniture or carving on the frames for framing the doors and windows of the houses, He made it in a beautiful country style. George was the best carpenter in our village with window and door framing. People from the other villages used to order his window and door framings for their houses and were always satisfied with George's work."

Zina was proud of her beloved husband and did not want to believe in his death somewhere in the camp. The misfortunate woman kept waiting for him.

Zina's voice sounded softer when she recollected her happy life,

"On Sundays, we used to go to the local church. Everyone was beautifully dressed, especially us women in our colorful shawls and sheepskin or fur coats. We were happy with our lives. We helped each other, celebrated together Saints' Days, weddings, baptizing of our children, and all the church holidays. Everything was going in accordance with the fair rules of the peasants' life, until the revolution reached the village."

Zina sighed deeply and kept silence for a while. Maria did not want to interrupt the silence, because she knew that Zina flew back into her happy life. Then a poor woman continued with sadness in her voice,

"One day, demons arrived to set our beautiful church on fire. Two large families near the church lost their houses due to that fire and became homeless. Since then, the children were not permitted to say their morning and night prayers, and no one was allowed to mention the word God."

Zina sadly told Maria,

“Our children lost their fear of God, because the new power had opened for our kids the gate into the world of sin, miserable existence and destruction.”

The Kurbatovs felt sorry for Zina. Her husband was imprisoned in 1937 as “a kulak element” (a prosperous farmer). The words “prosperous,” “rich,” and “wealthy” meant “enemy” to the dictatorship of the workers and peasants. The communist authority “expropriated” everything that families had earned through years or decades of their hard family work, they made them “peoples’ enemies.”

From the very beginning, the leaders of the communist revolution understood one thing: the middle-class people would not need any regime changes. Nationalization and expropriation made people impoverished and deprived. Only poverty-stricken people could follow in the direction the regime wanted them to go. One day, the communist authorities took Zina’s husband with them, and in four days, Zina was exiled along with her four children to Magadan. Since then she had not seen her George.

Zina’s children left the school after the seventh grade, and none of them graduated from high school. Once out of school, they started working in the local mines or factories. Her sons and daughters of did not try to escape or improve their lives. They worked, as most of the people around them, in order to get their minimal wages, so that they could drink cheap vodka for a week or two. When they did not have any money for buying bread, they went back to work. It was their reckless life cycle and their own hideous choice. The satanic forces could be proud, watching the results of their evil destructive work.

Olga was Zina's youngest daughter. She lost her husband due to alcohol overdose, when they were "celebrating" his 27th birthday. The death of a young husband frightened Olga, and she stopped drinking. She was pregnant at the time of her husband's death. Zina's granddaughter was born three months after her father's death. Olga moved into her mother's one room flat. She started to work at the local hospital and went to evening school for nursing assistants. Zina prayed for her daughter every day.

She told Maria,

"I ask our Lord, to give Olga willpower to live proper life and not to drink again."

Lord, have mercy! Lord, have mercy! Lord, have mercy!

Chapter 39

Sasha became the best babysitter of his brother. He substituted for aunt Zina every day after school. The parents could not afford additional hours of Zina's babysitting after 3 p.m. There was not a single day that Sasha was late. He took good care of Tikhon and enjoyed their time together.

Maria cherished her motherhood very much. Alexander liked to watch her playing with Tisha in the evening, giving him a bath, changing the bedding in his crib, and nursing the child. The whole picture looked so ideal, pure and magnetizing. Alexander knew that it was not the right time to think about the next child, but he could not interrupt the magnetic attraction. The only thought that sobered him in such a moment was the future of his family. He criticized himself,

"Why didn't I take any steps for a year and a half? Why did I allow myself to turn into a procrastinator? How come that I had not visited KGB office in Magadan at least once for such a long time, and had not reminded them that we were still waiting for our French passports? What stopped me? Was it the winter weather with daily storms? Weather had nothing to do with my hesitations. Was it Marie's pregnancy? The boy was born, and I still did not go."

Alexander tried to clarify for himself the true reason of not visiting the regional KGB,

"I should not wait until summer is over. The workers' train runs every day to Magadan. I need to find out what to expect and when. The worst scenario is if they forbid us to leave the country and do not allow us to move to the civilized part of Russia, but at least I'll find it out. Then I have to act in accordance with new information."

Alexander looked at Maria, who was nursing the child and tried to catch the words she whispered repetitively,

"Dear Lord, have mercy on us, sinners. Lord, have mercy on us. Protect us and save us. Amen."

Alexander smiled and asked in his hesitant manner,

"Who do you want to be protected from, Marie? Tell me, please."

He kneeled and kissed the head of his baby-son. Then he smelled Tisha's hair after taken bath and got lightheaded again. The wonderful smell of raspberry soup made Alexander a little bit dizzy.

"Marie, what herb do you use for bathing the baby? I cannot stop smelling."

Maria was surprised with his question.

"Today I did not use any herb, just the soup."

Maria smelled the child.

"There is not any special smell, besides the smell of a baby."

Alexander kissed his son again and hugged Maria's legs. He started to cover her toes and legs with kisses, repeating all the time

"What a smell!"

Maria burst into laughter. The baby gave a wide smile to his Mama, and the milk leaked from his mouth.

"Alex, stop it, please. Let Tisha finish with his supper and go to sleep."

Alexander got up and said,

"We also should go to sleep."

Maria asked, "What about doing laundry?"

Alexander replied,

"Mon Chere, you should not worry about it. I'll do it a little bit later."

Alexander left the room and Maria heard his steps to the bathroom. He was pouring some water into the basin with Tisha's clothing. She thought,

"He has changed his mind. He knows that later he could hardly get up to do Tisha's laundry."

Alexander closed the door in order not to disturb his family while doing laundry.

Maria was half asleep by the time he had finished with laundry and got into bed. She pronounced,

"I love you, Alex. Thank you for everything. Good night."

She kissed her husband and, in a minute, was sound asleep. Alexander was looking at his wife for several minutes, then kissed her and answered,

"I love you too, Marie. Good night, Mon Chere!"

The time passed by between work and helping Maria at home. The autumn was over. Alexander decided not to postpone any longer his visit to KGB. After the celebration of the New Year of 1958, he was ready to go and ask them one question about the state of their case. Alexander was serious about the repatriation to France. He did not want to mention anything to Maria, because his wife has always been afraid to discuss this topic. At the end of February, Alexander handed his request to the personnel department for three-day vacation. By that time, Alexander had many hours of overtime at the hospital. He received an approval at the time he made the request.

In the evening, when Alexander came back home, he made an announcement about his trip to Magadan. Sasha was excited and wanted to accompany his father. Maria did not like Alexander's idea of going to KGB. She found the reason for postponing the trip,

"Alex, you know how cold it is in the workers' train. The trip is rather long. You should think about your lung problem. The injury was severe, and you should not deteriorate your condition. This winter is the first one when you have seen an improvement with your unbearable cough. Why should you take a risk and go now? Wait until spring. In spring, Sasha and I can go with you and leave Tisha with Zina."

Alexander was joking about his trip.

"Marie, I am tired of a family life and prefer to run away in the cold night in order to have a rest from my disturbing wife and two disobedient children."

He walked around the table and kissed their heads. They laughed, but there was something that Maria could not determine with the words. She was always afraid of the demonic structure, like NKVD or, at the moment, it was already KGB. The thought of her Alex going to their regional office alone made her nervous.

Alexander tried to ease the tension, and asked Maria to write a list of products she would like him to buy in Magadan grocery store. Sasha asked for sausages. Maria mentioned flour for baking bread.

When the family was finishing with cooking of their supper, Zina knocked on the door. She entered the kitchen with a joke,

"I knew when to come. I knew that it was the right time to visit my neighbors for supper."

Everyone laughed.

The neighbor Zina liked to come to her neighbors for evening teas. Tea itself was probably not a major reason for her short evening visits. She enjoyed warm and loving atmosphere of Kurbatovs' family. She missed the warmth of her family life since 1937, but most of all, Zina liked the evening conversations with her highly educated and knowledgeable neighbors at the cup of tea when the kids were soundly sleeping. She learned a lot of beneficial things from them, and she liked the humor of Dr. Alexander and smoothness of Dr. Maria.

One day Zina came to a conclusion,

"A half an hour with both of you in the evening, and I can fall asleep quickly. Stupid thoughts do not disturb me at night."

Alexander told her about his trip to Magadan and asked, what she would like him to buy for her. Zina smiled and answered with shyness,

"Candies and honey cookies. I have always had a sweet tooth. In our store, they do not have anything except *sugar pillows*. I wish, you can bring some other candies with fruit stuffing."

Zina had her cup of tea, wished Alexander a good trip, and left.

"Alex, we have been living here for two years. Maybe, we need to wait a little bit longer, and they will change the laws. We got used to this life, didn't we?"

Maria looked with hope at her husband, but the last sentence did not sound particularly assertive. Alexander looked at her with disenchantment, and Maria read on his face that he had never gotten used to anything in this country. He looked straight in Maria's eyes and asked,

"Did we?"

He was short of breath again, and Maria knew: the topic was too painful for him. Alexander said with disappointment,

"I do not believe that you, Marie, forgot everything we went through and, please do not try to assure me that you have gotten used to this poverty and uncivilized life."

"I am scared, my darling. I am not, as brave as you. I do not trust them, and I am afraid of them. They are monsters, and we cannot expect mercy from them."

Alexander embraced his wife.

"You are afraid of monsters, and that's why you want me to postpone my visit, am I right? Don't you want to change our lives? You are a highly educated, professional woman that works for ten or twelve hours daily and is paid only for six. Is it fear?"

"Alex, but they do not pay anybody more than for six hours."

Maria stopped the conversation until Sasha had finished with doing the dishes and went to sleep. The parents went to the bathroom to give Tisha a bath. The boy was enjoying it very much, interrupting the emotional conversation of the parents with happy exclamations and the meaning of each howl only he understood. Maria put the child to sleep and returned to the kitchen.

Alexander was ready to continue their conversation, asking Maria:

"Nobody is paid, you said. Why? If you work so hard, they must pay for it. They fight against the exploitation of workers. They are for equal rights. Those people who are irresponsible, they are paid in the same way, as you and me. Where is their equality? It's only on their slogans, Marie. I tried to understand these people but could not. The majority is cattle with one-two leaders, who turn this majority in the direction guided by the communist shepherd. They do not even question, where they go and why they move in this direction. I know that one day, they will fall off of their artificially built communist empire, but I do not want to be here and wait until it happens."

Alexander did not except Maria's arguments and continued with the comparison,

"Marie, if we live in France and work, as hard as we work here, we would keep a housekeeper and a baby-sitter, won't we? After work, you will not need to run to the grocery store and carry heavy grocery bags, as well as you will not stay in the kitchen, cooking foods. In a civilized country, you will not have to carry heavy buckets with water from the street well for cooking, doing the dishes, cleaning the flat, doing laundry, and preparing hot water on the stove for kids and our baths."

Alexander got up and started to walk back and forth in their small kitchen. Then he stopped for a minute near the stove and continued,

"There, you will not clean the stove, bring wood, or start a fire at five o'clock in the morning in order to keep the house warm. With helpers at home, you will come from work and enjoy your time with children, books or friends. Marie, our mothers did not do chores but spent plenty of time with us. They were reading, playing different games or giving us piano lessons. When the weather was nice, the parents used to walk in the park, and we were running around, enjoying their stay with us. You know that the hours spend with parents are so important for kids' development. My darling, do you have time and possibility for these important activities now?"

Maria listened to her husband's comparison of two lives with admiration. Alexander took Maria's hands and kissed them.

"Look, Marie, at your hands. This life has completely changed your beautiful hands. I am sorry, Mon Chere, but they are the hands of an old woman. I want them to be rejuvenated with good care and less household work. What is wrong in my wishes?"

Maria leaned toward him and said,

"My dear, there is nothing wrong with you and your desires. But I am afraid of the soviet monsters."

"Don't be, Mon Chere. I must do it not only for us, but for our sons. I love you and them so much that this love does not allow me to sit quietly and wait. Pardon me, Mon Amour, if you can."

Alexander embraced Maria and covered her face and hands with kisses. She smiled with tears in her eyes.

"I love you, Alex. You are everything to me. Be careful, please. I beg you, my darling, stay away from arguing with them. Promise me that you go there just to ask a question about the status of our case and any possibility of repatriation. Nothing else, please."

Alexander did not want to let her go and answered,

"I promise, Marie."

Lord, have mercy!

Chapter 40

Alexander had to leave in a couple of hours for the train station. His train was scheduled at 1:15 a.m., but the train station was a forty-minute walk from their house. With Alexander's lameness and difficulty walking, particularly in winter, it could take longer than an hour to get there. The train usually stopped for a minute or two, so it was better to stay and wait on the platform in order to catch it.

Maria and Alexander sat down at the kitchen table. It was their ritual: to have a cup of tea after saying "goodnight" to their kids around nine in the evening. Zina usually visited them at nine and did not stay long. Just that evening, she was earlier, saying,

"I am here just to get my "sleeping pill."

All three of them needed the regular get-togethers and sincere human contact. Having a cup of tea with homemade plain cookies was not only tea hour. In calm atmosphere, they found the decisions of their everyday problems, dreamed about something delightful, and had fun of Alexander's jokes. The warm family contact rejuvenated the spirit of the house and filled the inhabitants with happiness and joy.

That evening, Alexander noticed that Maria was exhausted and upset with their conversation. He suggested,

"Marie, go to sleep. Do not worry, Mon Chere. Everything is going to be all right. They will release us soon, and we'll go to France. I am jammed between two lives. A person cannot be completely happy and satisfied, when he belongs to one life and gets stuck in another. It is like replanting a tree, when it's planted in a soil that is not compatible with this type of a tree, and then eventually the tree dies."

"What do you mean, Alex, saying that you are "jammed" between two lives?"

Alexander explained it in his usual pleasant manner, knowing for sure that she would understand him. Who else could do it, if not his Marie?

"Marie, I miss my previous life very much: our house, friends, and my highly skilled surgical team in the hospital. I miss my mother, and I worry a lot about her. She was as good to me, as you are to our kids. When I am watching you with our children, you remind me of my mother. I know that I am Russian, but I was born in France, because Russians chose another way of living. My parents did not accept their dictatorship of workers and peasants. They prefer the immigration to France."

He stopped abruptly. Maria sensed that he was thinking about something important and did not interrupt him with another question. In a minute he asked,

"Have we found anything human in this political formation?"

"What formation?"

Alexander replied,

"I mean their dictatorship. Dictatorship is dictatorship, and there is no difference between dictatorship of workers and peasants and any other forceful structure. Any dictatorship versus democracy. I was born in a democratic country with human laws and respect for people. I belong to another way of life, and I want to return there. Let them develop their dictatorship, or build socialism and communism, but without our family."

Maria could not hide her fear,

"I am afraid, Alex. They damaged us brutally, and I am afraid for our children and us to be tormented again. The monsters scared me to death more than once, and I haven't released that fear and pain. It stays inside of me, and it burns me all the time. I ask God to help me to deal with it. I feel sorry for my cowardice, but it's true. I am a weak person. Am I?"

Alexander was agitated with her question.

"Who could say that you are weak after everything you went through during the war and after? You are frightened, it's different. Don't be afraid, my darling. We need to leave this country in order to get rid of fear. Here, you would never release it. Every day, we are alarmed at work, and this is not because we have lack of knowledge or experience, but because they are constantly watching us. Any small infraction, as it could happen to anyone, will lead us not to France but back to prison."

Alexander stood up and moved to the stove.

"Will you have some tea with me, Marie?"

Maria could not recognize her husband. He asked again.

"Do you want some tea, darling?"

Maria saw a different person in front of her, who was strong and handsome again. His appearance had been completely changed. He stood straight and there was no more inflexible muscle spasm in the left side of the face that caused that ugly facial expression.

Only at that moment Maria understood, how hard it was for such a strong personality to mask his feelings and thoughts over the past twelve years. Maria's heart was tearing apart with sympathy and real physical pain.

"My poor Alex! He had never resigned. He bore everything for our sake," Maria whispered.

Alexander put a cup of tea in front of Maria, but the tears did not allow her to see it. They were dripping in her tea. Alexander noticed her crying. He embraced her shoulders and asked,

"Why are you crying, darling? Everything had to be resolved at least a year ago. I am a procrastinator. Now, I go to correct my mistake. Drink your tea, Mon Chere. You dropped your tears in it, and it could be salty. Try."

Maria tried to smile, but a new wave of fear had covered her body with goosebumps. She identified with her female senses that her beloved husband gave his word of honor that could not be overturned. He would choose death over allowing anyone to disparage his human dignity.

Alexander caught his breath and continued.

"Look, Marie, these people can enjoy their existence, but we were blessed from birth to enjoy a real life. My parents did everything possible to make me happy, educated, and secure in a civilized world. I want to do the same for my sons. Death is the only thing that can stop me from fulfilling my commitment."

Alexander went to the rooms, came up to the boys' beds and kissed his sleeping sons. He was staying for some time near each bed. Maria was sure, he was communicating with his sons, promising to make their lives happier. She did not interrupt her husband, feeling that the silent communication was vitally important for all of them.

Alexander looked at the clock and went to the vestibule. He put on his sheepskin coat. Maria followed her husband. He took both of Maria's hands and kissed them many times. Maria asked,

"Why do you kiss the hands of an old woman?"

Alexander whispered,

"Because they belong to you, my love. With their gentle touch, they bring happiness to everyone."

Then he pulled Maria toward him, pressing her hard to his chest and covered her with his coat from both sides.

"Marie, Mon Amour, I wish I can hide you and my sons from any misfortune in this life. Forgive me, if I was unsuccessful in it."

"I love you, Alex. I have deep respect for you. You are an honorable and brave man. Tonight, I saw and understood your inner struggle for long twelve years.

Remember, darling, you need to be very careful with monsters. You cannot leave us alone."

Alexander looked at her, and she read appreciation in his expression. He checked the time again.

"I know, Marie, that you are the only one, who always understands me. Forgive me, if I am not right with my decision to go and to insist in our repatriation to France. Forgive me, darling, if tonight, I have afflicted you in our conversation. You are my light and joy in this life, and I have never meant to hurt you, Marie."

Maria was about to cry. Alexander kissed her on her lips, opened the door, and disappeared in darkness of the night. Maria thanked the Lord for her remarkable husband. She kneeled and asked the Savior to protect him on his dangerous trip.

Maria returned to the children. The boys were sleeping soundly. She fixed their quilts and lay down in bed. She slept alone many times, when Alexander worked his night shifts in the hospital. Those nights, she was quite all right. The night Alexander left for Magadan, Maria could not fall asleep. She felt emptiness in the bed. She kept thinking about her husband, his severe emotional pain, and inability to stand any longer their life in the USSR.

In her mind, Maria agreed with her husband.

"How long they will keep us in slavery? We were released from the prison, but never liberated. Alex is right, we are not free."

Maria's frightened heart was racing,

"It's dangerous. What Alex decided to do is very dangerous. We need to be tolerant and patient. It's better to live quietly for another year. It's better..."

Her next thought contradicted the previous one,

"There is no way to be hidden forever. To hide my head in sand does not mean less danger, and it doesn't work for positive changes in our life."

From the bottom of her heart, Maria asked the Lord to support her husband in finding the possibility to 'unchain' their family, by receiving the permission to return home. Her mind raced together with the heart.

Maria felt exhausted and unable to continue fighting her thoughts and feelings. She pulled Alexander's pillow closer and hugged it, whispering,

"I love you, Alex. I hope, you'll win."

Tisha started moving in his bed.

"Be quiet, my baby. I love you too. I love all of you. Let us sleep and have wonderful dreams."

Lord, have mercy!

Chapter 41

That morning started like those, when Alexander was on call at the hospital. Sasha was taking care of the stove. Maria was cooking breakfast for kids, and at the same time, finishing soup for dinner. It was really good that her gentlemen brought water in the evening. She appreciated everything Alexander was doing in the house. He was thoughtful, and his example worked for Sasha very well. Sasha became a great help to the family. Zina appeared at the door around 7:45. It was her usual time to start babysitting. Maria and Sasha kissed Tikhon, he waved back at them, and they ran out of the house.

The work made Maria more balanced, and she was able to concentrate on a very complicated case in her department. She asked her assistant to arrange the consultations with two other specialists from the Magadan central hospital and invite them to evaluate the kids. Time was important, and she needed the specialists to do their examinations of the child, as quickly as possible. If they found it necessary, the hospital would transport the kid to Magadan.

Then Maria started the routine morning rounds with following up all the children. Some of them had noticeable improvement, and she gave the instructions regarding the decrease of their medications. That order made the kids always happy. There were few infectious patients, and she examined them thoroughly because in both cases the fever was persistently high, and the medications lowered the fever only for a couple of hours.

Maria stepped into her office. All her thoughts flew to her husband. The wave of fear came up again. She sensed it spreading out in the center of her chest, like something slimy, heavy and cold.

"O, Lord, what nonsense I keep in my mind!"

Maria was angry with herself, thinking,

"A woman of my age and life experience should not be afraid of anything."

She tried to read the charts of four new patients, but she could not focus her thoughts on the information. A new wave of fear and helplessness infected Maria. She experienced it twice in her life: once when she was raped in the house of her childhood, and the next time, when they threw her without a quilted jacket in the punishment cell with broken window and water on the floor at 40 degrees below zero. In both of the instances, it was the feeling of the end.

"Why am I so frightened? What is wrong with me? I have to prescribe myself the Valerian drops to calm down my nerves."

Maria closed the door and began to pray. She started with "The Symbol of Faith." Then she prayed several times "Our Father." When she was praying, she sensed some relief, but her mind interfered in a disturbing way, and she could not dive deeply in meditation in order to achieve the usual level of natural relaxation, enlightening and warmth.

"Maybe Alexander is in KGB office now," Maria thought.

She became angry with herself.

"Why didn't I stop him or go with him there? Oh my God, why did Alex decide to visit them?"

Maria recalled Alexander's words.

"They enjoy the existence. We were blessed to learn the real life…"

Maria did not want to think about scary issues. She tried to continue praying, but this time, her prayer was interrupted by her colleagues or phone calls.

She was ready to run out of the hospital, pick up Sasha from school, go home, lock the door, and sit still until Alexander arrived. She got a terrible headache. Maria was sure that her blood pressure was elevated with the anxiety attack. She imagined how her husband would laugh at her later when he learned about her behavior.

Maria called Dr. Belikov and asked for permission of the chief physician to leave a little bit earlier, due to her terrible headache and elevated blood pressure. She left at two o'clock, stopped by Sasha's school to pick him up after the last lesson. When they came back home, she was happy to lock the door of their flat.

Maria hugged her boys and smiled regarding her thoughts and fears. She asked herself,

"What was it? I must say the anxiety is not an easy condition. Thank God that my children helped me to calm down. They are my best medicine, and in half an hour, my anxiety attack evaporated completely."

It was not true. She fed the children with dinner but was not able to take a bite. Sasha was washing the dishes and Maria took Tisha to her bedroom for a day nap. Maria put him in his crib and lay down on her bed. Tisha was watching his mom and every time she looked at him, he smiled.

Suddenly, he started crying, like something or somebody slapped the boy. He stretched his arms to Maria. She jumped off the bed, pulled the child out of his crib, and brought him in her bed. The boy could not fall asleep. Maria was sure that he had picked up her nervousness. She tried to nurse him. The boy suckled for a second and burst into crying again. Sasha ran into the room. He did not remember his brother ever crying so badly and tried to amuse him. It worked for a while, and them again the baby was whiny. It took time for Maria to calm Tisha down, and to lull him to sleep.

If everything went smoothly at the committee, Alexander was supposed to stop at the grocery and buy some food. Sasha asked him about sausages, and Maria requested some rye and wheat flour. She continued to bake bread at home, because it was impossible to eat bread from the local bakery, so sour and heavy it was. There was a constant problem with homemade bread: oftentimes there was no flour in their grocery store, or it was sold in limited portions, like two pounds at a time. The family liked Maria's crunchy bread. Even small Tisha tasted it once and asked for more of Mama's bread. Every day after work, Maria had to stand in a long line in the local grocery store, in order to bring home some rye and wheat flour.

Maria looked for something to occupy herself, in order to turn away her thoughts of Alexander's dangerous visit to the Magadan KGB committee. She decided to greet her husband with fresh bread and his favorite supper dishes. She recollected her stay at Schulenburgs, when Alexander tasted her baking for the first time. The young man could not imagine his gentle wife, as a cook or baker. He tried her first bread with suspicion or hesitation, and he was greatly surprised and proud of his wife. He picked Maria up and circled with her in the kitchen, repeating the same words,

"You are my miracle, Marie. You are a true miracle, Mon Amour."

Maria saved leavened dough from the last time, and they had the last portion of flour at home. She quickly prepared the leaven for sourdough bread. While the dough was rising, Maria's thoughts took her again back to Germany, where they were also in danger, and the Lord was merciful to them. While cooking, Maria tried to understand the reason of her unusual behavior.

"What is wrong with me today? Everything is fine, thank God. We are blessed with two wonderful sons, who we love so much. We love each other even more, if it is possible to love more. And yet, I am panicky and cannot regain serenity today. It's not like me. *Help us, save us, have mercy on us, and keep us, O Lord by Your grace.*"

Maria looked back and found Tisha crawling into the kitchen. She exclaimed,

"Who is here? Who came to help his Mommy? What a boy! He wants to bake some bread for his Daddy!"

She quickly picked her son up and covered his belly and neck with kisses. It was ticklish, and Tisha was laughing. Then she called for Sasha and asked the older brother to take care of Tisha so that the baby boy wouldn't get dirty with some of the flour that had fallen on the floor.

Lord, have mercy!

Chapter 42

On that day, the bread dough did not want to rise fast, or probably Maria was in a hurry to start baking. She wanted to be occupied with work, and in the meanwhile, she went to do Tisha's laundry. She thought,

"When Alexander comes home, I want to be with him. My Lord, I cannot wait for his arrival. We'll sit and talk, and he'll share with me all the news from the visit to KGB office. I'll wash Tisha before supper. The tiny boy takes a lot of our time and attention every evening."

There were evenings when the parents hadn't seen each other until nine o'clock, being preoccupied with multiple chores and the baby. But after nine, it was their time. When Zina left after tea, Alexander and Maria were fond of staying together. Regardless that living together and working in the same hospital, they hardly ever saw each other during the day, and always experienced the deficiency of interaction.

During that cherished hour, Maria continued doing some work that was necessary for the family, but at the same time relaxing for her: spinning yarn, knitting, or sewing. Maria noticed several times,

"It's wonderful, Alex that we have our time in the evenings, when we enjoy discussing our work or home issues, as well as finding our mutual solutions."

Alexander used to remark,

"Did you pay attention, Marie that usually we start with our children - their progress, colds, interests, appetites, and things to buy for them? Then we talk about our work in the hospital, discussing the most complicated cases. We are blessed that we are able to assist each other in making the successful decisions."

They always touched on the topic of their future lives.

"Marie, my darling, can you imagine us being unconfined and returned home?"

Maria confessed,

"To tell you the truth, it's difficult for me to imagine, how we can enjoy our free life without somebody's watching, restrictions, and regulations."

They tried to imagine themselves in different parts of Paris after their desirable home-coming. Alexander wanted to be the first person who would introduce France and Paris to his sons. He asked Maria,

"Do you think they will love it, like us?"

Maria assured him every time, as if it was going to happen next week.

As a rule, 10:30 p.m. was their time to go to bed. The children were sleeping soundly by that time. It did not mean that the parents fell asleep at once. They enjoyed each other. They were blessed with real love. The tragic circumstances and years of hardship left deep imprints on their faces and bodies, but they had never paid attention at the wrinkles, stretch marks, scars, and other external imperfections. Maybe, they did not even notice them at all, or it was so insignificant to both of them in comparison with their real and never-ending love.

Alexander promised to return home on the eight o'clock train. In case he had to stay in Magadan longer, he would be back by eleven. Maria wanted to finish with baking bread, Tisha's bath, laundry and feeding the children by eight thirty. Then she had half an hour to put the kids in beds, and after nine, she would be ready to meet her husband. She was looking forward to seeing Alex.

Maria could not resist waiting for sitting with him at their kitchen table, feeding him supper, asking questions about his visit to KGB, and what to expect in the future after his visit. Maria's thoughts ran one after another.

"It's unfair, it's absolutely unfair. We were discharged, as people who committed no crime. Why do they confine us here? Why do they continue our slavery? When is our forceful resettlement over?"

Maria completely agreed with her husband regarding the necessity to go back to France. If not right away to France, then they needed to move to another region in Russia. She was as tired as her husband of living in poverty, lack of food, cold, and wilderness.

Maria sighed and sat down on a stool, waiting for the last portion of bread to be baked. She dreamt about her life before the war. That life always appeared, as a fairy tale, and it was a real pleasure to recollect what those pre-war memories brought to mind. On that time, besides the studies, Mademoiselle Kurbatov was always preoccupied with interesting books, music concerts, theater performances, art exhibitions, trips, and nice pieces of jewelry that matched her gorgeous outfits.

Nowadays, Maria concentrated on survival of the family, finding the foods, and pieces of the cheapest fabric to sew shirts or pants for children, her husband, or a dress for herself. She was knitting nearly every night. Otherwise, there was no way to find anything warm that protected them from the cold for nine months out of the year.

Sasha returned Maria back to earth with his question.

"Mama, are we going to have supper without Dad?"

Maria looked at the clock. It was a quarter to eight.

"Yes, Sasha. Bring your brother, please, and I'll serve your supper. Everything is ready."

Maria fed Tisha with some real food after he turned six months. A breast feeding was not enough for a boy. He had a good appetite, and the parents used to joke that one day, their boys would eat them up, if they did not find anything ready on the kitchen table.

Maria realized that it took longer for Alexander to be in Magadan. The boys were ready to go to bed. Sasha asked Maria not to go, he wanted to see Dad. Maria sent him to wash himself, put on his pajamas, and stay in bed, waiting for Dad to arrive.

She added,

"Sasha, your brother is watching you. If you are not in bed, he will not go either."

The reason was essential, and Sasha complied with mother's request. He was waiting and waiting for his father to come home. Finally, by 10:00 o'clock, he fell asleep.

Maria was sitting and knitting in the kitchen, when she heard a car stopped at their door. She looked out of the window. Two men got out of the car and moved toward the house. One on the men was caring a bag. Maria went to open the door. The men were in uniform of the militia. They were surprised to see Maria waiting for them in the doorway.

"How do you know that we are coming to your flat?" The older person asked.

"I am waiting for my husband. He went to Magadan last night. When I heard a car stopped, I thought, maybe, Alexander came back."

There was a long pause in the vestibule. Then Maria understood that something was wrong. She asked,

"Why are you here?"

She did not want to hear their answer and continued asking,

"Where is Alexander? What happened to my husband?"

The younger militiaman led her to a stool in the kitchen.

"Doctor Kurbatov, your husband was killed on the train."

Maria was looking at them with her eyes widely opened. Then she asked in a low voice:

"What, what did you say? My Alexander was killed? I do not believe you. Can you hear me? They should not kill him. Why did they kill him? My husband did not do any harm…"

Maria was in agony. She jumped up from the stool and rushed to the door.

"Take me to him, please."

The militiamen were watching her. The older one took her back to the kitchen.

"Doctor Kurbatov, please sit down. We feel sorry for you and your husband. We know that you work in our hospital, and that you are good doctors and decent people, but there are so many criminals in the area…"

Maria noticed a bag near the door.

"What is in there?"

The militiaman looked at her with sympathy and answered,

"You husband had this bag with him. They murdered your husband, but nobody touched the food. It is strange. Maybe somebody frightened them, and they did not steel."

Maria slipped down on the floor near the bag, touched it with her hands. Tears poured down her face. She repeated the same words,

"Why did you go, Alex? They killed you, my love. If they did not murder you in 1946, they have done it tonight."

The militiamen wanted Maria to identify the body and to sign the protocol. Maria got up and collapsed. They called the hospital. The doctor on call was at the house in five minutes. She was in a dead faint. The doctor injected the medications, one after another, but could not keep up her blood pressure. It was critically low.

The militiamen felt sorry for poor woman. Somebody in the militia station suggested not bringing the tragic news to the family until morning. Maybe, they were right. The doctor insisted in Maria's immediate hospitalization. He called the ambulance. The militiamen checked the rooms and found two kids, sleeping soundly.

"Somebody has to stay with children," said the older militiaman.

That 'somebody' was Zina. She opened the door of the appartment and walked quietly into the kitchen. She was surprised to see Dr. Maria on the floor and the men around her.

"I've heard your voices in my flat next door and decided to come. What happened? What's wrong with Dr. Maria? Did Dr. Alexander arrive?"

No one wished to explain anything to a neighbor. The village was small that all the inhabitants knew each other and were well informed about each other. The older militiaman said,

"Zina, it's good that you are here. Please, stay with children."

She wanted him to clarify, how long she had to stay with children, but did not receive the answer. The older militiaman added,

"The children cannot stay alone, do not leave them. We do not know, who and why attacked their father."

Zina followed the stretcher to the ambulance and covered Maria with her shawl. The ambulance left for the hospital.

The militiamen went to their car. Getting in the car the younger militiaman said,

"Her husband Dr. Kurbatov was murdered on the train. We brought her the news and it nearly killed her."

Zina was also shocked with the news. She grew weak and sat on the steps of the house, asking them,

"O, my God! Yesterday Dr. Kurbatov sounded so enthusiastic about his trip. Tell me, how it happened? Who did this?"

The militiamen shrugged their shoulders.

"Who knows? There were no witnesses around. He was found in a nearly empty train-carriage, killed with an axe. The bag with food and something else was near him. The killer left the axe near the bag. Dr. Kurbatov looked like he put his head on the table and was asleep."

"Who found that he was murdered?"

"Somebody from our village recognized the doctor and reminded him about his stop. There was no answer. The man came up and saw blood on the table. They called the militia station. We arrived, uncoupled the carriage, and our people took his body from the train."

"I cannot believe that he had money to be killed for and the person, like him, did not have enemies; on the contrary, he saved with surgeries so many people in the area."

"It was strange for us, as well, but they did not touch his money and a heavy bag with food products.

We brought it to Dr. Kurbatov and left it on the floor in the kitchen. I think that somebody scared the criminals, and they ran away."

The militiamen left, and Zina burst into tears. She was reeling from side to side, lamenting bitterly for her wonderful neighbor Dr. Alexander. The soul of the kind woman was tearing apart about his widow Dr. Maria and their small children, whose normal life without their father was absolutely impossible in the savage land.

She lifted her head up and, looking in the darkness of the sky, prayed: *"O Lord, grant your servant Alexander Kurbatov, who was murdered tonight, the remission of his sins and make his memory to be eternal. Amen."*

The woman returned into the warmth of the Kurbatovs' home, where two children were asleep. They slept soundly and did not know anything about the tragedy that occurred on the train with their father only a couple of hours ago.

Lord, have mercy!

To be continued…

Autobiography

I was born in 1952 in the Ukraine, part of the former Soviet Union. My father was a high-ranking military officer in the Soviet army, and my mother was a housewife. My parents tried their best to develop my skills and talents. From five years of age I remember myself in tight schedule of different activities, such as musical school, the studio of young actors with acting, dancing and reciting by heart long poems, as well as sport activities. Every Sunday I had one hour of real pleasure, playing chess with my father.

In 1959 I became a student of one of the best schools in our region, where the talented and knowledgeable teachers led us in the world of fascinating knowledge. I can be honest, saying that from ten years of age my teachers and parents motivated me to write. I was an editor of our school newspaper and in High school – Newsletter. Most of all I was enjoying writing my personal journal. My daily events were recorded in the form of poems and short stories. On Saturdays my parents arranged the family candle lit gatherings, where I read for them my first literary works.

During the school years I participated and won multiple Assay competitions in Ukrainian and Russian literatures. The language teachers encouraged me to undergo the University studies in journalism and creative writing, but I was interested in studying the foreign languages. In 1977 I graduated with Diploma and Degree, as a specialist of German and English languages and literature.

The years of under and post graduate schools were the most intensive in my life. I was married and became a mother of my son Roman. My schedule was three times busier, but still there was not any interesting exhibition, performance, concert or a book that did not reach my attention.

From 1977 to 1988 I worked as a teacher of foreign languages in Ukrainian high schools that was specialized in studying of several foreign languages. I would never forget my classroom of the German and English literatures. The talented artist painted wonderful portraits of world-known authors.

I tried to perform each lesson in the way that my students became the participants of a show and the question of discipline did not exist for me. Who could be bad in it? The world of words, phrases and grammar phenomena became as interesting, as a world of literature, history and geography of the countries, where people speak English and German. Throughout my professional career, I continued to enjoy writing the journal, exercising my English skills in creative writing. It was not only my favorite leisure interest; it became the preferred hobby of my best students.

In 1988 my family immigrated to the United States where for five years my husband and I were fighting for the life of our daughter Tatiana. Seven surgeries with numerous complications and one clinical death proved the words of my mother-in-law: "Ask the Father Almighty when nobody can help, and He will help in His miraculous way." Only God's miracles made out dream true and the child survived the hardships of those days.

Our life in the United States dictated new requirements and I added to my profession the Diplomas in Holistic medicine and Nutrition. God blessed us with over 20 years of successful international practice.

I consider my writing of family saga ***"God's Miracles in Lives of Regular People"*** that is an alternate historical and inspirational love story of a talented woman with thorny destiny, as well as its instant success in the USA and Europe at this difficult time is a real miracle sent from Above.

Author Angelic Tarasio
Florida, USA.

Bibliography

Encyclopedias

Encyclopedia Britannica Online,* *Encyclopedia Britannica, Inc. (2007-2008). Retrieved in 2007 & 2008, from https:save.britannica.com

"World War II"

"Western Ukraine under Soviet and Nazi Rule"

"Ukrainian Insurgent Army"

"The famine of 1932-1934"

"History of Organization of Ukrainian Nationalists (OUN) and UPA in 1920s"

"Bukovina and Ukrainian historical development"

"Transcarpathia and Ukrainian historical development"

"Munich Agreement between Germany and the USSR"

The Columbia Encyclopedia, Six Edition Online Encyclopedia (2007-2008). Retrieved in 2007-2008 from www.highbean.com

"World War II"

"Soviet army in Europe"

"National Socialism in Germany"

"Concentration Camps"

Columbia Encyclopedia – Wikipedia, The free encyclopedia. Retrieved in 2007-2008 from en.wikipedia.org/wiki/Columbia_Encyclopedia

Wikipedia: The free encyclopedia, (2007-2008) Wikimedia Foundation, Inc. Retrieved in 2007- 2008 from http://www.wikipedia.org

"Ukrainian History: Chronological Table"
"Soviet Invasion in Poland"
"World War II"
"Ukrainian-German collaboration during WWII"
"Eastern Front WWII"
"Kingdom Galicia"
Ukrainian Insurgent Army
"UPA and Germans"
"Collaboration"
"UPA and Poles"
"UPA's war with the Soviet Union"
"Soviet occupation of Latvia"
"Soviet occupation of Estonia"
"Soviet occupation of Lithuania"
"Soviet war crimes"

Andrew Gregorovich: Retrieved in 2007-2008 from www.infouks.com/history/ww2/

"Ukrainian History"
"World War II in Ukraine"

Forum: "A Ukrainian Review"

Leonid Sonnevytsky: BRAMA, Inc. Retrieved in 2007, from www.brama.org/sici?sici=0021

"Ukrainian History: Chronological Table"

"History of Ukraine – 20th Century"

"Annexation of Western Ukraine territory by the USSR"

Roman Kupchinsky: Retrieved in December 23, 2008 from http://www.ukemonde.com/mayday/partisan.html

"WWII – 60 years after: Mikola Leben and the Ukrainian Partisan Army"

Jamie Glazov: "The Voices of the Dead", February 2008

Michael Weiss: "Inhuman Power of the Lie: The Great Terror", February 2008

Ron Carpshaw: "Surviving Stalin", November 2007

Discoverthenetworks.org: Retrieved in December 2008

"Joseph Stalin"

"Famine"

Red-invasion.org: Retrieved in November-December 2008, from http://www.anti-communist.net/katyn.html

"Katyn Memorial"

Lituanus.org: Retrieved in 2008, from http://lituanus.org/1990_2/90_2_06htm

Soviet invasion in Lithuania

Yale University Press: Retrieved in 2008, from http://yalepress.yale.edu/yupbooks/book.asp?isbn=9780300112047

Geoffrey Roberts: "Stalin's Wars"

Harvard University Press Archives: Retrieved in 2007-2008, from www.hup.harvard.edu/catalog/HERJEW.htl

Jeffrey Herf: "The Jewish enemy: Nazi Propaganda during World War II and the Holocaust."

"Who is Who in World War II." Retrieved in 2007, from www.loc.gov/vets/bib-wwii.html
New York: Oxford University Press, 1995
Cambridge: Harvard University Press, 1984

Netfirms: Retrieved in Nov. 2008, from http://holocaust1.netfirms.com

"The history of Ukrainian- Russian and Ukrainian-Polish relations"

Macrohistory and World Report: Retrieved in 2008, from www.fsmitha.com

"Spain and Civil War"
"Stalin and Civil War in Spain" **Dictionaries**

Webster's Encyclopedic Unabridged Dictionary of the English Language. (1994) 1996 ed. USA, Random House.

Books

The Holy Bible, containing the Old and New Testaments, authorized King James Version, Red Letter Ed. World Bible Publishers.

Prayer Book, Fourth edition, Third Printing with corrections, Holy Trinity Monastery, USA, 2003.

Stephane Courtois, Nicolas Werth: "The Black Book of communism. Crimes, Terror, Repression". 1997 ed. France.

HOME-COMING
TABLE OF CONTENTS

Printed in the United States
By Bookmasters